FIRST
GENERATION

FIRST
GENERATION

In the Words of Twentieth-Century American Immigrants

June Namias

with an introduction by Robert Coles

BEACON PRESS   Boston

To Minnie of the first generation

and Robert of the fourth

Copyright © 1978 by June Namias

Beacon Press books are published under the auspices
of the Unitarian Universalist Association

Published simultaneously in Canada by
Fitzhenry & Whiteside Limited, Toronto

All rights reserved

Printed in the United States of America

(hardcover) 9   8   7   6   5   4   3   2

Library of Congress Cataloging in Publication Data

Namias, June
   First generation.
   Bibliography: p.
   1. United States—Emigration and immigration—History.
2. United States—Emigration and immigration—Bibliography.
I. Namias, June.
JV6455.F56   325.73   77–88345
ISBN 0–8070–5416–X

Acknowledgments

When this work was first begun, I had no idea of the great numbers of people and agencies who would be involved in helping me search for immigrants and verify information, read through drafts, help with the book's production, and encourage me to continue the work. I would especially like to thank John Higham, whose advice and example helped me throughout the entire writing of the book. Theodore Rosengarten has also extended himself many times in friendship and in good counsel. I thank both him and Linda Gordon for reading and commenting on the entire manuscript.

I would like to extend my gratitude to the following people for reading parts of the manuscript and offering suggestions, corrections, and comments: Orest Subtelny—the Eastern European selections; Michi Weglyn and Leslie Bedford—the Japanese selections; Bernard Wax—the Jewish selections; Francis M. Rogers—the Portuguese selection; Robert Mirak—the Armenian selection; Lilia Villanueva and Craig Scharlin—the Philippine selection; John Amoroso and Lanayre and Joseph Liggera—the Italian selections in Part I; Adria Steinberg for reading all of Part I; John Livingston for Part II; Howard and Roslyn Zinn, Allan Graubard, Natasha Anisimov, Martin S. Goldman, and Jan Lennon for reading and commenting on parts of earlier drafts. Of course, any errors in the text and any advice not taken is my own responsibility.

In terms of the book's production I must thank Lucille Kenney and Gale Halpern for typing many drafts, often from wretched copy, and Elizabeth Fenton for typing several early pieces. Barbara Doughty did much early proofreading. Daniel J. Borden contributed his photographic work, and Bill Ravanesi allowed me to use his photograph of Willie Barientos.

I would also like to thank those people who were kind enough to allow me to talk with and tape them, but who, because of space restrictions, could not be included.

Special thanks and affection to Rodolfo de León, Roberta Norin, Carol Nelson, and to Elliott J. Mahler, Patricia Miller King, Richard Mechem, the members of the Social Studies Department of Newton North High School, and the Newton School Committee.

To my son, Robert Victor Slavin, and my parents, Helen and Foster Namias, I would like to express my gratitude for their patience and their love. Without the free child care so generously given by my mother, virtually no interviews would have been taped. I would also like to thank other members of the family for their encouragement.

Finally, I wish to thank my editor, Charlotte Cecil Raymond, who has made herself constantly available for advice and direction. In the task of cutting the manuscript down to size, and in clarifying the numerous problems presented by the scope of this work, her help was invaluable.

Contents

Illustrations

Introduction

ROBERT COLES

In a letter to a young doctor who was doing "oral history" among white and black families in the South during the 1950s and early 1960s, William Carlos Williams (then rather ill, and alas, soon to die) had this to say: "I used to learn so much from the families I saw, on my house calls—so much, that I often wondered whose words I was putting into my poems, theirs or mine. Of course, we had no tape recorders then. But I wrote down what I heard, carefully, after I'd leave. The problem later is artistic—what to use and where."

I've kept that letter before me for years. I've stared, especially, at that last sentence. As June Namias, the author of this remarkable, accomplished, and quite compelling book, tells us in her introduction, oral history requires a novelist's willingness to select, emphasize, to give shape to words uttered, to use a spoken narrative in such a way that a particular person's character emerges and, not least, the drama of a given life history gets told.

In 1967, when working in an Appalachian hollow (Mingo County, West Virginia) I was given a lesson or two in "methodology" by a mountain woman who had asked what I was doing with my tape-recorded "material," as I was then apt to put it. I replied that I would go back home and listen and try to learn from what I had heard. She said that she hoped I didn't pay attention to her "every word." I assured her (and myself) that I did, I did. She smiled, then became serious: "It takes me a long time to say what's on my mind. I go around and around. My father was a man of few words, but my mother made up for it, and I'm her daughter, and most like her of the seven children who survived the bad times we had in the Depression years. There will be days I know I've talked too much; I can see it on my children's faces. I'll say one thing, and then another. I'll go in one direction, then another. Like the teacher tells my youngest son: you've got to try not to contradict your own remarks, if you can possibly help it. But if you stumble and fall, you've got to hope the person you're talking to has got the sense to know what you really want to say. That's asking some of another person, but if they know *you,* they'll sift and sort your words, and they'll get your story straight."

I was surprised at the time by her apparent willingness to have others "sift and sort" her statements—though, of course, we all are so inclined as readers and listeners; that is to say, we attend the statements of others, and hold closest what strikes us as significant, illuminating, suggestive, memorable—true not only in fact, but in spirit—true, that is, to a given person's intent as well as *sub specie aeternitatis.* Later on, as I did indeed work my way through her various utterances—her casual comments, her brief rejoinders, her longer declarations, pleas, interpretations, clarifications—I kept coming back to that word "story." I had never before thought of my work as working on *stories* and I set aside, eventually, the word. I now believe the speaker's intent. She was using a colloquialism; she was simply telling me to be an accurate and sympathetic recorder.

Years later, I found some of my books on the reading list of a Harvard literature course—English and American *stories.* Most of the writers were, of course, well-known short-story writers. What was I doing in their company? Well, the student who showed me the list had a simple, unpretentious explanation: I had been offering the reading public stories—in the sense of comparatively short personal narratives, or accounts of specific incidents, events, circumstances. Why, then, does one keep a little distance from that word *story*? Does it nudge one a little too much toward the "subjective," the "soft," the "unscientific?" Or perhaps there is the nagging suspicion, implied in a paragraph of this book's preface, that one is skirting fibs, exaggerations, distortions, deceptions: the storyteller as one who makes things up and thereby propagates legends—believed only by the gullible or the innocent, but certainly not by members of the well-educated, proudly skeptical intelligentsia of the twentieth century—for whom, incidentally, the varous myths of "science" and "social science" have a life and power of their very own.

Yes, some of the first generation people who talked with June Namias may well have forgotten things, concealed things, changed things around in their minds and hearts, as a few of her worried friends suggested. But what of those written sources, those diaries, the various correspondence, and even the official or semi-official records—do they not also present the same challenges to the scholar, the reader? People lie with the written word, too. People lie in courthouses and hospitals and schools. People even lie when under oath. Even the census and other official surveys have to contend with those who evade, who are out of reach, beyond the ken of the interested, the curious, the diligently observant. In our ghettoes, for instance, there are families who move about constantly, avoid various appraisals, enumerations. The same holds in rural areas. The point is to indicate that polarities like objective and subjective are not always as helpful as they appear to be. The author is right to stick to her conviction that the kind of work she does draws upon social anthropology, sociology, and fiction—if by the last of those three she has in mind the novelist's inclination to *relate*— Defoe's word. He had in mind not the contemporary banal, psychological sense of the word, but the desire some have to tell others what happened once, or what is happening, or what might happen one day, somewhere and to some people and under some skies.

This book joins hands with a growing number of others: in sum, a particular genre of storytelling. We learn what certain Americans brought to this country, no more, but no less. We learn what a sensitive, thoughtful, and compassionate listener chose to find instructive, evocative, penetrating, and not rarely, unforgettable. Let those so inclined argue endlessly where to place this kind of effort on some academic spectrum. The author knows (and tells us unashamedly) what she was about, what she hoped to achieve. She has done so brilliantly—and the result is a redemptive moment of sorts for the rest of us who have a chance, through these accounts, to rid ourselves of various abstract political or social pieties, and in exchange gain a sense of what this country has offered, has received, and not least, has through these lives, and countless others, managed to become.

PREFACE

The giant harbor woman, her torch raised, was on her island home by October 28, 1886. Emma Lazarus, a woman of Sephardic Jewish ancestry, had written a poem for the occasion. Placed at the feet of Liberty in 1903, its closing line read: "I lift my lamp beside the golden door."

Before 1900, thousands of immigrants from Ireland, Germany, and Scandinavia, from England, Scotland, and China had taken passage on sailing ships, and risked their lives and the lives of their families to leave Europe and Asia for North and South America. In the following century the steamer, the airplane, the automobile, the bus, the railroad, and even swimming replaced those tall ships as means of transporting the world's people to the United States. Between 1901 and 1930 over eighteen million came; from 1931 to 1945 a few less than 700,000; and between 1946 and 1975 over eight and a half million legally arrived. No one knows how many came illegally. Not all of those who came stayed, either returning to their original homeland or moving on to another country. Some who left the United States returned later. The process continues.

Essentially, this book tells the stories of a small number of first-generation immigrants and a few of their children who came to the United States between the 1900s and the 1970s. The book began as a personal quest. It grew out of a need to understand my own first generation. In 1973 Minnie Needle, my only surviving grandparent, was in an old-age home, sick and dying. I decided to buy a cassette recorder and to tape as much about her life as she would tell. Less than a year after I began, she died. As I transcribed her tapes the summer of her death, I became increasingly aware of that entire immigrant generation of which she was a part. I wanted to talk with other grandmothers—Irish, Japanese, Armenian—and grandfathers—Greek, Italian, Polish. I felt that time would not wait; in fact, the stories of most of this generation were already buried.

The first part of the book shares the histories of those who came before 1930. In the fall of 1972 I met Rodolfo de León, a young Cuban refugee. As I began to spend time with him and learn more of his experiences, I noticed the continuities and discontinuities between that earlier first generation and those men, women, and children who had recently arrived. The pattern of the book then became clear.

I knew the national groups I wanted represented, the time periods and some of the experiences I wished to include: those of mill workers, union people, Horatio Algers, domestics, political refugees of the right and left. It remained for me to find these people and to convince them to tell me about their lives.

I would have preferred to have talked with people living in all sections of the country, but this was impossible. The people with whom I spoke live mainly on the East and West Coasts, though many have lived part of their lives in the Midwest and the South. They come from over twenty countries in Europe, Asia, the Middle East, Latin America, and the Caribbean. Because of time limitations and the space limitations of this volume there are many national groups I was unable to include—Scandinavians, French Canadians, British, and Syrians, to name a few. I deliberately excluded Puerto Ricans. Their country's Commonwealth status affords them entry into the United States without going through Immigration procedures.

I spoke with fifty people and included thirty-one. This book can only begin to suggest the scope of even those stories. Although each person here carries a national and ethnic heritage besides an American one, each represents only his or her life, and only a selected view at that. Those wishing to understand the total experience out of which these histories arise will have to consult other books. Several are suggested in the bibliography and in the endnotes.

None of these people is "typical" in the sense that his or her opinion or experience is representative of a nation or background. Some might express views that appear outrageous to a reader of similar origins. The personal histories are here to suggest the diversity and individuality of America's first generations and to suggest the range of the immigrant experience during this century. To the extent that the lives included are not stereotypes, but rather complex human beings, the book accomplishes its purpose.

On the other hand, we all live in a particular historical time and place. We are all born into cultural, religious, national, and class backgrounds, which shape our futures, no matter how we come to terms with such "accidents of birth." In my selection process I chose people who, whether they realized it or not, were part of the massive economic, political, and social upheavals that have shaped the recent migrations to the United States, especially those upheavals particular to their national experience.

I have tried to let people speak for themselves, to tell their stories in their own words, keeping their language and syntax, except in those instances where it would be very difficult to understand their message. My apologies to those included if their meaning was in any way distorted. The interviews have been cut a great deal and edited for clarification. One of the greatest difficulties that a non–English-speaking immigrant faces in this country is trying to learn the language and being ridiculed along the way. Although many people expressed inadequacy about their English, I found the speech of the first generation to be direct, literary, and metaphorical, adding new richness to the language. The process of editing and selecting of both people and materials is not value free. I have tried to keep what I felt to be the essence of people's stories. The selection and order of the work tells something of my priorities and perhaps my prejudices.

The book is divided into three sections, based on three periods in American immigrant history: 1900 to 1929, 1930 to 1945, and 1946 to the present. Before each section there is a short summary of some of the historical and legal problems facing those entering the United States in that particular era. The personal introduction suggests something of the individual and his or her background, and notes the date and place of our meetings.

Several people who read selections of the manuscript have asked me, "But are these stories true?" How do I know these people were not lying? This is a problem with any source of information. In a few cases people have asked me to leave out some matters they felt were too damaging to themselves, to friends, or to members of their families to be published. This often happened with political refugees from rightist or leftist countries. It was also true of several adolescents. We discussed this and reached a mutually acceptable agreement. In several cases a person wished the protection of a pseudonym. In some of these cases their residence was kept intentionally vague.

Oral history is both a new and an old form. Its originators were probably closer to Homer than to Thucydides; its modern version must pay homage to the technology of the tape recorder. Basically, it involves the narrating of one's own experiences. It is part of a recent movement among historians to find out what people think about their lives while they are still living, through conversation rather than depending primarily on quantitative data or written sources. It borrows techniques from social anthropology, sociology, and from fiction.

Telling the story of one's life is not easy, especially when talking with a stranger. I would like to express my deep gratitude to all of the people with whom I spoke. It was often painful for them to share certain experiences, and without their openness this volume would have been impossible. Their histories demonstrate that it is not only the famous, the powerful, and the wealthy who build a country, but men, women, and children from every stratum of society. It is my hope that I have faithfully rendered the sufferings and the aspirations of this first generation.

June Namias

Cambridge, Massachusetts
September 1977

FIRST
GENERATION

I. New Beginnings: 1900-1929

Moving. The theme is an American one. It can be found in Twain's story of Huck Finn along the Mississippi, and in Bob Dylan's ode to Highway 61. Between 1890 and 1930 four major migratory movements changed the location, the destiny, and the color of the population across the American continent. In 1890 came the close of the frontier and the forcible restriction of America's native population to reservations. The other three migrations resulted from the industrial growth experienced by the United States from the end of the Civil War through the 1920s. With the nation's growing need for labor to mine its resources, run its shops, and build its factories came the movement of Americans out of farms and out of small towns, the movement north of rural southern blacks and whites, and the movement to the United States of European and Asiatic immigrants. These last three movements had the same destination—the city.

This new mix of rural blacks and whites and immigrants met in the city with earlier immigrants and descendants of pre-Revolutionary Americans. The problems of mixing a highly heterogeneous population in an urban setting of the early 1900s has modified in the late twentieth century but the changes are those of degree rather than kind. Housing, poverty, the need to find work, the education of children from a variety of linguistic, religious, and cultural backgrounds, the question of who has political power, and the hopes and anxieties for one's children—these were and still are the problems facing America's urban population.

Of the four late nineteenth- and early twentieth-century migrations, it is the ingathering of immigrants which, in sheer numbers, left its greatest impact on the American metropolis. By 1900 there were over ten million foreign-born people in the United States out of a population of close to seventy-five million.[1] Between 1901 and 1930 over eighteen million immigrants legally entered the United States. From 1908, when figures began to be kept, to 1930, over eight million foreigners left, perhaps to return another time. The in- and outflow of people before World War I is staggering. Immigration topped the one-million mark in 1905, '06, '07, '10, '13, and '14.[2] By 1912, forty percent of New York's population was foreign born, as was thirty-six percent of Chicago's and Boston's, thirty-four percent of San Francisco's, thirty percent of Milwaukee's, twenty-nine percent of Minneapolis's, and twenty-four percent of Portland, Oregon's.

Why did these people come? The European mass migration of the nineteenth century was largely a result of the Industrial Revolution, which rendered an agrarian peasant base obsolete. As it hit Britain first, early nineteenth-century emigration contained many English, Scots, Irish. Another important factor in early emigration was the doubling of Europe's population between 1750 and 1850.[3] Historians have also noted that the peak years of immigration between 1800 and 1930 correspond to the ups and downs of the U.S. economy. During America's prosperous periods immigrants arrived in large numbers; in periods of depression fewer people came.[4]

Other factors contributed to immigration. Interest groups within the United States encouraged it. In the nineteenth century the railroads advertised in Europe to entice people to populate lands they had been given by the federal government. State governments, especially in the Midwest, sent recruiters to Europe, and steamship lines competed for immigrant services, driving down the price of passage. By 1897 steamship travel to the United States was cut to five and a half days; in 1850 it was forty-four days by sailing vessel. By 1882 fare from England to the United States was between $12 and $15, a passage often paid by a relative who had already made the voyage.[5] There were also political and cultural reasons for emigrating: conscription, denial of cultural or religious rights, political persecution.

The early and mid-nineteenth-century immigrants tended to come from northern Europe. The two largest groups, from Ireland and Germany, were followed in the later nineteenth century by Scandinavians and French Canadians.[6] Chinese came after 1849.

The industrialization and population growth which struck northern Europe in the early and mid-nineteenth century struck southern and eastern Europe by the late nineteenth century. Northern Europeans continued to arrive in large numbers after 1880, but that date signals the beginning of a shift to large southern- and eastern-European migrations. This "new immigration" was predominantly Roman Catholic, Eastern Orthodox, or Jewish, and did not speak English. Italians came in the greatest numbers, with Jews second. Violence against Jews in Russia was a major factor in their emigration after 1881. Poles, Russians, Slovaks, Slovenes, Serbs, Croatians, Bulgarians, Ukrainians, and other Slavs made up one-quarter of the new immigration. Poles made up the largest number of people in the Slavic category and had over one million immigrants in the United States before World War I.

Other Asian peoples also entered after 1880. Another distinguishing feature of much of the "new immigration" was that it was overwhelmingly male and between the ages of fourteen and forty-four years old.[7] Many post-1880s immigrants intended to, and in fact did, return to European or Asiatic homelands.

Reading the stories of the early twentieth-century first generation, one sees that some already had family here, some were caught in the economic and social changes of their native land, some fled minority status or conscription, and some were too young to remember the real reasons why they came.

Prior to World War I entry into the United States was not difficult for most Europeans. The reason was the relative openness of United States immigration policy. By the early 1900s there were restrictions on criminals, the insane, the destitute, the diseased, and the "anarchistic," and also significant limitations placed on Japanese and Chinese. In 1917 literacy tests were passed by Congress over President Wilson's veto as a growing restrictionist movement gained national power. A "Barred Zone" was imposed on most immigration from Asia and the Pacific. These restrictions and more imposing ones which followed in the days of '20s isolationism were generated by a complex of factors in the prewar and postwar periods. But what was made difficult by legal restrictions was eased, at least until the quota laws of the '20s, by the accessibility of cheap transportation. Steerage was not glamorous but few people died on the steamers, as many had in sailing ships. One could, for a modest price, be ferried to a magical land where reportedly gold littered the streets, land was free for the tilling, and political and religious freedoms came with the air one breathed.

MINNIE KASSER NEEDLE—
Jewish Grandmother

Mina Kasser was born in Galicia in the late 1880s. She was one of two million Jews of eastern European origin who entered the United States between 1881 and 1914. Of the thousands of years of Jewish history this was the greatest period of mass emigration—greater than the exodus from Egypt, the dispersion from ancient Israel and Palestine, or the forced exile from Spain in the late 1400s. Eastern European migration, like those earlier migrations, followed the devastation of the lives, villages, and some of the culture of the Jewish people.

Galicia was a province in the northeastern portion of the Austro-Hungarian Empire, with a large Polish population. Jews had lived in Galicia for centuries. Like other eastern European Jews, Galicians had a history of both torture and stature. In the mid-1600s bands of cossacks raged through the Ukraine west into Galicia, slaughtering thousands of Jews en route, often giving them the choice of baptism or death. In the early 1800s, when the "liberal" Francis I ruled as Emperior of Austria, a few Jewish families enjoyed both status and wealth. Major attempts were made to "educate" Galician Jews forcibly into "enlightened" European society.

In the eighteenth and nineteenth centuries important Jewish movements emerged in Galicia, and in the late nineteenth century the crosscurrents of Chasidism, Zionism, socialism, and traditional Jewish life made it a breeding ground for great Yiddish writers of fiction and politics. But economic life in Galicia was in a state of change, disrupting life for Jews and non-Jews, and the Jewish existence was continually and violently attacked. Between 1881 and 1890 sixty percent of the Jewish population emigrated from Galicia. Between 1870 and 1914 over two million Jews left eastern Europe for America. Twenty percent were, like Minnie, from Austria-Hungary.[1]

Minnie's mother, Rachel Leah Bock Kasser, married at the age of fifteen and had thirteen children. The family was brought up on the land just outside the village of Mosciska, near Przemysl, today, on the Soviet side of the southeastern Polish border. Her town being directly south of Lublin and directly west of Lvov places it within the boundaries of a rich Jewish heritage. Minnie, her mother, and most of her brothers and sisters came to America. She came to Boston in her early teens on the *S.S. Ivernia* in June of 1904. Her father, Israel Kasser, died shortly after she left.

Minnie's future husband, Joseph Needle, was born in Russian Poland.[2] He came to this country via Glasgow, Scotland, with his brother Harry, also in 1904. Both were in their midteens. They left their small village to flee conscription into the czar's army. Minnie and Joe married in 1911 and shortly thereafter made Boston, Massachusetts, their home. At the turn of the century Boston's Jews clustered in what was then the West End. Minnie and Joe followed a common migratory pattern from the West End to Roxbury. Joe became a machinist in Watertown.

Poker was important to Minnie. Other relatives indicate that games played at her house were not a universally welcomed facet of the Roxbury neighborhood. Games were played two and three nights a week, often until one or two in the morning, with eight to ten people in Minnie's house at any one time, most being Jewish women from the building or nearby. Small apartments, transoms, and summer heat made for noisy meetings. At least one Sunday night, police broke up the games, which were in violation of the state's blue laws.

The family took varying views of these card games, mostly dim. Nevertheless, they did help with the rent, and with the rakeoff Minnie got from her baking for the guests she pocketed more money. Some relatives thought her "gutsy" and "revolutionary." Others felt disgust or shame; one person went so far as to say that she was "a horrible mother," always out hustling a game rather than doing the things good women should do.

During the '20s Minnie ran a small-time survival operation with the help of her bathtub. There is a hint of some brush with the law on this matter, and fear ended her breach of Prohibition. A number of Jewish mothers in Minnie's building took routes to survival other than home brew and cards. In early Depression days, one relative commented, "There was a lot of action in that place." After one neighborhood wife got certain material goods and services by working "the oldest profession," her husband found out and beat her up. Those neighbors soon moved out.

My grandmother never told me these stories and neither would have anyone else if I hadn't kept calling, writing, and plying the sisters, cousins, and aunts. Perhaps she wanted to appear to her grandchildren as she had not to her own children.

Fall 1973–Spring 1974
Walmont Nursing Home
Roxbury, Massachusetts

I only remember when my father brought me to the train from the small city where we lived. He brought me to the train to go away to America. It was in—let me remind myself. See, I forgot—so many years, how can you remember?

In the old days my sisters were writing to Europe for my others to come here with my mother. I had nine sisters and three brothers. My name was Kasser.

My mother came with five children, four girls and a brother. Every two years my mother had a baby. They came to Boston. They had an apartment in the West End. Don't even remember where. So she didn't like it because she was very pious. She made those peruke they used to wear in the hair when they were getting married.[1] She had a place. She had a few girls with her. So she says, "I don't like it here." So they all moved away to New York and she took an apartment. From there the girls worked at something; a couple of them worked at her place. I never saw it, but I know that was the idea.

I worked in an overall shop. With the coats. With the overalls. A big shop. I was a buttonhole maker on a machine. I had to learn how to do my own everything, how to fix the machine. And I had to know how to set it and how to sew.

My sister's husband was in [the] furnishing business. He was buying goods from the man who owned the shop. So he told him to take me in. He took a girl for a couple of days to teach me how to sew. Then I worked in there three years, till I got married. I worked every day, like they work now, from eight to five. I used to make $25 a week. All the people that was sewing worked by piece—section work. I only worked buttonholes on everything, and on a machine, but that's all I remember. After I was married I never worked.

I met my husband to a private wedding in Cambridge. She worked with me in the shop, the girl that was married. I'm from Austria, so they didn't call me Minnie or anything. They didn't know me. They only knew from where I come. They asked me so I told 'em. So they called me *Galitsiana Maidle*.[2] So I served on the tables and I served on them. And then, when they all got through three or four boys they were all around me. You know, when I was a young girl they liked me. I wasn't handsome, but still. So they said, "Miss, *ich vays.*"[3] [Laughs.] "You sit down and we gonna wait on *you*, now."

They waited on me then. But when we were going home, they took a cab. They took everybody home. When I came to my home so my husband took me up to the doorway. And that's all, and said goodnight.

On a Sunday I was on Cutler Street in the West End, where my sister lived. I was living with her. I was standing in the window looking out. It was in the afternoon, I think. So he was walking around on the other side sidewalk and looked around if he'll see me someplace. So he happened to see me in the window. And he came over to this side and he said, "You remember me?"

I says, "Who are you?"

He says, "Don't you remember, I brought you home?" So he asked me to come down. I took a walk with him, and that's what happened.

One day, on a Thanksgiving night—it was pelting, this I remember. He rang the bell. He had tickets to go to a show. We go to a show and then dinner, I suppose. So he rang the bell I should come down. My brother-in-law, my sister's husband, said, "Who is this?"

I says, "Oh, this is the boy that I go with him."

He says, "If he's good enough to walk in the street in the rain, he's good enough to come up to the house."

Since then, you know how it is, a boy and girl. So, you know everything.

Woman friend: You fell in love, eh?

Fell in love! I went with him two years. I liked him, but he was *too young*, he was only nineteen years old then.

Woman friend: And you were older than him?

I was older a year or so, I don't know. I don't remember exactly.[4]

Finally I said to him, I says, "Go, maybe you get a girl, her father might be in business. He will make you something." He didn't have no job or anything, a young fellow. He had a father in Hartford, Connecticut. He was a junk dealer. He had a house and everything.

So I says, "So what you in a hurry? You too young."

I went with him for two years, and then I told him my family wanted me to get married. I says, "I'll go to work, I'll keep working."

He says, "You wanna work, work now." He says, "You not gonna go to work when you get married." He didn't like it. Men wouldn't *let* the wife work! He says, "If you want to work, work *now*." You gonna write this? [Laughs.]

I got married just like all girls. I got married a Friday afternoon in North Russell Street Shul. In the West End is a North Russell Street Shul, and I got married there. And I was dressed. I got pictures, you saw, like all brides, everything. In a Friday afternoon, June.[5] At the supper I had from New York an uncle, and my mother was yet living then.

I took an apartment before I was married. My sister says, "So what do you want to go to an apartment? Go on a honeymoon."

I says, "Where am I gonna come home then when I go for a honeymoon and spend the money I have?" I says, "No, I've got to have a home to come back. That will be my honeymoon." So I had an apartment and I furnished it and everything, and that night I went home to my home in the West End.

Your mother was born nine months to the day.

What did you think when you found out you were pregnant?

What should I think? I got married, so I knew if it happened it happened. *Then* I got smart. I waited five years till I had my son. Five and a half years.

How did you get smart?

This I can't tell you.[6]

Those years we lived on Charles Street. I lived there when your mother was born. She was five-and-a-half years old when Gilbert was born. That was on Humboldt Avenue in Roxbury. Both kids were born in the house, and I nursed both kids of mine.

How did you learn how to cook?

I learned how to cook when I got married. A landlady lived downstairs where I took my apartment. Whatever I didn't know I used to go down and ask her. And she told me how to put up pickles, how to put up wine, everything. Many times it didn't come out good. Two, three times. That's why I made the best good that could be. Over here [at the nursing home] whatever I eat I don't like because it isn't the way it's supposed to be. And I learned from my own mother-in-law. When she came from Europe, they came to my house. She was in my house for

Minnie Kasser and Joseph Needle
Engagement photo, 1911

two or three weeks. She went home because my father-in-law, the junk dealer, he has a house for himself. I learned from her how to make strudel. She was a good cook.

[Later on] I had a little delicatessen store in Dudley Street—not for long, though. The women in the neighborhood used to play cards, come together. And Grandpa used to work and when he came home he was tired. He played with Gilly. He lay down with him to play. So he fell asleep. I took away the baby, and put him in his bed, and I left him asleep. Next door was a neighbor, very friendly, I told her, "Listen, if you hear him cry, come and tell me." Then I used to go out in the evenings to play cards. This was after Helen was already eight or nine years old. Not when they were kids. I never left them with baby-sitters.

I was very attached to my children. I loved 'em. When my Helen was a little girl, when she cried I cried with her. I was afraid she's sick.

Do you remember anything about my mother or Gil when they were teenagers?

Sure I remember. I remember you mother was very young when she started to go with boys, from in high school. She went out with a lot of nice boys. They had their fathers' cars, they used to go to college. I told her, before twelve o'clock she should be home, because I never went to sleep until she came home. I used to take very good care of her, don't worry. I was afraid. She was too pretty. [Laughs.]

She used to go out with a lot of fellows, but on New Year's night she knew a girl. Helen didn't have nobody to go with so she told her, she was seeing someone, a doctor. She says, "A fellow's coming up too, without a girl, so you'll meet him. So that night, New Year's night, she met your father. And he brought her home and since then he made a date with her once, again, a second time. So when he was coming up to see her, she says to me, "Ma, this fellow that's coming up to see me tonight, you'll like him."

And when he came up I did like him, right away. So he never left her. He brought her an orchid for the first time he had a date with her. And he looked *stunning,* your father. He was very nice-looking too, he's dark. I liked him right away. He's got such a nice little nose, your father. Nobody has such a nice little nose like him! *Oy!* I always liked your father. Of course his family, he only had a brother, and his father and mother was old. They lived in Fall River.

They went a whole summer, from New Year's to Labor Day. And between the summer they made up to get married. Helen told him I couldn't afford to make a wedding. I *couldn't* afford. But still I wouldn't let Mommy go out just like that—because I was old-fashioned. I says, "No sir. I got only one girl, and she's getting such a nice fellow. He's a doctor.[7] Let her out like that! Nothin' doin'."

So Grandpa, another few men in the neighborhood, they started a organization. They saved up money. They called it an "Auxy."[8] I went in and somebody endorsed for me, and I borrowed five hundred dollars. I made her a nice wedding. In Kehillath Israel. A very nice wedding. They were such a beautiful couple. The two of them. And I had Rubin the caterer, and Rubin the musician. Beautiful wedding she had. I let her out very beautiful.

Your husband died soon after that. How did he die?

My husband had a heart attack. He had it from young. And after all he got older and he worked, and he climbed steps. He worked in shops, so it's a factor.

So he took sick and sick and sick. He worked, he only wanted to go to work. He was very sick. I didn't let him go to work, but he didn't want to be home. He was only in the forties when he died. It was no shock, he was sick.

When my husband died I wasn't a citizen of the United States because those years *he* was the citizen. When he died I wasn't a citizen, so I took a lawyer and he looked me up everything. He looked it up because it's there in the history, everything—my steamer, my when I came, my parents and me, everything. And then when I applied for citizenship papers I took a friend of mine for a witness. I got a little booklet. I had to learn, you know, how many presidents, a little history, before I took out my papers. And I got my papers.

After your husband died, you were still quite young. Why didn't you ever marry again?

The first thing, I wasn't interested in some man because I wanted to be free. Just like you. And I had a bunch of women that didn't let me be lonesome or worried. We used to play cards and they drove 'em a car. We used to enjoy ourselves like that. So that's why I didn't care. I never cared to get married. I was busy with Mommy, cookin' and bakin'.

I remember somebody wanted me to meet somebody—the butcher.

The butcher, the baker, the candlestick maker. [Laughs.] They want me to meet some man. I didn't want to meet them because I lived by myself. I didn't want anybody to come to my apartment. I lived by myself for so many years, I don't know how many years, maybe thirty years? A single man never came to see me. Men came with women to play cards, with their wives. But a man to see me never came because I never dated anybody. I figured, if I date him he's going to come to my house. I don't want him to be here. My neighbors will see a man coming up to my house by himself. So only when they played cards. [Laughs.]

My son Gilly was seventeen years old when his father died. He worked. He worked in town—that's why he knows how to talk Jewish, because he used to work in the stores with the Jewish women, delivering things. Whatever money he picked up while he was working, I put on Mommy's name. I didn't want him to go into the army. So I thought they wouldn't take him because he was my supporter, but I couldn't save him. They took him to the army just the same—Germany for four years.[9]

He was fighting against Hitler. You really didn't want him to go into the army?

Well, I didn't live in Germany. That was in Germany. That wasn't in Austria. Galicia. That wasn't there.

In Austria too.

It was? Well, I was here. I wasn't there no more. I came here, I came here I was sixteen or seventeen years old. I married here in North Russell Street Shul.

He came home after the war. So this boyfriend, he was in the pants, he was a rich boy. And my son Gilbert had a new car when he came. The boy said, "I'll take care of everything and we go to California." That's the time he came home and he says, "Ma, my ten fingers will work for you and me, but I gotta go away from Boston, because I wouldn't go for nobody to work. I wouldn't go to have a boss over me. I'll try to make a living by myself. Over here in Boston I can't do it. There is nothing to do for me. So I gotta go and see what I can do."

So one day he was going away, and he had no money. I wanted to give him some. He wouldn't take it. He says, "Ma, I don't want it because you've got to have it."

He went away and he wasn't there very long before he met Ruth. They went around a few weeks, not too long. And he wrote me, it's too expensive they should live apart. They decided to get married. He wanted me to come, but I didn't.

Where you happy about his getting married?

Yeah, Mommy and I cried plenty. [Laughs.] Happy I was. I can only tell you that Gilly, I'm proud of my son. His wife didn't know nothing about Jewish. She didn't care. She didn't like Jews, she liked *Goyim*[10] all the time. And she didn't even care that her boys should go to Hebrew school. But my son wanted to bring them up Jewish and by the way I like. Until this day he had 'em in school, and he had 'em in Hebrew school and gave them *Bar Mitzvahs,* just the way it's supposed to be, just the way I gave him.

Thanks the Lord I didn't have no trouble from my children, that's why I love 'em. They didn't shame me, they didn't do nothing to me! Gilly was four years in the army in Germany. Whatever he did there I don't know. But he came nice and clean with his hands and his feet and face, and if I saw him it was enough for me. I looked him over. And I still love the two of them, just as good as I love all my children, all my great-great-grandchildren. I love youse all, 'cause they all come from me. If not for me none of you were here. Isn't so?

I only know you'll always remember Grandma when Grandma's gone. If you talk about Grandma you'll say, "I had the best Grandma."

CATHERINE MORAN McNAMARA— The Life of the Irish

Catherine Moran was eighteen years old when she docked in East Boston in the spring of 1903. Close to 340,000 other Irish with "Immigrant Alien" status arrived in the United States in that decade.[1]

In the first great wave of Irish immigrants between 1831 and 1860, almost two million Irish came to the United States.[2] The agricultural and industrial changes taking place in England and Ireland a hundred years before had set this mass migration in motion. Technological developments had made it profitable for English owners of Irish lands to put an end to the centuries-old communal agricultural system and its Irish peasantry and to replace them with pastures and a caretaker work force. In 1838 the Irish Poor Law, by taxing the peasantry out of their ancestral lands, contributed to future emigration. During the late

1840s the blighted potato crop dealt death to over half a million Irish peasants. With no relief in sight, millions were added to the original exodus. Sailing vessels that arrived from the Americas with timber, tobacco, and cotton returned with a large Irish cargo.[3] Landing in America, the Irish settled in large numbers in New York, Chicago, Philadelphia, and Boston.

Unlike their cousins in other cities, Irish were virtually the only major foreign-born group in Boston from the 1840s until the latter part of the century.[4] By the 1850s Massachusetts was a center of the nativist, anti-Catholic movement, the Know-Nothings, and in 1854 a Know-Nothing party candidate was elected governor. In Charlestown in 1834, anti-Catholic, anti-Irish feeling resulted in the burning of the Ursuline Convent.[5] Burnings and other harassments were not soon forgotten; they were too similar to English attacks on the Church in Ireland.

A grandiose Victorian Boston was built in the years following the Civil War, but not without cost to these first immigrants; for the city's advances they were paid poorly. The men were concentrated in the building trades; the women, like Catherine Moran, did maid service in Yankee homes. For more highly paid jobs, signs read "NO IRISH NEED APPLY." The struggle to gain political power became a means for the Irish to settle economic and social scores. By 1903, the year Catherine Moran arrived, Irish outnumbered the "native" Yankee population in Boston. With the combination of numbers and political know-how, the Irish had taken political hold of the city.

I spoke with Mrs. McNamara one morning in her room at a Catholic old-people's home in Somerville, Massachusetts. Her independence impressed me. She said that she did not like people telling her how to dress or wear her hair, and that she would prefer to make her bed each morning rather than have someone else do it for her. She sat close to me, looking me straight in the eye. She is a bit hard of hearing, and I would often have to repeat questions the few times she paused.

Many immigrant men died at an early age, leaving their wives to care for large families on their own resources. Catherine's husband died young, leaving her with five children. She had lived with her eldest son, Ed, for the last twenty years. Talking of Ed's life and recent death, she cried. "I'm really very very sad after him. Oh, very. Oh, the day I don't cry." But her humor and her faith have kept her going.

March 25, 1976
Little Sisters of the Poor
Somerville, Massachusetts

There was twelve in our family. The oldest died and the other one went to Australia with my uncle. I was about five when she went. So there was ten of us, you might say, in our family. We had to pay *every cent* we possibly could produce to taxes. Every war England had she had you pay her part, even though you just had nothing, and you had to pay on your land some expenses out of it.

My father, before he married, a house was built for him. I guess it was his father built it. We had a good big house, we had a big family. We had boarded ceilings and up above you could sleep there if you wanted—they call it an attic here. We had a big open fireplace.

We wasn't put out of our land because I had brothers. Some of them was old enough to work and just pay back the rent. Just *exist*, try to exist.

My mother kept house and my father had no work but just the bit of land we had, to work it, and give the cream of the milk to England for everything. They had to get the big rent, and then if the year was bad and the stuff didn't grow, we suffered on that.

The Irish lived under awful stress. I've seen the family thrown out. I recall that distinctly because we took them in our barn. They had no place for their bed, for anything. I seen the little child, this is God's truth, I'll never forget this, it was just about a year and a half, put out in the little cradle. I seen the pots put out and the coals of fire put into the iron oven they used to bake with. Everything that they had, put into the yard. If they were caught in that yard that night they'd be shot or somethin'.

England did this, of course, and her regime. She had certain ones to do it. The landlord, he was English, and the English owned Ireland then.

My father and two other men built about three rooms or so—our barn was big—put all their furniture and their beds and fixed a place for a fire for them. It was six or eight months when they were building. I was five—maybe five and a half, going on six. They hadn't nothing. They hadn't a cow. Everything they had was sold trying to pay the rent. They lived there and he went out to work everywhere he could for a few pennies. Just dragged along until the freedom come.

I had the pleasure of goin' back and seein' the lovely house built by the Irish government. Upstairs and down and everything modern and lovely, right where they were, where my father and the other one built the cabin. And they have land back and operating it all in full bloom. Ever since the new government, everyone got back what was taken away from them. I went back and I was tickled to death. I said, "Well, glory be to God!"

It was *awful hard* on them poor people. There wasn't much and they paid hardly nothing, for they had nothing. England had *everything* they had. She took all their churches and knocked them down and burned them. Took *everything* they had. *Six hundred years* she had Ireland. And now you'd never know.

Trellick was the name of my village and Kinvarra was the next town. We went to school to the convent there, in Galway. But they didn't bother that somehow. They did at first bother the convent and the churches. They wouldn't let you go to church or nothing. In my time there was nothing in that for them, no money in that for them, so they let you go to school.

When I went to school, we couldn't have any shoes; we had to save and give it to the rent. For a while some of them had no stove, course most of them hadn't in the country, just open fireplaces. Some of them had little stoves and grates. They had nothin' to cook in the first place, but were taught to cook. They taught you to make puddin' and custard pie.

There was nuns living at the school. I suppose they had no place to go and they left them there. Nuns, of course, all they do is pray—the poor things—and wear their habits, you know. The nuns didn't hurt them. The nuns used to tell us, "Pray for them to direct them." Instead of cursin' them like most of the Irish done, the nuns said to pray for them. [Laughs.] One girl come home one day. She told her father, "The nuns want us to pray for the English, to direct them." And he says, "If someone knocked them all together I'd be glad to hear it," he said. "Pray for England. Well, pray that she may do justice, which she never done." And, of course, he was angry at that. But he was a man that prayed himself, you know, and wouldn't hurt anyone.

This was goin' down six hundred years—imagine being under anyone's thumb for that length of time! But one consolation, when America opened up. It took an awful lot of needy people here and it opened a gap for them, like God done at sea, otherwise they had to be on their knees for England. Either shoot them or kill them if they went and do the least thing, you'd never see them again. May God forgive them.

It was only about ten dollars or somethin' to come here at that time. It was cheap. I'm here seventy-three years. My sister's here seventy-five. Once she's here she sent for me, see. There was five of us out here.

The one who come here first was a brother, and he would be out here six years, and he went back home. Then there was my sister, who is dead. She died here four or five years ago. She was here many, many years. These sisters of mine died here: Nellie died here, Margaret died here. So I've been alone for many years myself here now. I'm one of twelve in my family and I'm the last one of the twelve.

The trip was very bad. We were sick all the way, throwin' up all the time, throwin' up and, ooh, and the smell of the water and everything. It was awful. But when I went back the last time, it was beautiful. They had beautiful food and everything. 'Course comin' over here and then they couldn't give you much of it.

I came by myself, except you might meet someone on the boat was from nearby, but you wouldn't know them at home. I was eighteen in April, and I come, I think, May or June.

I landed in East Boston, and the man that met me asked me did I know such a girl? "I'm the girl!" I said.

They had a lovely home in East Boston then. He was a blacksmith, and they had one child. They took me from the boat for three or four weeks. Then my uncle's daughter come after me from Natick, and I had the life of Riley for a couple of months. Bought me nice things to wearin'.

I went to Southbridge for a job there. I think the pay was two a week or so—work in the house. Well, of course, the lady was a very nice lady, to be sure. Very fussy. And I told her the circumstances. She said she knew it was terrible. "Wonder the Lord would allow this to go on."

"Well," I says, "it's awful hard to come to that conclusion. Why, we don't know."

She was very nice. She made two or three nice dresses for me, but oh she used to have a lot of company! She said I had a natural ability for cooking. [Laughs.] I said, "I had nothing to cook home," I said. "The milk and potatoes and whatever you have," I said.

I'm sorry I experienced that because it was too bitter.

I worked there about a year, and then I come back to Worcester,

Catherine Moran McNamara

where my aunt was. I went to work in a factory, it's in Framingham now, with the paper napkins. I done pretty good there, made five or six dollars a week, just to press your foot and cut the paper napkins. They still run it—big pay now. But then it wasn't bad either, you would make five or six a week and that was great. And the board was only three. You had three or four dollars for yourself. I was there for a year, I think. It was a nice factory. You could sit down and just count the napkins, see. But then if you would've put too much napkins in, they didn't like it, and you didn't put enough in, they wouldn't like it. So you had to be careful to count the dozen in each roll and roll it up. It was a nice job.

Then I went back to housework and stayed there for a few years. Nice people. This lady and her mother and her husband. She was very nice. I could go out every night, every afternoon if I want to. It was right in the plain streets of Southbridge. They paid only then two dollars a week to the maid of the house. Two and three. For three you had to be a great cook and everything. But now they have to pay sixty and their own room and none of this *scrub* work. Now I guess the workin' girls is in with the union, like. Hahaha. A long road that hasn't a turn in it, very long, You have to go a long road before you'll be turnin' somewhere.

How did you meet your husband?

Oh, at a dance. I forget now. I think 'twas a wedding.

He had a pretty good job, my husband. He was a nice fella, the Lord have mercy on him. Nice lookin'.

He was a boilermaker—they haven't got them now at all—in the roundhouses. They've cut them all out. It's all now some invention of electricity or some other method they have. In Lowell, had a round-house, big, round, and inside it with the boilers that was comin' in, the boilers that was goin' long distances be leakin'. They had to go in sometimes. I seen his skin burned. Then they had to go again on some other place. Their morale gone for years.

We lived first in Somerville. He got a better job with the same company in Lowell. In Lowell he had the six days, and after he went to church, he could work Sundays. On Sundays they would get more pay. We lived there for seven or eight years. I was all alone out there. Then I come back with my sisters in Boston. The last place we lived was in Somerville.

I was married in January and in next November I had my boy. He's still my boy. He don't look forty, but he's sixty-six. Six I had. I buried one with diphtheria. Two years old she was.

I had an interest that my children would do well, and I made my own bread, to cook and everything, and to clean my house and do all the work like that. They went to high school, but it was a pity because they were pretty bright, the two boys. They didn't have any desire to go to college, but they would go if I could afford it, but I couldn't afford it. Had no money.

I had four daughters, but they just sew a button, fix a dress. They went to high school, that's all. They hadn't any great ability, you know, just ordinary. They could make a dress and fix a dress and like that, and they're married. One of them lost her husband ten years ago. Left her with four—three boys and a girl.

The boy that died last year on me, oh God be with him, he was lovely. He had a time with cancer. Poor fella, he was just a fireman, but he could have been the head of the firemen, but he wouldn't take it. Humility was his motive. He was so humble. He was sixty years, but he was single; he never married, never went with a girl. He lived with me, but he's dead and buried here, over a year. He was a *wonderful* son. He sent me to Ireland.

My son went over, the one that died of the cancer, gave them one thousand dollars for the ones that's gettin' their freedom—oust the Orangemen, we call 'em. They're fine with England, you know, oh, first-class.

He'd give to charity. Protestants and Catholics alike he'd give to. "Ed," I says one time to him, "you givin' more to the Protestants, I think." "When a Protestant child is hungry," he says, "they are hungry as a Catholic child." And that is God's truth I'm tellin' you now, he had a bag this width—thank-you notes from every organization.

My husband died forty years ago. I could've married again if I wanted to in a year after. God no. I didn't want to. It was in the family, none of them ever married again.

I had five—one died with diphtheria as a baby. This is a strange thing, but God is my judge, that I never had any more desire for sex than that spread that's on the bed there. That's the comparison. I had three years between them. I had five years between the two boys, yet I had six 'cause I married young, twenty-two. But I didn't have 'em through desire. My sister said, "You're a liar. You couldn't have them if you didn't." I told the doctor that. "Oh, yes, you can," he said. "At certain times," he says. "Oh, yes, you can."

There was a time was terrible if a girl had a child. God help us. There was some woman goin' through a farm one time, I remember. Someone took advantage of her. Everyone knew they did, but still it used to be thrown at her, a life obstacle. That's sad. Not so now. They just have every privilege the men have and they have their jobs and they're gettin' back their own.

Oh, forever she'd be down. It would be terrible disgrace if she had a baby, terrible forever. But the old man could go around and marry any girl. They had a terrible lot. Some of them that take a dose of salts after get rid of it, some can't no matter what they do.

The pill? Don't you know dang well they have all those things in Ireland now, too. Dublin, my dear, was always pretty smart in that way.

Were you ever involved in politics?

I wasn't interested in them things at all. I had nothin' to gain from them, whatever I had to lose. [Laughs.] Ah, they was lovely when they was running for office, but then they give themselves away when they got the office. I'll never forget the one time I was lookin' for a job for a friend and this fella that I done so much for him, helped him a little bit financially, said, "Oh, ten minutes now, I'm due in Boston."

"Ain't it funny," I says, "You get elected, you're always due in someplace, to get away from the party that ye owe the obligation to or the favor." I says, "How convenient. I know that story."

"Do you?" he said. Then he starts laughin'. "Tell the truth," he says, "this is a bluffin'. They tell you to say that."

"Ah," I said, "If I tell you to go steal something, and you'll do it? You'll be dishonest in your word, your action is similar." But he was a nice fella. He's dead now. I don't have nothing at all to do with them now. I've just got the old agin'.

Were you a member of the Church?

I went to my own church, Catholic Church. We were all Catholics. They went to Saint Joseph's School, my children. And the boys, they had the Brothers then teachin' them, which was great teachers.

The Irish is brought up as good Catholics, good God-fearin' people. No matter how poor they were, they went on their knees every night and say the rosary, I remember that. We *never* seen a night when the rosary wasn't said in our house.

They had great faith, and they held the faith. Just like the Irish have suffered for the faith. Terrible too. The English wanted them all to abandon it. Did you know they used to burn their churches? If they'd be caught goin' to churches, they'd be jailed and shot dead one at a time. Imagine what my father seen when he was small. Imagine. He wouldn't describe it.

Of course the ordinary people in England couldn't help that. There's some very nice people, English, decent people, and there's some good people to work for. This is the government. They're like God, you know. That's the way they are with the kings and sirs and all. That's all folly, vanity—of the most foolish degree. That had to be *upheld* in Ireland. They had to take their hats off, and any Irishman wouldn't do it, they'd be jailed. Most of them wouldn't. I hope God will forgive them, because after all how could you help what your grandfather done? Their great-great-. What good is it for me to have someone else suffer? I think it's no good.

NICHOLAS GERROS—
Greek Horatio Alger

Nicholas Gerros first came to Cincinnati, Ohio, from a rural village in Macedonia in 1912. He arrived young and poor, and in his lifetime became the owner of a $300,000-a-year clothing business.

Greek immigration to the United States began in large numbers after 1890. The majority of Greeks were young men who left rural areas such as Macedonia that were still under the rule of the Ottoman Turks. They left Greece mainly for economic reasons. The area was poor, family obligations many. Brothers had to pay for their sisters' dowries before they could start their own families. Taxes were high under both Turkish and Greek rule and debts in the rural setting constant. Some young Greek men planned to go to America and then return to their native land, rich and respected. Between 1900 and 1930 a large percentage did in fact return to Greece. Greek men also emigrated to escape Turkish conscription. In 1908 the Ottoman Empire began to require military service for non-Turks. The historical oppression Greeks experienced under Turkish rule did not make this prospect a pleasant one.[1]

Immediately after Mr. Gerros arrived in the United States, his father returned to Macedonia. Those first years of the Balkan Wars were peak years of return to Greece, and national recruitment within Greek-American communities for this war of emancipation was common.[2]

While many of the Greeks who settled in the United States moved into Chicago and New York, after some years in Cincinnati, Gerros moved to Haverhill, a small factory town in northeastern Massachusetts. There were over seven hundred Greeks living in Haverhill by 1908,[3] and in the nearby city of Lowell an Eastern Orthodox Church was built in 1893. Small clubs, coffeehouses, and pan-Hellenic organizations became popular in most Greek-American communities by World War I and served as social gathering places for young Greek émigrés.

In the years following the Armistice, many new national organizations were formed by Greek-Americans. Mr. Gerros was a local president of AHEPA, the American Hellenic Educational Association, one of the most important ones. Organizations and business play a key role in Nick Gerros's life. His other memberships and offices include the Kiwanis Club, board chairman of the Haverhill YMCA, president of the Haverhill Chamber of Commerce, and chief coordinator of fundraising for the town's Greek community center. He and his wife also worked with Greek War Relief Aid and AHEPA to funnel funds into Greece during the Fascist occupation.

Among all immigrant groups there were Horatio Algers, men who believed that with hard work they could become successful in America. Nick Gerros "made it" in American terms, but never forgot his Greek origins.

September 20, 1975
Cambridge, Massachusetts

My mother died when I was nine years old. My aunt and my uncle took care of me. I had a brother who was three or four years younger, then still another brother when my mother died of childbirth.

My father was in the United States previously to my coming here. He moved to Cincinnati, Ohio. When I came to the United States, I came direct to Cincinnati. I came alone with other boys in a similar age bracket with me, from the same village—Menopilon in the Macedonian part of Greece, Kastoria province.

The way life in the village was the men always had to go out of their homes into other lands to make a living, come back, stay with the family a length of time till the money was gone. They used to have little farms around, that didn't produce enough to live on, so naturally they had to go to other countries. My father had been working in industry. They have some farming in Macedonia, but he was in lumber. When he came here he sent for me, sent me money and everything else.

I was at that time fourteen years old. Our village was 'way up in the mountains. We didn't use anything with wheels to carry things. We always loaded the backs of different animals. When I went to get my passport at this Kastoria place was the first time I saw a wagon with wheels. From there on we went south to Thessalia. We stopped in the city by the name of Trikkala. From there we left for Athens.

We were in Athens about three or four days. I was with some distant relatives, no brothers, but they were all the same age. They were all leaving Greece for the same purpose. There were about half a dozen or so of us. On the boat we stopped in Naples. We were there about a week some reason or other. It was just like a big armory, just plain buildings, not much accommodations. I remember reading all kind of writings on the wall, how bad this place was, get away from it as soon as you can. Some were in Greek and some were in Yugoslavian, all kinds of languages. Then we got into an Italian boat by the name of *Saint Georgio.* It took us two weeks from Italy. We left the village March first; we left Greece March 15; then we arrived in New York April 15. It was a little rocky. Most were a little seasick. I was a little seasick, not too much.

We got to New York, a place they call in Greek *Castn Gare;* in English it's comething called Castle Island.[1] We used to unload there. From there we go for examination, for eyes, for sickness of all kinds so it would not get into the United States. We stayed there couple of days, I think.

The first thing shown to us was some [church] pamphlets written in English. We couldn't read them. Some man came along. He gave us a box containing food of some kind, a little bit of everything, and [a nurse] gave us the food and a Bible.

We had a ticket on us because we couldn't speak English. They look at you and tell you, you go there, or you go there. Traveling was easy because it was prearranged by the agents. We took a small boat from New York to Norfolk, Virginia. Some of us went somewhere else. I remember three or four of us was together, all young men and boys. We were waiting on the train and begun to look in the package to see what we had. Each of us had a banana to go with the rest of the food that was given him. We didn't know how to eat it. We'd never seen bananas. Finally somebody realizes that on the train and showed us.

When we went to Cincinnati, there were some people there waiting for us. They showed us [how] to go direct to the apartment. When we got into this apartment they treated us with ice cream. It was the first time we all had ice cream. These people before us organized a room for us. There were more than a half-dozen rooms and a big kitchen.

I stayed with my father for a while, for all the while he was there. He was working in something concerning furniture. Just before the Balkan War started, he went back to Greece.

Those years there were no Greek woman coming to the United States. Mostly all the Greeks were young, between twelve and thirty. They had to kinda stick together because none of them knew any more of the English language than they did themselves.

I remember how hard—this you can put with a line under the words because they mean so much. The young people in America, they've got it so easy and they don't know how easy it is. I was asked to go out to buy something. I think I was in this country for two months. It was late spring. It was still cold, and I had to go down from the second floor. There were stairs going right straight down to the door. There was a bunch of young fellows there talking to each other and having a lot of fun. I was their age, but I couldn't speak any English. I didn't want to get into any trouble with them so they're sitting down on the stairs and I tried to pass by to go do what I wanted to do. I didn't want to step on their clothes, so I was kind of careful and they realized that. One fellow, he wasn't sitting down, he was talking to a girl. I didn't know what he was saying. As far as I was concerned, any language was English to me. The only thing I could speak was Greek. I surmise now that he told me, "Let's have some fun with this fellow." So he came to me and talked, "Blah blah." The first thing I know he gives me one upper cut and down I went.

Right in front of there was a bakery shop. This man is selling bread as well as cakes. He came out and the kids run away. He took me in. He asked me if I was hurt. Well, I [looked] and there was no blood so I says I wasn't hurt.

Right there and then I made up my mind. I'm going to go to school nights, learn the language, read, write, and spoken, and go to the YMCA to prepare myself to defend myself.

Here the oldest boy is supposedly boss of the rest of us living in this particular apartment. It is up to him, the rules and regulations and how to behave. The boy was about ten, twelve years older than I was. The older ones felt certain responsibility for the younger ones. They thought that they should keep us as close to them as possible, possibly as ignorant of life in the United States as possible. They thought that everything in the United States was out of proportion, was too free. They thought that I was going to school because there were girls. There *were* girls, from other countries because they moved here, from Hungary, from Italy, from Austria. So when I announced it to the crowd what I was gonna do was go to school and go to YMCA they told me, "Look, you didn't have a YMCA in the village where you come from. What do you want to go to YMCA for?"

"Exercise, take baths, and meet people."

"No, you can't go."

"Can I go to night school?"

He said, "No, you can't go to night school." He said, "You don't go there for an education, you go there because girls are there."

I says, "No." I says, "I learned my lesson. I go there for an education." And I remember, he tried to stop me.

He says, "You can't go. You have to be in bed at nine o'clock, the latest."

I says, "I can't be [in] at nine o'clock because school doesn't end until nine o'clock or quarter past. Then it takes me time to walk from there to here. The earliest I can be is nine-thirty."

He says, "I don't care what time it takes. As far as I'm concerned, you shouldn't go."

For the first night I went and I found the door closed. I made a lot of noise and he opened up and we had a big verbal fight and he says, "Well, I'll let you in this time, but tomorrow, nine o'clock."

I couldn't get back. I came late, same thing. I was the only rebel. He told everyone not to say a word to anybody and to keep on pretending they were asleep. I knocked on the door and nothing. I knocked and knocked. So I looked around and there's an old broken-up chair in the hall and I says, "There's an old broken-up chair here. I'm going to pick it up and break the door down." After that he opened the door and gave me heck. Right there and then I decided to move. Some of the boys came with me and we went to another apartment.

In the meantime, we were working in the shoe shop. They all made a small living in wages at that time. Like for instance, I worked from seven o'clock till six o'clock, and one hour in between for lunch. We got work. We used to take care of ourselves, no mother, no father, no uncles, no aunts, no nothing. You have to earn a living, take care of your clothing. You could eat, cook, and go to school. All this we did together, maybe six of us, but we were all over twelve then, fifteen, fourteen, and to twenty.

After a year or so I was going to school nights in a different school. At that time, TB was the biggest killer of all the diseases, and people were scared stiff no matter if they just coughed a bit. This teacher noticed that I was sweating. She says, "You should go to a doctor." I went to this dispensary. At the end of three weeks they told me there was nothing wrong with me. In the meantime, though, I was totally scared of all this business and lots of my young fellas, they afraid to be with me.

I was determined to get well. I quit my job. I had saved some money. The salaries those years were $4.75 to $7.50 a week. Image what you had to figure on to eat. I also shined shoes on Sundays to make some extra money. We applied ourselves to the necessity of times.

I left those boys. I left them because first of all they didn't want me anyway because they were afraid and then because they didn't contribute anything to my life. Then I went to the farm. I figured I would get well out in the open. I was going to get well in spite of anybody. I used to take a trolley in Cincinnati, go the end of the line and get out and walk out on a farm. I remember I used to go out on both sides of Cincinnati. Cross the Ohio River from Cincinnati and you are in Kentucky. I went there just at the beginning of World War I. I stayed there on [different] farms until April or May the following year.

I had a cousin in Manchester, New Hampshire. She knew I was there and she wrote to me and she says, "Come here." She says, "The climate is better in New England. You come here and you be better off." So I came to Manchester, New Hampshire, and I got a job in one of the shoe factories.

When I lived in Manchester I used to love the men's clothing business. Even in Cincinnati I used to admire the good clothing stores and look at the way they kept their merchandise. That was my idea—sometimes to have my own business. When I come to Manchester, I went to get a job in a store, part-time. They were hard to get, those jobs. I went to this place to a German. He said, "What can you do?" He says, "Well, I don't need you today." For four or six weeks I went every day for a job. He says to me, "Why do you want a job here?"

I says, "'Cause I like your store".

He asked me more questions and he said, "All right. You can work Thursday evenings and Saturdays." I think it was $1.75 for a week. Three hours on Thursday and eight hours on Saturday. Then he went up to $2.25, then he went up again. He had me sell on the floor.

In this process I met some people and they told me there were a lot of shops in Haverhill. That was 1917, 1918. I went there and I got a job in the shoe factory and was doing pretty well. I was doing finishing, pressing the shoe all around, finishing the job so it will look nice for the customer. They were all small shoe companies; there were hundreds of them. The foreman maybe Yankee and all that, but mostly Italians, Greeks, Irish, French, and all nationalities. The hours were not bad. Seven o'clock in the morning until twelve, then you go and come back at one, and then one till five. I made a lot of friends here in Haverhill. They were all in just three or four blocks around. We had a center and we felt at home. Lacking a home life, you have to be with people, naturally, and so I stayed in Haverhill. I was in the shoe shop, then I was in the life-insurance business. In Haverhill, I was selling to anybody. I earned quite a lot.

A couple of fellows, one was in a shoe factory and the other had a small business, wasn't doing too well, and they wanted to go into the clothing business. They went in the clothing business and they found they didn't know a damn thing. In fact, they couldn't even speak English very well. I had a *little* experience, more than they had, so they convinced me to go with them. I was making about $75 a week at the insurance and I wanted to go in the clothing business for myself, so I went with them. I had $600 to invest. I put that in there with them. Later one didn't want any part of it any more. We paid him off with $300 and we kept the store between the two of us.

The younger man, he was my age, he didn't care much for the business either. In fact, he didn't know the difference between beautiful and terrible. This is my partner. I was about twenty-two, twenty-three. I told him that if he wanted to sell, to get somebody. So he finally got somebody and he sold his share to him. The new man spoke much better English. They are from one of the good families in Greece.

My dream was a store of some kind. I worked with this man for about three years and I gave him a proposition: "Either you get out of the factory and come with me," I says, "or I have to do it alone." He tried to convince me. He tried the hard way and the easy way. I told him, I says, "The only way we can do it together, we got to be within the family." In the course of talking back and forth for about two weeks, three weeks, in February I said, "Look, the time's late already for spring. We've got to get ready." He says, "All right, you buy me out." I bought him out with $6,750 for his share. From there the business grew up.

I borrowed the money from the bank and I put on a Dissolution of Partnership Sale, and I took in more money than I gave him. I went to the bank and paid 'em up. I had borrowed for five months, and I paid 'em up in five weeks. When I had the big sale on, people were coming in and out. He was across the street watching it and he felt that small, He wanted to buy the place back. Of course, I wouldn't sell.

How did the Depression influence you?

In 1931 [the building was sold and] I had to move to another place. When I moved it was three hundred percent better location. I was paying $150 a month rent and had two people working. The Depression did influence me and I'll tell you why. The prices went down, and I lost some money at that time, not too much. It didn't bother me too much because I was young in the business and I also was young. My future wife, she had to wait quite a few years 'cause I couldn't make up my mind. I wasn't secure enough in my business.

She was from Haverhill. She was born in Greece and came here when she was four years old. She was working for an office where they used to sell oil burners. She was the bookkeeper there. She was an orphan from her father. She came here to this country with her mother alone. She was very, very smart and a good bookkeeper, and had a very good personality. She meets people she makes friends.

Her mother used to come quite often to the store. She got friendly with me and all that business. At that time you couldn't go out with a girl and not be engaged to her. In order to get to know her better, I had to get engaged to her. I used to go up to her office on my break quite often and talk to her. We decided to get married. I proposed to her and to her mother. This was the way it was. I got married in 1935. We had three children, all three girls. We lost the first one. That was also a girl. The years went by and we were associated in the business. She's got a very good business head. She's very easy and she's got the gift of gab. She can really move people and their friends.

Me and my wife, during the World War II we tried to help with Greek relief. The poor people are suffering too much. After the war was over, the people who were with the Nazis were put *back* in power. Why should you award the people who did wrong for the country? That's just what they were doing. The government destroyed the church, bombarded the village, my village where I was born.

In 1946 I went to Florida, St. Petersburg, around there. I was reading the newspapers. I see where a Greek prince was visiting some port in the South and they give him a reception. I wrote a letter to the newspaper criticizing the United States, the government, especially the cities. Why do they do that when we don't believe in kings and princes? It was quite a nice letter.

Naturally I took part in supporting the leftists in Greece. I did all kinds of support. This fellow from Athens was representing the leftist newspaper in Greece. He came to New York to Boston, Boston to Haverhill. I introduced him to the newspaper in Haverhill. The city accepted him for the *Gazette* to go to work for them.

Quite a few years later, they went over to my house, I don't know, FBI, CIA. They said this, "We're going to ask you a few questions regarding the security of the United States. Why you have joined this particular organization?" It was some organization to help poor people when they die so they can be buried.

"Well," I said, "I see no reason why I shouldn't support that."

They said, "But you're not a member of that."

I said, "I know it. I'm not a member." [aside] Because they just didn't know how to organize. "But I see no reason why I shouldn't do it. The United States Constitution doesn't bother me for that."

He says, "Well, you were in Florida such and such a year such and such a month and this is what you wrote in the paper. Why'd you do that?" And one of the men is a Greek. He asked me that question.

"I tell you," I said. "Democracy was instituted first in Greece, and I'm proud of it, and you should be. The United States is a democracy. We don't believe in kings or princes. Why should we give such an honor to them? My Constitution does not tell me anything like that at all." So he shut up.

We sent a lot of stuff to Greece. I had a Greek committee, and we sent four tons of clothing and $6,000 in money during the war. So they called me on that. I said, "Since when does the United States forbid charity?" I wasn't afraid. "I'll do this right over again," I said. "I see nothing to stop me from doing this." They run out of questions so I say, "If you people got anything else, out with it fast because I work all day long here and I want to go out to get my supper." They never bothered me again.

What ever happened to your store?

In 1936 we changed the name to my own name—Gerros' Mens' Shop Incorporated.

I don't have the business today. I work part-time now. I was in business with the other fellow, it was $12,000 dollars for the year. When I got out of the business, it was $300,000 dollars a year. Some difference.

To what do you attribute your success?

Just hard work—that's all. You gotta be young. When you're young you've got to have ambition with no limit, because otherwise you are satisfied with small aims. You've got to have a challenge, feel inside of you that really you *could* do it without anyone else discouraging you. Don't begin to ask too much advice from people that haven't got that problem in their hands. You've got to listen to them, but do your own decisions. Most of all, you gotta be fair with the people you do business with. Nobody can move you if you are right, and if you know you're right and if you stick to it and fight back. Nobody can move you, no matter how strong they are.

This maybe is the only thing that stopped me from being even better than I am or was, because my dreams were not big enough or long enough. I should have dreamed a bigger business, and I would have had a bigger business. I should have gone to school further when I was much younger. I should have gone to work for a big store, like Jordan's, for instance, for a little while.[2] Go to school, to Harvard, if possible. First of all, you've got to get a goal. You have to have a dream of what you want to be. You can find it. It will take time, like everything else takes time, the sooner you dream the better.

Many immigrants who came when you did didn't do well. Perhaps they had too much to overcome?

No. Let me tell you something. Don't forget, everything in your life. *you decide,* nobody else decides, unless they come with a gun at your head and say, "Look, decide my way or else." Even then you got a choice, either die or do what he says. [Laughs.] You see what I mean? But most of the time you're free to decide. Everything else we bring as alibis, that's all. They can't stop you from going on your own.

There was discrimination on account of different nationalities. They did discriminate, no doubt about it. There is a Greek organization in America called AHEPA, the American Hellenic Association. I was chairman of that, president in my city for about a year. At that time, as I told you before, there was too many Greek boys from twelve years old to thirty. Well, naturally they would be interested in girls. They couldn't speak English, and they certainly didn't meet the right kind of girls anyway, and they created a very ill name in the United States. With so much against 'em at that time they decided that they couldn't get justice anywhere, even if they were right. Certain people began to think what should we do? They organized this AHEPA. They did that to offset those impressions that the American people had. This same thing happened with all the nationalities at that time. Naturally, there were some obstacles, but listen, we have rainy days and we have sunny days and how we gonna know the difference if we didn't have them both?

You were born poor, so what? But it's all up to you. You're free to do what you want. You've got to gain it within the law. Not only political law, but natural law. You've got to know the truth. This is what I say to my daughters because they expect things to be easy; they don't want to sacrifice much. We spoiled 'em. There is actually nothing in life that you cannot do if you plan it, but it takes time.

PHILIP AND THERESA BONACORSI—
Children of the Lawrence Strike

Pan e lavoro—bread and work: these were the forces that propelled millions rooted in the peasant life of southern Italy to journey to America. Leaving Italy was not desired, but for the peasants, artisans, and urban poor of the *contadini* class it was a matter of family survival.

Of the over five million Italians to come to these shores between 1876 and 1930, eighty percent were from the south, the Mezzogiorno.[1] In Italy's history, the south was something of a stepsister; northerners often considered southerners racially inferior people whose territory was good for annexation and exploitation. After the unification of Italy in the mid-nineteenth century the south was alternately ignored and terrorized into subservience. In the last quarter of the nineteenth century *contadini* income went down, population went up,[2] and the cost of living doubled. As life became economically more precarious, nature contributed to the disasters besetting the *contadini* families. Volcanoes, earthquakes, and tidal waves struck southern Italy in 1906 and 1908. Land continued to pass from the hand of the *contadini* to the control of the *signori,* or gentry. The dying economy left the *contadini* both landless and jobless. Deprived of any means of subsistence and intent on preserving their families and whatever they could salvage of their way of life, millions of *contadini* decided to send their menfolk to the Americas.[3] In 1907, the peak year for Italian immigration to the United States, over seventy-five percent entering were men and boys between the ages of fourteen and forty-five.[4]

The families of Philip and Theresa Bonacorsi were part of that *contadini* migration. The Bonacorsis have lived virtually all of their lives in or near Lawrence, Massachusetts. Philip was born in Sicily in 1902 and came to Lawrence with his family at the age of two. Theresa Campagne was born in Lawrence in 1905, her father having come from Sicily in 1900 or 1901 to work in the Lawrence textile mills. The rest of the extended family followed about a year later. In both Philip's and Theresa's families fathers or uncles came first, the rest of the family followed. Many other Italian men who came returned to Italy or went to Italy in the fall and came to the United States in the spring to work on the railroads or in construction.[5]

Lawrence is one of several once-important mill cities along the Merrimac River. The mill towns, with their growing foreign-born populations, produced the textiles which fed mostly into New York, making the United States a highly productive ready-made clothing producer. The New England mill system as it developed after the Civil War utilized the "family system," in which immigrant men, women, and children all worked, and some of the worst abuses in the history of American child labor occurred. Almost everyone in the Campagne and Bonacorsi families worked in the Lawrence mills.

When Philip and Theresa were children, one of the most important strikes in American labor history occurred in the city of Lawrence. In 1912 Lawrence had a population of 86,000, of whom approximately 60,000 worked in the mills. The immediate but not underlying cause of the strike occurred in January when the American Woolen Company's hour and pay cuts to men, women, and children hit nearly every working family in the city. This cut was accompanied by long-standing grievances caused by low pay and poor working conditions at the Lawrence mills: malnutrition, abnormally high infant mortality, rickets, and premature death, plus patterns of work and hiring systems that encouraged favoritism and exhaustion. Between one-sixth to one-third of the mill workers were Italian. There were over twenty-five other nationalities involved in the strike.[6] It was the first major American strike in which foreign workers were organized, in which the revolutionary Industrial Workers of the World (IWW, or Wobblies) were the organizing union, and where women and children played a vital role. The strike was won after two months.

I spoke with Theresa and Philip Bonacorsi in their ranch house in Methuen, Massachusetts. Listening to their story, it was clear that the strikes and struggles of their childhood continued for many years after the country forgot Lawrence.

When I asked, "How many children did you have?" Theresa replied, "One, but there was a whole family structure, nephews, and nieces." "Funny," said Philip, "her father with two wives had twenty; my father had fourteen. . . . You gotta remember this. When you go through Depression like we did, hard times like we did, the fear, you know, of trying to do something. . . . Bring another kid, God sakes, you don't even know if you can feed this one."

March 23, 1975
Methuen, Massachusetts

Philip: My father was from Trecastagne, which is a small town near the province of Catania. My mother was born in Catania. My father carried merchandise from town to town and then became a middleman. In those days they used to do a lot of bartering. He used to get a commission.

He had some people who were here in this country and he figured it was a better place to come and make a living. Plus one time my father had beat up the mayor of the town. Some woman was crying that the mayor owed her money for her husband's work and he didn't want to pay, so my father gave him a lickin'. It might have had something to do with it. But he came here because he could make a better living.

He had a big family. When he left he had seven children. Then, of course, there were seven more when he came to this country.

Theresa: My mother came from Termini, a small city in the province of Palermo. My father died when I was a little girl, ten years old. My father came from Leonforte in the province of Syracuse. He was a shoemaker. He had a little shop, but I guess there wasn't enough money. When he used to make a pair of shoes, if they were a farmer, they'd give him food.

My father came here first. I don't know how he landed in Lawrence— I guess like everybody else. The mills were just starting at that time. The Wood Mill was the biggest whole mill in the world at that time. It must have been a couple of years later or so when my mother came. They had two children. He left them in Italy with the intention, like everybody else, that they were going to make some money and return. But that didn't happen; they never returned. I was born here.

Philip: I started work when I was eleven and a half years old. I was born in 1902. It was about 1913 when I started work. You could work if you were thirteen years old and forty weeks. You were supposed to be fourteen, but they used to discount vacation time, the summertime. Now when you came from Italy and you've got brothers or sisters working, we used to work with *their* papers. Like I worked with my older brother's papers. He was two years older than I. He worked with my older brother's papers. The only one who worked with his own papers was the oldest one. Then there was always eighteen months or two years between us.

At the time they used to work fifty-four hours, so we used to work forty-eight. You think that's much. My father used to work sixty hours when they came to this country. We never used to see him till Saturday afternoon.

People congregated together because of the language barrier. They can't go in and buy something. So they go with their own communities.

Theresa: The Naples people and the Sicilian, they kind of stayed by themselves. The Sicilian took the section of Lawrence near the lower end, near the Everett Mills. And the Naple people took over the side after the Common. Then there was this thing that the Naple mothers would say, "Don't go over there! There's all the Sicilians." And the Sicilian mothers, "Don't bother with them, they're Naple people. You know how they are!" Us children, we didn't know any better, so we just stayed together. [Laughs.] The rest of Lawrence was all different groups. The Polish people was congregated by themselves, the Lithuanian, the Syrians.

Philip: Everybody lived close. Kids died of diphtheria, measles, tuberculosis. In them days they were poor, but believe me, they understood each other. They were friendly to each other; one had a problem, they all felt it. They were very close, helpin' each other any way they could. Families were pretty good size, of course, but there was always somebody sick, or dying and dead. All you could hear was women cryin' because a child died. I remember one time there was eight of us laid up, but we came out all right. We were pretty lucky; I know whole families who were completely wiped out. In those days there used to be big homes, three tenements. But they had yards between them. In the summer the men used to put a table out there, play cards, rush in for a can of beer—the only thing they could do. They never had no money. We were lucky we never went hungry, eh, Theresa? A lot of 'em did. I don't know how my father did it. They were tough times.

My mother never worked. My father worked in the Everett Mill a short time only, and it figures why. He stopped as the boys start workin'. My father was always feeding. We had sixteen to feed, plus we had always a cousin or something in the house. So there would always be eighteen people to feed. I always remember my father with one of these orange boxes on his back, goin' to the store to buy food. And every day he'd be with a box. And for my mother there was the cooking, the washing, and the laundry.

I went to four grades in four different schools in Lawrence. As the family got bigger, we'd have to move, so I was always in a different district. In high school I *quit.* What happened was we were workin' overtime at Davis and Ferber's Machine Shop since my family could use the money. I went back to work, which was a mistake I made; I should have gone back to school.

What do you remember of the Lawrence Strike?

Philip: There was a strike in 1912; there was one in 1919; there was one in '22; there was one in '31; and there was one in '41.

Theresa: The worse one was 1912 and 1919.

Philip: Yes, 1912 was the worst. It hit a lot of people. Things were really tough. See, I was ten years old. I remember I had to read the paper for my father. I remember the bread lines. On Common Street they set up a place for the strikers. They used to give 'em a loaf of bread and some salt pork. That's what you had to have to eat. Things were pretty damn bad.

Theresa: I remember one woman coming to my mother, not that we were rich, but my father had a store, so it was a little bit different. Coming to my mother, she says, "How can I just eat this?" Bread and salt pork. My mother was always cookin' so she gave her a hot dish of whatever it was.

And that strike was in the winter months. It was terrible. The Polish were used to cold more than the people that came from southern Europe. Half of 'em weren't provided with warm clothes.

I was going to the first grade or second grade at the Walton School. I remember there were the cops there, with the bayonets. When you're a child if there is a soldier or a cop near you, you feel so safe, and they didn't do anything to anybody.

My father had the store. It was like a clubroom mostly because he had pool tables and he had a couple of tables to play cards, and then in the front of the store he had this showcase with sweets, candy, chewing gum. On the other side there used to be a shoeshine parlor—this is all in the same store. The store was opened till late; but when the strike happened, he had to close very early.

Philip: There was a curfew.

Theresa: In fact, not even two people could be in the same spot. We had to close all the curtains so there wouldn't be no light showing out. We had two large rooms; one was for us, the children, and one was for my father and mother, and always a little one besides, in the same bedroom. At that time my mother was so scared to be alone with just us that she put the two beds together in one room. She locked the outside door and then locked the bedroom door. Even though we had no connections with the strike, we had the effect of it, with all these things going on.

Philip: I don't remember too much, only my older brother was very active. He was one of these guys they used to call, not comrade, socialists. He was a Wobbly. He was eleven years older than I was.

That 1912 strike, the Italians were pretty strong. They were really the spearheads of that strike, but every group—the Polish had their area meetings, the French had their meetings, and the Lithuanians. The Italians were picketing, and going to homes, "Don't go to work or you'll get your head bashed in."

Theresa: We were all with the strike. One of the things I remember—of course, this was with the later strike, 1919—they decided *not* to send the children to school so that [the company] would give in. I don't know what the purpose of that was. I wanted to go to school, but one morning my brother says that we should stay home and we didn't go. Right away the teachers knew *why.*

One of the incidents I remember very well was when my sister made a dress for me. The material was a khaki dress; it was on the same line as a uniform, only there was a skirt and there was a blouse with a belt. She had all these buttons of the IWW. They used to screw on. So she thought she'd use them, but not with the exposed part, with the IWW— with the other side, the brass.

When I was at school, everybody admired the dress. The teacher sent me from one room to another. "What a beautiful dress!" For some reason, things get unscrewed by themselves. One button unscrewed and the side with the IWW fell on the floor of the school. Somebody picked it up. I think it was the teacher in my room that got hold of it. She wanted to know "Who had that button! Where's the button!" She looked around. She has an idea she saw my brass buttons on my dress. "Where did you get this?"

I said, "I don't know. My sister made the dress and they were around so she used them."

That sort of made it bad. There was an embarrassment there all the time.

Philip: I remember some beatings in picket lines, 1919 strike. Some of them were scabs; the strikers were beatin' 'em. Some of the strike-breakers were with the cops. Oh yeah, there were clubbin's.

You know what I was makin' when I worked forty-eight hours? I started out after the strike, I'll never forget, $5.03. But wages had got *better* when I got in. Because during the 1912 strike things got better.

Theresa: The inside of all this—the 1912 strike—the people a little older than us know better.

Philip: Many are not alive.

Do you remember when you first started working?

Philip: I first started work at the Wood Worsted Mill, which was the biggest mill. I got fired in one week. I was an oiler boy, oiling up the machines. What do you think I got fired for? I'll never forget. I was only a boy, eleven and a half. American Woolen had a building here and another building here—there was like a big space in between. I borrowed a mirror from one of the girls there, and I was just flashing it on the other building with the sun. What the hell. And he fired me for that. This man Constantino, his father picked up the section hand and he threw him [pushing his hands] for firing me. He quit too. Well, he knew he was going to get fired or arrested.

Theresa: I remember then that people would just leave their jobs at noontime and go look for a job at the other mill.

Philip: The Italians used to say *a'look'are*, to look for another job. Well, I did that many times. I was always lookin' for a better job. I came to the Ayer Mill and I became an oiler boy. It was the same company but different mills. All I had to do was put oil in the motors at the back. Them days there weren't electrical motors. I'd oil the rollers.

I started work in the Arlington Mills after the '22 strike, 'cause I wanted to get in and learn my trade. Before the union, they used to have what they call a pink slip. I don't mean a firing slip. This was a record that they used to keep on every worker. Does he drink?

Theresa: The CIA. [Laughs.]

Philip: Does he go to church? Does he have any bad habits? How does he work? Doe he talk unionism? Big lists like that. But we never knew that. Even in the thirties. We got to know when a friend of mine was in the office. They kept a record. And you know, from what I've heard, they used to pass that in between different companies.

They played rough.

Philip: [Softly.] Sons of bitches.

Theresa: I was sixteen when I started work. I was born in 1905. We started at $15.55 for forty-eight hours. We used to work Saturday for four hours, then they stopped that. I worked there, and I worked in the same place until it shut down, and then from there I went to work in a sewing factory, men's clothing.

At American Woolen I used to do spooling. It's when the threads come out. They've been twisted; they've been spun; they've been wound on another spool. Then we used to get them and they used to put them on spikes like in forty threads. We had to watch them; it was like an inspection to see that the yarn was all right. While the threads were coming down, if there was any bad yarn, you had to take that out. Then they used to take it to the dressing room. All these threads used to be made into cloth. I worked there right through till they shut down.

The other kids, they were out working. One was working in the shop; he was doing the same thing that my brother Joe was, he was a wool sorter. My older sister she was working in the cotton mill.

We were paid on a piecework basis. [Later] I sewed sleeves. In the woolen mills we started out with hourly pay. But then they started this piecework business. But once you got used to it, you could swing pretty good pay.

Do you remember what the factory conditions were like then?

Philip: This is one thing I always remember. Having a drink of water. In them days, there used to be a faucet on the wall, and the water was terrible. You'd even hate that you'd have to go for a drink, but you'd be so dry.

Theresa: I don't remember drinking. In fact they had these signs, "DO

NOT DRINK THIS WATER." I remember, the water used to be terrible. It was a ten-gallon tank.

Philip: Lighting wasn't as good as it is today, of course, but the ventilation was terrible. They'd have windows they'd open up in the summer. The machines give a lot of heat. You sweated enough. Now where she worked, the garments—I used to see 'em through the window—I said, "I wouldn't do that. I'd rather be a burglar than do that." I like always to move around.

I seen some get hurt. I've seen this young Syrian girl, about seventeen. Each machine had a belt. They all had their own pulley. These belts were about maybe four inches wide. And they used to have one where they'd hook all these belts to an iron buckle. They used to join them and whack the points in to hold the belt together. Once in a while they used to break. One broke, the Ayer belt, and it hit this young girl with the buckle right in the eye. I never knew what happened, because I quit right after that. I never knew what ever became of her, whether she lost her eye or not.

I saw one girl, also a Syrian girl, nice girl, combin' her hair. In them days you had five minutes to go and wash before quittin' time and that's it. They used to allow lunchtime, ten minutes, but you had to eat it on the fly, you'd eat it while you're working. Well, this girl was combin' her hair. She was in the spinning room with the little wheels and they caught her hair. It tore her scalp right off. Made me sick to look at her.

And I saw a fellow at the Print Works lose that much of a finger, in the folding room, where your sister worked; he was workin' there. He was jacking rolls. That's a job I had. You see these little rolls of cloth, like bolts, but rolls that you put in the machines, and they're inspected. These iron brackets would stick up like this. Guy would say, "Jack up the rolls!" There was a piece of pipe stickin' out from the rolls, and two men would get a piece of pipe, put it in there, and lift it. This guy's finger even got caught under there. I see it go, chum, just down on the floor.

Do you remember any kind of discrimination against Italian people?

Philip: Oh sure. The Irish worked in the better mills. One time the

Irish weren't allowed at the Arlington Mill, either—there used to be a big sign, just before my time I was told, it's in the history of Lawrence: "IRISHMEN AND DOGS, KEEP OUT!"

Theresa: The better jobs were held by Scotsmen and English, the English especially. They were all the bosses.

Philip: You know why, Theresa? The textile mills were from England, and they figured that nobody could do that but an Englishman. That's the way they felt.

Theresa: I remember some of the bosses from the Wood Mills. There was Barton, Case, Whitehead—all English names, no Italian names. There was probably a few section hands that took care of just a small section of the room; there were some Italians doing that. But bosses, never. Not even till they shut down.

William Wood, he went to Italy and I think he went to Poland, gettin' workers to come over here, which is true. Wages were very small, but they was better than over there.

Philip: In places, if you were an Italian, you'd never get a job.

Theresa: Even in the stores, in the dry-goods stores and things like that, that's how it was. Maybe an occasional one, but maybe the father was a doctor or something. You could number them on your fingers; you couldn't get a sales job, even if you were born in this country.

Philip: You know why they did it eventually? It got to be such a big Italian population, well, they want that business. So they're going to have someone who can relate to them.

Theresa: My sister got a job, she left the Print Works. So she went to get some work in the New England Woolen Mills, the Cunards, which was one hundred percent, I think, Scots and English. So they hired her—because she was light and she could pass. But after they hired her and read the name, the following day they fired her.

Philip: The mills closed in '52. Lawrence was actually dead. It was the best thing that ever happened.

MOSE AND JOE CERASOLI—
Stonecutters in Vermont

Thomas (Mose) and Joseph Cerasoli, first cousins, were born in Abruzzi, Italy. Their fathers were both stonecutters. Joe was five years old when he came to Websterville, Vermont, in 1901. His father had come in 1899 and then sent for his mother and their three children. The family moved from East Barre to Barre in 1911. Mose arrived about 1905 at age six or seven. Both Mose and Joe began work grinding tools in the sheds at fourteen. By fifteen they were being trained as stonecutters.

Granite was Barre's major industry. Cutting stone became a profitable industry in the 1880s and continued to be even more so with the greater use of the railroad. Scottish workers were the first major group to cut stone in Barre in those years; they were later joined by Swedish, Italian, and Spanish cutters. In 1886 the Granite Cutters International was organized. By 1900 there were fifteen local unions in Barre. By 1907, 1,750 cutters belonged to the International.[1] This was the union for which Mose and Joe later became organizers.

During the early years of the twentieth century, the Italian population of Barre grew to one-third of the town's population. Unlike the Cerasolis, many of these Italians were from northern provinces: Tuscany, Lombardy, Venetia.

The Italian-Americans I spoke with were working people, brought up in an era of violent strikes and horrendous working conditions. They talked of the men and women like Elizabeth Gurley Flynn, Eugene Debs, Joseph Ettor, Arturo Giovannitti, and Bill Haywood, people they remembered speaking at rallies on their town commons or in their public halls. Even so, the stigma of radicalism from the McCarthy years made politics difficult to discuss. Mose briefly and sadly mentioned a union man who committed suicide after blaming himself for a tactical error resulting in the loss of a five-month strike, and the role of anti-communism in the 1950s in purging the union. But these issues were not dwelt upon.

Mose began by talking of the first strikes in which his parents were involved. Many times the family survived only on potatoes and flour brought to them by the union. Some strikes were for higher pay, and some were related to the installation of a pneumatic tool called a "bumper," brought into the Northfield sheds in 1908. In 1910 the workers of Northfield refused to use bumpers and were locked out of their jobs. His father and other workers were against these tools as they discovered that along with the increased speed in which jobs could be accomplished, the machines brought on silicosis, a dangerous lung disease caused by breathing certain quartz particles.[2]

Vermont stonecutters suffered a terrible mortality rate. "Workin' by hand you got more dust. The old days, ya know, lotta stonecutters died of TB. Silicosis. You got dust in your lungs. My father was one of 'em," Joe said. "My father committed suicide because of work," added Mose."There were seven of us in one year; all went to cut stone about the same time. . . . I'm seventy-seven, and the oldest one that lived was forty. . . . They all died."

Joe, Mose, and I met together upon two occasions on Joe's front porch in Barre. Occasionally Cordelia, Joe's wife, would join us. Joe rocked back and forth in his chair. His eyesight was poor. He usually listened to Mose, the latter being the more excitable and talkative of the two. When Joe spoke it was with a rather laconic, distinctively up-country Vermont twang. Both are retired. Mose lives with his second wife in Lake Placid, Florida.

July 18 and 24, 1975
Barre, Vermont

Joe: I was fifteen years old in April and I went to work for Joe Martell grindin' tools. This was in August. Come Christmas my boss, French-man, Martell, said to me, "My boy, how'd ya like to cut stone?" I said I'd have to ask my father. I asked my father and my father said, "What else you gonna' do 'round here?" I cut stone till 1960; I'm retired fifteen years now. We worked in the sheds.

Mose: In other words, we were skilled men. They brought the stone by cars or trucks or railroad, even horses. Stonecutters lived from hand to mouth. They worked four, five months, then they'd be laid off.

I think the Italians came from a more militant background. Remember what helped color their ideas. If it wasn't them, it was their fathers, and grandfathers had fought in the revolution, about the time of the Civil War.[1] That war, if it went against the established hierarchy, had to be against the Catholic Church because they owned most of Italy, as well as Austria and France. They had become radical in those days so their ideas were much advanced.

Joe: You know, in the old days, down here some big guy go down to the stone shed, he asked for a job, he couldn't get one, because he was Italian. Scotsmen wouldn't work with Italians. I'm talkin' back, fifty, sixty, seventy years ago. But now them people all dead. I travel 'round with all nationalities myself. We all good friends. We never think of that, callin' each other dirty Wop. You ever hear that word? Dagos? Dirty Wops? Ol' Frenchmen? But now you don't hear that no more. The young people got more education.

Mose: The bitterness was more basic than that. The background of that particular kind of hatred was in the working, in the plants. That's a story in itself. Of course, I don't know whether the background of this sort of stuff was something that was cooked up, figured out by the employing group, or that's the way it worked anyway. There was always jealousy between them. Just like they started fear, hatred, as much as they could, between blacks and whites today. There'd been fights and struggles where there was turmoil in this town. People were, well, they were driven out. Dozens and dozens of stonecutters could not come back in here and get a job. They were blacklisted. I think the worst of this started after the First World War. But it was awful bad before. Remember the fights on the street?

Joe: Yeh, sure.

Mose: Well, this has something to do with one of the strikes for better conditions. You can correct me. I think this will give you an idea, because this started much sooner than the First World War. Something that wasn't healed for years. There was bitterness in this town.

The way that it started, the A. F. of L., they were out on strike, before World War I. [The workers] had been loafin'[2] a little while, but this has happened other times too. Finally a meetin' was called to take a vote on whether they'd accept the latest offer by the granite manufacturers, or whether they'd reject it. It was basically wages. They voted to return to work, to accept the conditions. It seemed to be the Anglo-Saxon section that voted to go back under their terms, in those days, a cent an hour, or two or three cents an hour. A cent or two an hour was a big win. Who ever heard of twelve cents?

It seemed at that time, however, a clean split. The Italians, in the vast majority, refused, not only refused to accept that decision, but called it a sellout. It wasn't exactly money, it was a lot of things besides that. So finally, they were going to take another vote, on whether to go back to work or not.

I remember that day very well and maybe you do too. They voted in the hall. It was on Main Street here just below the post office, on the same side, third story up, 'cause you remember when the fight started on the stairs. Then we were to have the whole membership vote. For the sake of becoming more accurate, we'll call it the Anglo-Saxon side and the committee.

We never heard of a secret ballot before that. Secret ballot is not necessarily democracy, you know that. One side used to take one end of the room, those for or against, and that's the way it had always been. That took care of the weaker ones too, because some of 'em would have been ashamed to vote against keepin' on fightin' if they had to show themselves. On the other hand, when there's a secret ballot they vote to go back to work. The Italians refused. Perhaps it wasn't one hundred percent Italian—Italian, some Spanish, maybe a few—but we were split right down the middle. They said, "We want to see who is who. We want to *see!*"

On this day, the day of votin' came, the Italians organized down at Granite Street. That's where the parade started. The Italians came up the street with red flags. The vote box hadn't been counted yet. Then the battle started. Mostly Scottish. They defended themselves on the stairs by pullin' off the rails, wrenched them off. The Italians, driving up the stairs, they got there. They grabbed the ballot box, then they came up through the streets, singin'. There was music, a band, a ballot box, and the red flags.

That caused a bitterness and a natural hatred. It was too bad. And even amongst the kids, which don't usually go in for things like that, but they're hearin' their folks. You could hear the kids sayin', "the white men," in description of the Scottish. Now they say, "white men," that leads you to assume Italian and Spanish were black men; that's the insinuation if not the intent. And you know, it took years before the old wounds were healed, till the '30s.

The most active crowd was anarchists. Anarchists were good people. They are the ones that most of 'em were blacklisted, driven out of the city. There was a lot of sentiment for socialism, Eugene Debs. Barre was one of the two most radical towns in the country. It was quite famous for some of its struggles. The woolen mills, that was the thing before stonecuttin', before they even had quarries here. These woolen mills came out solid, so there was a militant background.

The dramatic part was in the early '20s. It was part of a national movement to destroy unions. It wasn't a local issue. [The bosses] had speakers come around from other parts of the country. The owners of these places used to come here and speak at meetings, why we should get rid of the unions, it's unpatriotic. They were for the American Plan, "where everybody gets what they earn."[3] That was a nice name. "Unions are a foreign importation," and all that stuff. But the bosses wanted it.

Joe: That's when the Canadians came in this country. We had a few Canadians before that, then they called people in here from Canada and they worked American Plan; that was about 1922. That lasted four, five years, didn't it?

Mose: Till '33. The French Canadians were ostracized.

Joe: As time went on one shed would sign up with the union, then another.

We'd get together. The head man of the flying squadron, they'd send me up that way one time then, "You do down here tomorrow." I think I went to Montpelier once, not sure. We had carloads, three, four pleasure cars. Just brought pickets.

The papers then, they was against us too. They were the big shots here. The guard, they came in. They were no trouble. They'd just watch.

Mose: About the military, the national guard, it's not so that they were no trouble. In fact, there was a clash that took place near the school on Ayer Street. That time there was quite a little bit of force used. When the military told us to disperse, we didn't disperse, so they picked up some, and put 'em in the truck that they had. Joe, that day I said,

"Look, don't let these people get away with that." I said, "Then let's climb the truck." Before we got through, the officer in charge was very glad to give up, let everybody go.

Now you remember the troubles down the North End. There were a couple thousand of our people down the North End. And also that Eureka plant down there. You weren't there, Joe, you were a family man more than I was, you did your work around here. But down at Eureka, there was a *real* battle. We barricaded the street. I put my car, the first one, across the street. Was a new Ford. Some of us were pretty well hurt. But somebody pulled me out just in time. I'd fallen over with gas. They used a lot of gas. My kid that went to Ayer Street School came home cryin'. Tears runnin' down their faces where they'd got the fumes of it.

They don't take national guard from the hometown. They could never have depended on them so they'd get outsiders. There were three or four companies from three or four places.

We organized all over the state, but we didn't get paid for it like they do now. It was voluntary. I was part of a group that went around. Remember we went down the marble to help 'em and up to Woodbury to help?

Joe: I didn't go out of town. I done guard duty here. Made sure nobody got into work. And when they got out of work, we threw stones at 'em and tried to break their tires.

In 1933 I was workin' as a picket. I didn't go to work that year till June 7. My baby was born the day I went to work, first day that year. That's the year I done a lot of picket duty. At seven o'clock in the morning when you start working, American Plan schedule, ya know.

Mose: Call 'em what they are Joe, scabs.

Joe: We'd go there, the bunch of us, and we would call 'em names. We didn't throw stones or nothing at 'em because they could pinch us for doin' that. We'd just call 'em names, "Bozo, Bozo." Nobody got arrested, Mose, right? Police never arrested any of 'em.

Mose: As I say, it was militant. There was no holds barred, from then on in particular. And then we won. This was to reestablish the union. Because there was a nucleus here anyhow. Some manufacturers said they wouldn't work without union men, and they, two, three of 'em, stayed union all the way through. So with that nucleus, the idea was to organize them all. Sure, say, "Violent! Violent!" Well, so are *they* violent. They's legal violence and ours was for protection of your job, and your life.

During the strike the newspapers around here start comin' out, "Communists do this, Communists do that." We didn't know any Communists. One day we were up the park, [a] Scandinavian background stonecutter, we got talkin'. I said, "Communists? Are they like us or what?" I said, "Where are these Communists?"

"Oh," he said, "they're from New York City."

He had a brother. I said, "Can you write to him, tell him if he can send an organizer up here or somebody?" And remember, they did. Remember that fella? He came up on the brakes, coal dust all over him. He came here and five of us joined the Party at that time. Later on there were others including the women. We were quite prestigious around here.

Of course, the big mistake the socialists made of that day, was that they never passed on their ideas to their own family. Sometimes they were even disowned by their own family.

They always used to ask, "Aha, who wants unions? It's something that came from Europe. Americans work differently. Don't need any unions." Our fathers knew better, and we did.

"MOSHE LODSKY"*—
From Russian Poland to the Lower East Side

"Being I'm a Stranger"

Moshe Lodsky was born in Lublin, then part of Russian Poland, in 1893. He arrived in the United States in 1912.

In the late eighteenth century a geographical ghetto confined Jews to a section of eastern Poland and the western Ukraine known as the Pale of Settlement, where they lived in small Jewish villages or *shtetlach.* The Pale's grip loosened somewhat by the end of the nineteenth century, and many Jews settled in the major cities of Odessa, Kiev, Mos-

---

*"Moshe Lodsky" is a pseudonym.

cow, and Warsaw. In larger cities like Lublin, they populated their own sections of the city. Lodsky, like the Sholom Aleichem folk hero Tevya, became something of a traveling salesman within the Jewish community.

Although Mr. Lodsky does not mention them, from 1881 through the first decade of the twentieth century cycles of communal madness known as pogroms struck randomly throughout the Pale. These acts of mob violence, often government supported, hit Elisavetgrad, Odessa, the towns of Kiev province, and Warsaw all in 1881, Balta in 1882, Kishinev in 1903, and Bialystok in 1906. Whole villages, sections of cities, and synagogues were destroyed. As these pogroms struck the Jewish community and as economic hardship and inferior status became more unbearable, waves of Jews from the Ukraine, Bessarabia, Lithuania, Byelorussia, and Russian Poland headed for the European ports and ships that would take them to America.

Besides persecution and economics, foreign policy also played a role in this Russian exodus. Jewish men had served in the Russo-Japanese war at the beginning of the twentieth century. With an impending world war in sight, Jewish men fled conscription like an oncoming plague. As Lodsky said, "Anyway, the Jews didn't have much privilege there."

When Mr. Lodsky arrived at Ellis Island, the Lower East Side of New York City was the cultural and social center for America's newest Jews. German Jews who had preceded eastern Europeans by many decades were already fairly prosperous and Americanized. They occupied the "uptown" areas of the city. The newest Jews were conspicuous by their dress, their poverty, and their Yiddish language. Heavily concentrated at the tip of downtown Manhattan, Russian Jews shared the area with co-religionists from Hungary, Rumania, and the Middle East. A uniquely Jewish-American literature, theater, and life-style evolved from this mixture.[1]

Mr. Lodsky found his first major job in New York as a stitcher. The clothing industry had been manufacturing coats like the ones on which he worked since the 1880s. By 1913 over 16,500 clothing factories existed in the city, employing over 300,000 people.[2] In March of 1911, one year before his arrival, the worst industrial fire in the city's history—at the Triangle Shirtwaist factory—killed 146 women workers. Pay was often low, working conditions dismal. New immigrants often sewed clothes in small tenement rooms with their children by their sides or in overcrowded and dangerous sweatshops.

Mr. Lodsky later became a butcher. As meat and poultry require ritual slaughter and separation from dairy and nonkosher foods, the Jewish butcher became both a necessity and something of a folk hero in many Jewish neighborhoods. Lodsky opened his own butcher shop during the garment industry's slack seasons after World War I. In his later years, he lived in Miami and Israel. After the death of his second wife, he moved to the Boston area to be close to his daughter.

I met Mr. Lodsky on a summer day in his daughter's backyard. His Polish-Yiddish accent has a strong overlay of the Lower East Side: "girl" was "goil"; "plucking," "plawkin'"; and "family," "famila." His hearing was poor, but he knew what I wanted to know and what he wanted to tell me. His daughter forewarned me that I should expect "a lot of blarney from Poland," but then, there are many kinds of truth.

August 15, 1975
Brookline, Massachusetts

I left Poland. They called me to the First World War. I never dreamed to go here. I had it very convenient there. I had a business and I had seven sisters, and we were a very good family, very happy. But in Russia it was like this—you weren't permitted no education. Even in Hebrew, [we] had to [study in] a basement. When the police got us, they gave right away a summons that rabbi.

My father was an elderly man and he was a poor provider. He tried to get along 'cause that time in Europe, if only you had a cellar with potatoes and a barrel with cabbage, you don't need anything else. Rent you paid ten dollars a whole year, firewood you went to the woods, pick. So soon I went out from the Hebrew. I saw how it is so I started to help out in the house. I started first to go to the woods to bring my mother should have wood. I used to then go get water in the pail. Later around when I saw anything that happened in the house, it's a shortage, so I took a little basket and I took cigarettes, matches, candy, and I went to the Polacks.

The Polacks liked me. When I came to them so I told them, "If you have no money to pay me for that, could they eggs? I could take a chicken." I was already fourteen, fifteen years, so I went ahead and got a horse and wagon and I started to deal.

At home my mother, she should rest in peace, she made a little bakery. She baked rolls. Later on, when I went with a horse and wagon, I took along for the Polacks, rolls, kerosene in a barrel, and I brought to them everything. They were so happy. But they didn't have no money so they paid me with stuff. I took a calf, I took a sheep. And that's how I was growing and growing.

Meantime my sisters grow up. They were beautiful girls, all handy. But in Europe you had to give a *nadan*.[1] So I try it. My sisters got married. They married very nice.

I started to deal with the secretary in the little city, Zacksherik. I used to bring hare. I used to bring them little chickens, and he was very satisfied, especially his wife.

In the meantime, you know, the years are flying like a dream. I came to seventeen, eighteen. I was nice established, good name, everything fine and good.

I came to the secretary once and I brought him some stuff. So he said to me, "You know, you are a very handy boy and I know your family, a very nice family. But I'm sorry, I have bad news for you. You know they gonna call you to the army?"

I said, "Well, I figure that I am the age but being I'm one son, maybe they'll release me."

He said, "I don't believe. I tell you what I'll do. I'll give you a letter and you'll go to the mayor. And I'll give 'em a good recommendation and I ask him maybe if he can do somethin' for you."

"All right." I came home. I told the parents. Oh! When my parents heard that they called me to the army, oooh, it was terrible.

I came into that mayor with that good recommendation. I came two weeks later and he said, "I'm sorry to tell you, they wouldn't make no exception because we expectin' a world war. Bein' you such a handy boy and you want to be saved, it's goin' to be a terrible war, so you should go to the United States."

"Well, " I say, "I'll take your advice because I don't care for myself, but how could I leave them all and go to the army and fight?" Anyway, the Jews didn't have much privilege there.

I went home, and when I said that to the house, honest, my mother was knocking her head and she was crying. But what would you do? You got only to go.

This was 1912 when I started. I left them all alone and I went away. But before I went away, they had a nice rabbi, a very good rabbi, religious. I believed in him. They called him Moshe Letritchke. I came to him with my mother. She couldn't talk, she was only cryin'. I told him everything. So he shaked his hands to me and he said, "Listen, my dear child, maybe, of course you feel terrible. You all alone and you leave everybody, but maybe someday they all envy you, because we expect it's goin' to be a world war. I don't know what's going to be with us."

So he went ahead and he shaked the hands with me like this, "*Shalom*. And you should be lucky. In case you should be sometimes in a pickle remember my name and you should say in Hebrew: *Tsuris, Rabbis, Chutzi, N'chuma.*"[2] Then I went away.

When I had to go to cross that border line, that wasn't permitted because I belonged already to the army. So I went to a Polack to his house. I told him, "Being that you live here at the border line, could you give me an advice how I could come to the other line, to the Austrian, and then I'll see and I'll pay for it?"

And he took me over. When I came to the Austrian border line the Austrian was talkin' a little Jewish, a little Polish. They asked me if I have a registration. So I had a registration, of a horse. [Laughs.] He said, "That's all right. You could go."

I was in Austria, then I was in Germany.

I took along money. It was very cheap. When I gave a Polack two rubles he took me where I wanted to go, and I was goin' in Germany. In Germany I went from the port, Bremen. I was at the port and I bought a ticket for $20 and I went.

What was the boat like?

Oh, don't ask! To tell you the truth, when somebody'd come at that time when I was on the boat and told me, "Come, I'll take you back, I'll take you home," I would jump and go.

The name from the boat was *Klist* and the boat took four weeks to travel. And the waves were shaking so, a lot of them took sick, *terrible*. They were vomiting, everything. I was strong enough and took it, but there was such a suffering on that boat, I only figure even if I paid somebody for my family, how will they travel on a boat like this?

I slept downstairs. It was like this—here one bed, here another bed, here another bed. I'd walk on a stepladder.

When the boat left, there were hundreds. I got familiar with the people. Mostly they were Polish people, Polacks, Jewish.

When I got to New York, the light shows. So right away they say, "We are in New York already." So the boat stopped, and then the boat went into the port and they took us to Ellis Island.

In Ellis Island there was standing doctors, select 'em which one was all right, send 'em here; which one wasn't all right, even if he wasn't so well a bit, here. When it came my next, he took me like this: "Go ahead! You all right." So that's the way I came to New York.

Is a lot to tell. Later when I came around, it was terribly hard to get a job. Only the Immigration on East Broadway,[3] first I came there and they gave me a meal and they told me, "Have you got any family in New York?"

I said, "Ya, I got a neighbor, he went a year ago. His real name is Avram Rosenfield."

They said, "All right, we gonna bring you there." That was in New York, in Broom Street. So a man took me into that house and knocked on the door.

"Avram Rosenfield?"

"Yuh."

"Here's a man from your city, a boy. He's here to see your husband."

"We have no room for nobody! My brother should be glad I keep *him,* but we have no room for nobody."

So I said to her in Jewish, a little Russian and Polish, I said, "Listen, my dear lady, I didn't come to stay with you, and I don't want to taste of you a drink of water. The only thing is, I would to see your brother, Avram Rosenfield. When he'll come home, he'll help me to go somewhere."

"*Nu,* so all right. I have regards for Avram and for the family." So she says, "Sit down and when my brother will come from work, he'll take care of you."

I was waiting and then the brother came. "Oooh! *You* are here! I never believed that you are gonna come here!" I told him the story and he said, "Sit down and you'll have supper."

"No," I said. "I can't eat because your sister says she has room for only you, not for somebody else. The only thing that I would like from you—take me to a restaurant. I'll get familiar with somebody to rent a house. I got money, I could rent a room."

When I came in the restaurant they all recognized me. I didn't know

so many people that they know me. "Oh Moshe!" "Moshe!" and
"Moshe!" "Where are you?" and "When you came?" I tell 'em the
story how I came, how it was. "So where are you gonna stay?"

I said, "I'm lookin' for a room."

"You could stay in the same house where I stay." When he took me
up to the lady where he lived and he said, "That boy is from our town
and he's lookin' for a room. A very nice boy from a nice family, maybe
he could stay here?" She said, "Why not? I got empty rooms." I gave
her three dollars, got a room.

I got up in the morning. I *daven*.[4] I go out in the restaurant. I had a
coffee. A coffee was five cents. For five cents you could eat of bread,
rolls, herring, as much as you want to. I ate up, then I go. Where shall
I go? All of a sudden I meet a *landsman*.[5] I used to deal with 'em.

So, "Oh! What are you doin' here?" I told him. Same story. He said,
"You've got to learn a trade here, be able to work. I'll tell you what
you should do. You buy a *Morning Journal*[6] for two cents being you
can read Jewish, then you can see advertising. Some of them needs
boys." So I went ahead and I bought the *Morning Journal*. All of a
sudden I see a butcher advertised. He wants a boy to work he should
pluck chickens. So I went over to him with the paper.

"You advertise for a boy?"

"Yeah," he said. "You could pluck chickens?"

I said, "Chickens I could pluck."

I sit down and work and work. Oy! The chickens were so filthy, so
lousy. But what shall I do? I was workin' till twelve o'clock. Lunchtime his wife brought me something to eat. Then he said, "I see you are
a handy boy. You'll be able to work here. You'll get three dollars a
week and you'll get a room to sleep and eat."

A bargain? When I saw a bargain like this. Three dollars, that means in
Russian six rubles. That was a lot of money at that time. I took the job.

I was sitting and plucking and plucking and plucking until eight
o'clock. Eight o'clock I was full of chicken. Oy, what will I do? She
brought me in something to eat supper.

She said, "Here's a couch. Here you can sleep."

I went. What shall I do? Where shall I go? I lay down on the couch. I
was a little tired. Something bites me *terrible*, like you would strike me
with needles. I light the gas. The whole couch were full of *vantzin*,[7]
mosquitoes and red things. When I saw that I didn't go no more on
that couch. I went in the store and I was sitting in the room.

In the morning the man came in. "Well, how were you?"

I said, "That job is not for me. The lice and the mosquitoes, they eatin' me up. I'm all scratched."

"Ah, all right." So he paid me fifty cents for my day's work and I went out.

What shall I do now? I stayed in the corner Rivington Street. A *landsman* came over. He knew me.

"Oh, Moshe! What are you doin' here?" Tell 'em the story again. He said. "They making boys' jackets. A friend of mine has a shop with a partner and he could teach you how to sew on the machine, so you become an operator."

"Good. I appreciate." He took me in. Very very nice people, both partners.

He said, "That boy is from our town, he's a very good boy and a handy boy. Can you do something for him?"

He said, "Well, we could make him for an operator but he has to pay $10 and work four weeks for nothing. Then, later, we'll start to pay him."

I said, "Yeh." I took out right away $10 and gave him.

He said, "All right. Now come to the machine and I'll show you how to handle it." He shows me the cotton, the needle, everything. Soon he showed me I knew how to handle it. Then he said, "You step with your foot here, the wheel will turn. You put with your heel here so it will stop. And that's how I started. Then, it didn't take long. I handled the machine.

It was sectionwork—everybody doin' somethin' else. One makes a pocket, one make a sleeve, but when I finish out all the sleeves he didn't hand no more sleeves to me, so he gave me something else. I finished this, he gave me something else. Little by little I became an all aroun' operator.

It came to the end of the week. Friday, four o'clock. He comes over. He gives me back my $10, and he takes out two dollars and gives me. "You'll work, you'll get a raise. It wouldn't take long and your raise will grow up to five dollars." Oh! When I heard that I was jumpin' high as the sky.

They came in all together we were about sixty operators. Every operator on another type of work. They made boys' coats. No children, only from seventeen, eighteen years boys and girls. The girls was sittin' and sewing buttons, sewing all kinds, and mostly the men were sitting by the machine.

Did you join a union?

I got familiar in the union, became a union man there and a delegate for Amalgamated Clothing.[8]

So I was workin' and I made five dollars a week. All the women *looked.* "A foreigner, just came and he makes five dollars a week."

It was goin' nice and smoothly but all of a sudden the Russian head of government, he gave out an order that all the Russians, they called to the army. If they couldn't go home now, they never be able to go home.

When I heard that, I got scared. I'm goin' to leave my family? I ran and I bought a ticket to go back to Russia.

When I came back and I told the bosses that time I'm goin' home because the Russians gave out that order, the boss said, "Show me the ticket." I show him the ticket. He took the ticket. "You *not* goin' home. You be lucky that you are here." And he grabbed the ticket and he went back to the bank. They gave him back the money.

I didn't go back. I wrote a letter home every week. They said, "We gonna have now a war and we happy that you are there. We don't know what's gonna be with us." They called us to the local board. They asked me if I am willing to go into the army to fight Germany and Austria. I said, "In this country, you don't have to ask me—I would go right away. But for Russia, I don't wanna fight." I actually came here on account of that war, not to fight for Russia. So they said, "Let's put him in the fifth class in the meantime."

Meantime the time was runnin' and the fight was goin' around full speed. It was already disconnected, no mail, no connection, nuthin'. Pass by another two weeks I got a letter from the local board, I should come. Again they put me in the fifth class. It passed by another couple of weeks. So in the evening I'd go out, I liked to talk with the chairman [of the local board]. He said, "They're goin now to draft *all* the boys. The only thing is, which one will be married. This will be the exception. You got a girl? Go get a marriage license or you'll be taken."

So I saw a *landsman.* He said, "How you makin' out? I see you're tryin' all kinds of tricks but I don't think that will work now. They gonna draft now without any reason, all the boys. But you want to get married, I have some daughters."

I went with him to his house. Nine girls. One was 'bout nineteen, one was 'bout seventeen, one was about fifteen—that's how they were goin'. So he said, "Which one you like? Tell me and go get your marriage license."

The first one I didn't like. The other one was a very nice handy girl, but my mother's name and her name were the same name, and our religion don't permit that the daughter-in-law and the mother-in-law can be the same name. It only come out the third one, so I said, "So what, so I'll take the third one."

So he says, "So what, so take the third one."

She was fifteen and a half years. She was born in Poland. He brought here his wife and six girls, three was born here. Then he said, "Ziva, you go tomorrow with that boy and get the marriage license." Her parents came and went to the clerk. We went into court and got married. I was twenty-two.

Another two, three weeks I got another card. "Bring your proofs. If you have any reason now, everybody has to go the army." So I went ahead and I took my wife and I came there. They knew me already. [Laughs.]

"What kind of reason have you got now?"

I said, "The only reason that I have now, I am married."

"Married! How come you got married?"

I said, "Being I'm a stranger and I work a little, so I got familiar with a girl and I got married."

The chairman looked. He knew what was going around. [Laughs.]

I was working. At that time I already made more money. I made $19 a week, and the boss gave me a raise because I got married. He gave me $20 a week, so I was a millionaire.

I went to work and she was running the house and this how it was goin'. It was more than a year my daughter was born. Oh fine! Good! Very nice. The only thing, the *landslayt* was *kibbitzing*[9] me is that, "You gonna be like your father-in-law. Soon was born first a girl, you gonna have straight girls."

I said, "Well, we'll see. I don't believe in that."

I had in Poland, I had a friend, a doctor, a very great man. And he liked me so, you have no idea. He was talkin' many times about nature, about gettin' born boys or girls. He said, "When a man have intercourse with his wife, when it goes on the right side it's going to be a girl, and the left side it's going to be a boy." So the next time we had intercourse she was layin' on the left side, came out a boy. The whole neighborhood, the whole block, "Oh! We thought that she's gonna be like her mother." It came out a boy. Then, took time, another boy, lovely boy.

All of a sudden, that trade that I was working started to go out. Mostly they went in Italian, coloreds, they took over the work, and it wasn't much work. It was stoppage and stoppage and stoppage. So what shall I do? That was when the war was goin' down. There was no work in the shop, I got a job in the slaughterhouse. I had to get up very early in the morning. Later on I said, "No matter how it's gonna be, I have to go back to the butcher life."

So how will I go to the butcher life? I looked into the *Morning Journal*, I saw a butcher wants a helper and I went in and I said, "I'll tell you the truth, I am handy to the butcher line. I used to, in Europe, skin the carcasses and I could do it again. But I want to learn the trade, and in chicken-plucking I have no interest."

I learned the trade, then I said, "I must go for myself now," because he didn't pay me much. He only paid me $10 a week.

At that time Armour and Swift were running everything. They had a fat-house, sent out drivers to collect fat from the meat from the butchers. So if somebody wanted to have a butcher store, and he didn't have no money, they fixed up for him a butcher store and you pay it out with the fat, and that's how I went ahead. I rented the store and I paid out with the fat. When the war stopped so they got 'lectric. Oh! When they got 'lectric don't ask. The machines go *dddddddddddd,* so its clean, everything. It was goin' very very good.

At that time already there was a new law, they didn't permit everybody to come, so it was hard for me to bring somebody. My father died. I received a letter from my mother. "I only want to see my son. I should have a chance to take me to the United States. I don't know if I'll be able to travel on the boat." I was afraid that time if they died, they throw 'em right in the water so I was afraid for that. So I went home.

I went to Poland a couple of weeks. I saw the family. It was everything upset already. It wasn't the same Polacks. They had such a wild, like teenagers around here, they were running around, it was terrible.

When Hitler stepped in they destroyed, they killed, they didn't care—all the elderly, young children, they drived them all in the fire and they burned them. They didn't care. All of my family got killed, all of them—only their children. I brought here eleven nephews, my sisters' children. And there are some in New York, some in Israel.

My wife died, I think in '48. It was a little my fault. I loved her too much. She was very nice. I appreciate that she saved me from the army. I appreciate that she gave me such lovely children. I didn't know what to do for her, but when I came home from work she was jumpin'. Later we started to argue.

I married another woman. Such an angel you wouldn't believe. [Cries.] She was so nice, she was so good to me and every step she watched. When I took a shave, "Let's see your face. Are you all right?"

Then New York started to get spoiled. It started to be colored and everything. I had in the neighborhood all my customers. My friends had to move away. Their children came home from the school beat up from the colored. They couldn't stay. But they liked me so, I used to make them kosher the meat, and everything. So where they moved they called me and being it was electric I used to bring them meat, chicken. I used to have a car, I used to deliver them.

Some moved to New Jersey, some moved to Long Island, some of them moved very far away to the Bronx and I had to run with the car like this when I went away with an order.

"When will you be back?"

"Listen darling, I don't know when. I have to park my car, I have to deliver."

"*Oy*, how will I stay all alone?"

I tried my best. When I came home she was still standing at the door, "I still wait."

But nothing is forever, my dear child.

VALERIA KOZACZKA DEMUSZ—
From Catholic Girlhood to Dorchester

Born into a Polish-Catholic family in the village of Dgbrowa Tarnowska in 1911, Valeria Kozaczka is a child of the twentieth century. In the first fifteen years of her life she lived through the horrors of war, the separation and death of many members of her family, and life in an orphanage before she was reunited with her parents in Rhode Island.

In those same years her village, Dgbrowa Tarnowska, near Krakow, became Tarnow, a small city. Tarnow occupied an almost-border position on the northern Austro-Hungarian Empire when Valeria was born. During World War I it became a Russian-occupied area. When she left Tarnow, it was part of an independent Poland; when she returned recently, it was part of a Poland in the Soviet bloc.

Because of Poland's loss of independence in the late eighteenth century, and because of the scattering of its peoples in eastern Europe, it is difficult to obtain accurate figures for Polish immigration to the United States. Large-scale Polish immigration began as part of eastern-European immigration in the latter part of the nineteenth century. Due to the transition from an agricultural to an industrial society, the traditional Polish-Catholic life of the peasantry became disrupted both socially and politically. Millions of Poles began coming to the North American continent prior to World War I. Many returned to Poland, seeing the United States as a temporary home. But by the time Valeria's parents settled in Rhode Island, large Polish communities existed in Pittsburgh, Detroit, Buffalo, Milwaukee, and Chicago, the last being the third-largest Polish-populated city in the world.[1] Her parents, like most Polish immigrants, settled into *Polonia,* the Polish-American community.

Valeria's parents came to the United States before World War I and before immigration legislation became highly restrictive. They expected to be able to send for their two daughters shortly thereafter. But first the war, then the quota acts of 1921 and 1924 interfered with their plans, leaving Valeria and her sister Emily in Poland. The family was separated for over a decade. They were reunited in Rhode Island in May of 1926.

After living in Rhode Island for several years, Valeria married an immigrant of Ukrainian origin and moved to Dorchester, Masachusetts. She spoke at some length about her church activities and the importance of her earliest experience with the Polish-Catholic parish in Boston. She mentioned her forty-two-year membership in the Polish National Alliance and the Women's Alliance, and her involvement with a community "fair-share" organization. Since her husband's death, she has worked as a home nurse.

August 20, 1975
Dorchester, Massachusetts

My mother was here four years before she married. Then she got married back in Poland. They had three children, two girls and a boy. The boy died. My father just came out of trade school and he opened a business for himself. They had an old house in the small city, Dgbrowa Tarnowska; it's Tarnow now. So they tore down the old house and built a new house. It wasn't finished; they needed more money and my father just new in business, two children, one buried, and my mother knowing it's easier to earn a dollar here than over there.

And then the war broke out, 1914, and my grandmother says, "Take your husband."

She borrowed money, I guess from my grandmother, and she came over here, not knowing that she was pregnant. She came here and she barely made enough. She had a terrible job in a die-house someplace. She's tellin' us how she had to step all day off a chair and hang the threads. Oh, my God, what a job! My father came a week before Mary was born, so my mother was happy.

They both came with the idea that they're both gonna make a little money and go back, finish that new house. And of course we were there with my mother's mother, our grandmother, in Poland.

But the children kept comin' every twenty months here; then the war broke out. So they stayed and they figured, "Oh, let the children stay there, they get a better education." It didn't turn out that way at all.

When the war came, the Russians weren't occupying, they were just passin' through. Our house happens to be one of the new houses, though it wasn't completely finished. Beautiful tiles and bricks. The kitchen was still dirt floor. The living room had a beautiful tile stove and the roof was beautiful, curly and red slate, so we had Russian officers stayin' in our house during the war.

Four or five officers stayed in our house. I remember sittin' on one of the officer's laps, and Emily on the other officer. Like today I see him, tears in his eyes, and I heard them say to my grandmother, "We left children like that at home." So nobody likes wars.

The Polish soldiers were passin' through when they came. They took everything. I remember seeing how he pushed my grandmother, she was holdin' her elbow on a trunk. She had a last loaf of bread in the trunk for us. He pushed her and took that last. They were taking bread and hot rolls out of the oven. I was all alone with my grandmother.

I remember, it was just like a dream, how [me and my sister] were runnin' [with my aunts] away from the town where we were. And I remember the bullets shootin'. They were takin' the straw for the cows and we're behind that, and the bullets be just like over there in the ground, and we were runnin' away and we were prayin'. They took us some way out and my grandmother was sick in bed. [She was left behind.] When we got back she was dead. Dead in bed, and nobody to attend her. It was 1914. I must have been between four and a half and five years old.

[When we returned my grandfather took us.] My folks, supposedly, were sending money to my grandfather. My grandfather didn't use the money for our schooling. Sent us to work and whatever we earned he collected. He was a big overseer for the church. The government would give 'em so much land. This was church land, hundreds of acres and a forest. Of course, things were going down already. He was illiterate, he couldn't read or write, but my mother tells me, he was just like a lawyer. Very smart.

My grandfather, God rest his soul in peace, he used to be very religious. He had us pray together all the time, especially on Sunday. The church bells would ring and no matter where we were, he'd call us together and we prayed. He reminds me of one of the apostles. He was tall and handsome, and you'd kneel and he'd pray with us. And evening prayers the same, before he'd retire at night. In the morning, no, because he used to go to watch the people in the forest, or the people would steal the needles from the pines to burn. They only took care of us for a while, then they gave us to people out in the country to work in the field. We were children born in the city, me and my sister Emily.

In the country we were minding cows, workin' in fields, runnin' the house, takin' care of babies. Somebody reported that my grandfather wasn't sending us to school. My mother kept asking. Then people got aroused because his own children were going to school. I was ten before I went to first grade.

I came back to the city and lived with my godmother and my sister for four years. This godmother named me and everything. She was a very beautiful person. She was the real mother that I had. Even though I had my own mother here, I never had a chance to be with her. [I had an aunt, the sister of my godmother,] she was a redhead, and you know redheads are very rare in Poland and she's full of fire. She liked me but she didn't like my sister. She was educating us and her own daughter. But then everything stopped. Christmas Eve we came from midnight Mass and [my godmother] just died. I grabbed her and she gave the last breath in my arms. She was the one who really opened our eyes to the world that there is somebody that cares for us. And she used to fix my hair. I had hair, long to here. But when we came over there I looked like the dogs that's not combed for a week. She used to comb out my hair every morning and braid it till she got it shiny. She got my hair so beautiful and she used to braid it and wrap my hair around.

That was still a small city, Dgbrowa. Still they kept one cow for the milk 'way in the back of the buildings. And I used to take that cow into the ditches to feed and the women from the country be comin' and say, "Who combed your hair?" and "How pretty you look!" I used to be her pride and joy because her daughter would be away at school.

You know, I thought I'd never live. I got the black diphtheria and scarlet fever together. I almost died. I didn't care whether I lived or not. I was sick three months, and that sister of hers—we called her "fire"—she took care of me. A doctor came and he was fresh out of school from Warsaw. He said through the hour I was supposed to be dead. And they gave me the last rites of the Church and I'm supposed to be dead, and they locked the door—as they call it, sealed the door. But my sister, she's twenty months older, she sat behind the door and she cried, bitterly cried. Somehow I heard her cry and I started to moan and with that she came, the sister of my godmother.

They came and they cooked mashed potatoes, cooked salt pork, mashed them good so they're good and greasy. They put it in a cloth and made a compress out of that, put it around my neck. Then they went in the chimney because they had this stove that burned wood and the blackest soot and boiled milk and, little by little they had this 'round my neck and poured the milk and soup down my throat and *they* brought me to life. The doctor, specialist from Warsaw, left me to die. They cared, those poeple.

I was fourteen years old. I worked as a governess for two years after that. I took care of one child because the mother had TB.

How come your parents never sent for you?

Somehow they couldn't. My father said they closed the immigration or something after the war. We had to wait, especially because my mother wasn't a citizen. We came on his first [citizenship] papers. His [final] papers, I think we were here already. It's different before than it is now. Emily was eighteen and I was sixteen. My parents sent us the ticket. In 1924 my mother stopped sending the money. There was a big uproar over that, and again we have to go somewhere else.

In 1926 I was on a boat. You know it took us twenty-five days to come here. I don't know why. We waited so long. And we were so dumb and so frightened. Just the two of us. And not knowin' any other languages but Polish language. It was terrible.

I was sixteen on the boat, and I was very seasick, and they thought I was gonna die and they gave me examinations, oh all kinds of gymnastics I had to do because I was so sick. And my sister started to cry terrible because she was frightened. She was the older one, but I was more forward.

We docked in New York. Nobody came to me. I remember we took the World Travelers' Aid. They switched us right over and we went to New Bedford. We went by boat. Then we docked. Then we went by train from New Bedford to Providence. In New Bedford somebody comes and takes us off the train. [They] were policemen before we came to Providence. We had to get off somehow from one train to the other. And he come and he's smiling and we look half scared, me and my sister. We were sixteen and eighteen and honest to God we were frightened. He's talkin' English to us and I got so mad. I was so bewildered, I figured that everybody would talk Polish because we never heard any other language but Polish. I looked at him and I figured that he should speak Polish and I said, *"Mow po Polku?"*[1] And I was mad. And with that he started laughing worse. And then he sees that I'm really put out with him, and he started to talk Polish. He put us on the train, and in Providence my father and mother were there to meet us both and one of my sisters, the second born in this country. We came on Mother's Day, on a Sunday, 1926.

I was twenty months old when my mother left, and I didn't see her till I was sixteen and a half, so I didn't get my mother when I needed her the most. They say when I was sick and delirious with the fever I was yellin', *"Mamoshu, Mamoshu."*

I told everybody when I was coming here that I'll go to school. I had to go to the factory, nights, and work in Woonsocket. I went three weeks after I went here because was depression and my father and mother didn't know other kind of work and there were six children here and us two the oldest ones, so we have to go to work.

I went to the wool mills, working on machines as long as the two rooms. You know how they running? Fast. And you have to catch the threads. My hands be cut up. And nights—the only time you could get a job is nights. This was lucky. There was a Polish woman that helped me translate and tell me what to do.

If my mother would give me the message and tell me to go back to Poland, I would have flied. I cried for a solid year. I came to my father and mother, they was perfect strangers. They were so happy to see us and all that but, finally from there I went to another wool mill. I couldn't last there. The pay was very little. I was disgusted. So I went to the rubber shop with my father and mother—one of the biggest rubber shops in Woonsocket. Woonsocket was a big mill town in 1926, '27. They begin to close too. My father and mother made good money there. My mother made more money than my father, really. I'd been doing spinning. There weren't many Polish workers there. Woonsocket is a French town. You go on the street and you think you are in Canada. My mother could make overshoes. She used to make them. She was smarter than my father. Then they got the conveyer. My father couldn't take that.

I was cuttin' out the shapes out of the rubber, the pieces for the overshoes and with electric knives. That finished me. I was on the verge of TB. I'd come home and I wouldn't eat. My mother worked all her life in a rubber shop. She could eat. She'd come and prepare lunch. It was so near that I could come home for lunch. I was just like a toothpick, being so sick and cold, so my mother saw that I really couldn't work.

I just begin to make $25 a week. I just begin to get big pay, everybody was happy. I guess my mother was going to give me a dollar a week for spending money. In those days you turned in your spending money. You don't do what my children do, give me $10 for room and board [laughs]. My health was just givin' away so my mother was talking to different people and she found me a place.

He was a manufacturer. He still is. They're both beautiful people, and I would travel to the beach with them. I spent five years there and that saved my life. Went to New Hampshire. They didn't have any children, and they treated me like their own little girl. They didn't call me a servant. They really began to be my own speed, the way I want to live. People used to talk because I used to go with her and still it was those times, you were a servant. I never was treated as a servant. They were very, very nice and I spent five years. But I was also very lonely. Have you ever heard of Watch Hill, Rhode Island? It's beautiful. A lot of millionaires used to live there. They had a beautiful summer home there. That's where I learned English. This was only the second year I was here. I cooked, I washed. It was also like a family.

My home was just down the hill. I used to come home every night, but I used to sleep there as their companion. That's how I learned to nurse because he was diabetic and she was weight-watching. I learned a lot about cooking.

When I got married she got so bad she didn't come to my wedding. He came and he cried like a baby. They didn't want me to get married, because I didn't get married to too much of the luxuries. I would have been better off if I'd stayed. But somehow—I was twenty-four years old—I wanted to get married, have my own house. And for some reason I wanted to come to Boston in the worst way.

He had a job here in Boston. His uncle's people were friends of my father's and mother's. He was born here, but his mother took him and she died over there. You see, we were sort of *tragic* people. And we had so much in common that we met and we fell in love just like that. Neither one of us had anything to get married on.

He was living in Boston. He was just coming visiting me back and forth. So he begins complaining, and it wasn't quite a year traveling back and forth and he used to complain in the letters all the time that you know, he don't got his sleep, he has to go to work. Imagine what a chance I took—he just had a big accident, he fell. And little did I know that I'd have to baby him for thirty-two years of our married life. He never had good health after that fall. He fell thirty-five feet. He was cleaning windows. You know how they hang like a bird? That's the way those old buildings were. He fell thirty-five feet and he was out of work. He was six months on a farm, about two months in a hospital. And he didn't even have a steady job. I said, "Gee, how loony I must have been." We had so much in common the two of us, we felt sorry for each other. And he told me, he says, I look like his mother.

He had $300, figured that was an awful lot of money in 1934. He says, "I'll spend all the money and go on a boat and I'm gonna become a bum if you don't marry me." Believe me, I'm still green, I got frightened. [Laughs.] And I married him.

We got married in a terrible depression. I followed him here because he had a job and he was making $35 a week—then was a good week's pay.

Have you ever gone back to Poland?

I went back to Poland after forty-five years to the home where I was born. I'll tell you, Dgbrowa, it used to be dirty. They used to be sellin' everything open market. [Softly.] You should see it now. It's all roses, trees from different countries, brand-new post office, all new buildings. It's really beautiful.

The Church functions but if you belong to the Catholic Church you don't have a good job. My aunt is an editor of a paper there. [She] belongs to the Party, but she doesn't go. My uncle went to the Church.

Let's hope to Russia, but maybe they'll come to, they'll have a United States. Will be wonderful, that they unite. But that never, never come. The Polish resent terribly to belong under Russia or Germany. If they rise again, they're only gonna be slaughtered; they're too small. They've got to belong under some bigger nation, because they are too small to survive. The Polish people are not real fighters but they are very noble people. They have nothing, but they're very proud people. Very proud. They hate to be beggars. They are a proud race, which I admire them for.

Here Polish people were slighted for a long time. They never spoke up. There is awful lot of smart Polish people, big people, but nobody knows about it. They've lived in this country and they've done a lot of good, they've lived as beautiful citizens.

No, I wouldn't want to live there. I'm hoping that they'll straighten out because they have a good foundation. But I'm afraid Europe is soaked with blood. I don't think I'm gonna see any peace over there. But here, we've got a problem here.

I live not too far from Roxbury and I have Carson Beach here.[2] That's the first beach when my husband brought me to Boston I went to. The black people had that beach for years. Why all of a sudden, they say there is people from New Jersey and New York comin' here. Two buses. And they stirring up trouble. This friend of mine she went to nine-o'clock Mass and she said she saw buses from New Jersey. It's not our people who live around here who are instigators. They get instigators brought in here. But it's scary.

And yes, I feel sorry for the parents that have to send kids to school.[3] We're gonna have a home war, that's all that's gonna happen. This country is peacemaker for everybody but it can't handle it. The country is goin' broke trying to help everyone and the more you give 'em the more they want.

But I'm telling you, the people have heaven on earth here, and they don't know it. I don't care—the poorest person lives like a millionaire after what I saw. There people stand in line. Here you're not that poor. If you're that poor the city or the state government will help you. If you don't have enough for a loaf of bread, that's your own fault, that's the way I feel. If you go hungry you don't know how to manage. For goodness sake, you can go buy a bone and buy some potatoes, or get a box of oatmeal. That's considered the main meal in many places. There is an awful lot of waste in this country.

It's a country of opportunity, milk and honey. All right, I word hard, very hard, but right now I'm going through a very difficult period and it's the best thing for me to be busy. As long as I'm healthy. It's ten years since my husband's dead. People are not as strong as we were. For about ten years I felt persecuted, but you've got to educate yourself how to live but keep it busy.

No, I don't want to live there. No. If my father and mother were there I would, oh, after my husband died, definitely. The children thought when I went for the trip, they were hoping like—because I got boys and when you got boys you don't have much company. A mother-in-law is out of place. So they thought I would stay in Poland, but no, a visit. It's too many sad memories over there and why would I want to go there? Even though I don't see my children too often. But here are my roots. My children are born here.

Like they think I'm gonna go out of Dorchester. I'm trying to improve this house. Everybody afraid that the black ones, we got 'em across the street already. Especially the Irish people, they're so afraid of the black. And here I am left by myself and, I don't know. I have no place to go. I have a beautiful family and my sisters and my brother. They have their own lives and their own children to think about and their grandchildren already. What should I go there for? It's nice to go visit, but I tell you this is where I belong.

RICHARD O. LIM—
From the Laundries to San Francisco

After the Mexican War and the Gold Rush of 1849, white Americans pushed west to claim gold and land. Chinese male workers were imported on a massive scale to mine, build railroads, and after the completion of the Transcontinental Railroad in 1869, to build levees expanding land use for a growing agricultural economy.

In the mid-1800s, as the Chinese population grew, anti-Chinese agitation began to reach hysterical proportions. West Coast politicians were able to pressure the U.S. government into passing the first piece of exclusionary legislation in American history—the Chinese Exclusion Act of 1882. By the late 1880s anti-Chinese hysteria had spread to several other states. Chinese were murdered, burned out, and thrown out of towns throughout California.[1] Many men returned to China. Most of those remaining took shelter in the Chinatown section of San Francisco or in similar Chinatowns in other American cities further east.

Richard O. Lim came to the United States in 1929 at the age of seventeen. His father was born in this country but returned to China both to marry and to have children. Mr. Lim's father was a farm worker on the West Coast. When he returned from China his wife did not come with him. Richard and his brother were able to come into the country because of their father's American birth, even though by 1929 quotas and restrictive laws closed immigration to most Asians of both sexes.

The male society in which the Lims were forced to live dominated the Chinese immigration and subsequently the American Chinatowns. It began out of economic necessity but was later enforced by legal statute. From the mid- and late nineteenth century young Chinese men left their villages to aid in the survival of their families. They expected to make money in America ("Gold Mountain") and return to their villages later. Many, like Richard and his father, returned home to marry and assure the continuation of the family line. They then would return to America.

The Chinese Exclusion Act legally put an end to the entry of Chinese laborers and was extended from 1882 to 1892 and then, in 1904, indefinitely. After 1884, Chinese wives of all but merchants and American-born Chinese were barred from entry.[2] In 1888 the Scott Act forbade the return of Chinese laborers. The Immigration Act of 1924 forbade the entry of most Chinese women into the United States for the purpose of living here permanently.

Illegal entry of Chinese laborers and women occurred despite the legislation. In 1943 the Chinese Exclusion Act was repealed by Franklin D. Roosevelt.

— our allies

The earlier statutes effectively reduced the Chinese in this country to a single-sex society. If the racial intent of these laws had been in any doubt, in 1906 California's miscegenation statute, passed in the 1870s to stop white-black marriages, was extended to include "Mongolians." Miscegenation statutes existed in other states with Chinese populations as well. The California statute remained on the books until the late 1940s.[3]

Richard Lim did have some family ties in America, since it was his father who sent for him. But unlike his Greek counterpart, a young man like Nick Gerros, he had no other family here nor was he allowed to build his own. For men coming out of a society rooted in family and clan life, the impact must have been enormous and terribly lonely. Some "wives" left in China saw their husbands once every twenty or thirty years. Mr. Lim returned to China in 1936 and married. When a son was born, he was not allowed to bring him or his wife to America.

March 12, 1976
On Lok Senior Health Services[1]
San Francisco, California

My father was born here and he wants me to come over, help him out and maybe go to school. I take a boat out from Hong Kong to this country. By that time, 1929, was still $90 for the transportation.

I arrive in the Depression. It is hard times. First I go from Seattle, Washington, to my father's place in Walla Walla. He's working in the potato farm. I worked for the other ranch, not the one he is working. I picked potatoes. That time you had to bend over to pick up the potato in the ground, but now you don't have to. I did it maybe a year. Then there were maybe a hundred Chinese. Now I think no one is up there—maybe a few, that's all. They don't work the farm anymore.

Those years I go around all those towns to the east: Chicago, Indianapolis, all those places, looking for a job. I took the train. I go by myself. I have some friends over there. Maybe some friend can find me a job.

First Chicago, not much luck. My father have friends there in Hammond, Indiana. Not much luck there, either. I go to the school. I worked in the laundry. They don't pay you much. I didn't know the people before. They are Chinese. They need someone. They want me to work in the laundry and go to school. By this time I finish, they pay about five dollars a week. They have room and board over there, so I don't have to pay expenses. Sometimes I do cooking, ironing, all those things, rough linen. Gees! Long hours. Wake up in the morning about six o'clock and you have to cook for them and eat it and go to school at nine.

When you come back from the school after three, you have to work for the laundry—maybe sometimes it's at night, twelve or two o'clock. You have four or five hours to go to sleep. When my teachers tell me, "Why you come in here and sleep?" I don't know what to talk to them. I say nothing. But see, the teachers don't know I'm working so long hours.

I make the money. I go all around the country, like a hobo I am. [Laughs.] It was lonely. Some people write down from Chinese to English and tell me the right train route so I come out of the East. After that I stay in Stockton, California, maybe a few years.

In Stockton, they gave me about three dollars a week in a friend's laundry. If they knew you so well they hire you; otherwise they don't hire you. I have to work for them in the morning till night at eleven o'clock. What do you think of that? Three dollars a week! Gee! I did that because I could find no work.

Did you ever see your mother again?

There are just us two brothers in this country. My mother stayed in China. I don't think they let Chinese women come in country after 1924. I just been back in China in 1936 or something. I saw my mother then. After that, never saw her again. She died.

At that time I married. My wife cannot come over here. She died during that war in China. We had children. They were in China; after I don't know where they were.

When I come over here, I learn my barber trade. Very hard to get a job. After a year I got a job working for someone else in Chinatown. So far so good. Not so hard job. A year and a half later I got my barber license and then I am drafted into the army, '41 I think. I try to go but my number is too low, so I go working for the naval contractor—those

mess-hall jobs, boy cook jobs, everything. You know what boy cook is? Make up the rooms and all of that, next, mess hall for the contractors over there, over two thousand men.

They sent me over to the Midway Islands. I been over there little over a month. The Japanese start war. I nearly be a prisoner.

Those Japanese submarines with the guns were out there. I was staying, and then later, going to sleep. The submarines was shooting. I said to myself, I take a look. I hear yelling. If the big guns explode I die, but they didn't. Now I got *this*. [Laughs, pointing to his paralyzed side.]

At the time we go over there was $90 a month for wages. Nothing to spend the money on over there. Only maybe get hair cut, buy something to eat.

How did the contractors treat you?

The contractors all come from this country. Some good, some bad, especially those coming from the South. I don't have much to do with them. They say something I don't like, I go away. No use in getting up to that. Maybe they gang up, what you gonna do? No use, If you can get away, get away better.

I go back to China in 1947 and get married again. There was fighting in Shanghai and Manchuria. The Japanese were in the south. After that, I think it's '48, people go Hong Kong. Chinese Communists came. I get out before they took over China. My new wife came with me after that time.

When you went back to China in '47 did you ever think of staying there?

In a way I want to go to China, go there and learn something in '47. I try to get my last little kid to come over here, but he didn't like to come. Nah, I wouldn't go back there no more. Can't do anything. Nah, I wouldn't go back there no more. Even if I go back there, nobody know me. This country end for my life. [Laughs.]

What happened to my life? All things bad luck. When I came back to San Francisco after the war, I took up barbering again. I come back and collect my wages from Honolulu. So I go buy the barbershop in San Francisco. In a few years later they want back the store, so I have to move.

My wife divorced me by that time, then every two years something go wrong. I lost some money and now I lost myself in half three years ago.

Now is no more use. I stroked, I cannot even clean up myself. The whole side. I usually work on my right, half right side is numb. Can't raise my right hand, see? If I stand up with this one I fall down. No use. [Laughs.] I never thought of spending my life here [motioning to the room in the Center] . I got back luck. I don't know why.

This is the year of the dragon. It's supposed to be a good luck year.
What good it is to me? [Laughs.]

NATSU OKUYAMA OZAWA—
A Japanese Woman Remembers

"So the Big People Will Know"

Natsu Ozawa is a Japanese woman in her seventies. She came to the United States in 1924 to join her husband, who was working as a merchant in San Francisco.

Not only Chinese, but the majority of Asian immigrants who came to the West Coast between the Gold Rush of 1849 and the Oriental Exclusion Acts of 1924, were contracted or encouraged to come to fill a labor shortage. They were overwhelmingly male and under thirty. They were seen by many Americans as drones, first to build railroads and drain land, and then to become the stoop labor necessary for a growing agricultural industry.[1] It was not intended that they should stay, raise families, and become citizens, and laws excluding them from entry and from naturalization were part of their American heritage.

Between 1900 and 1910 only one in ten Japanese immigrants was a woman; this figure was up from the previous ten years.[2] In 1910, between four and nine hundred women arrived, increasing the total Japanese female population roughly from 500 in 1900 to close to 26,000 in 1920.[3] Although this is not a large figure in a period when millions arrived annually, "Yellow Peril" hysteria inflated both the figures and the "menace" of entering Japanese women who, it was said, threatened to overrun the white population with a mass production of babies.

This hysteria was heightened by the "picture bride" controversy.[4] Traditionally, Japanese marriages are arranged and a matchmaker consulted by the families of both bride and groom. A combination of this practice, immigration restrictions, and geographical separation resulted in women having marriages arranged in Japan and arriving in San Francisco without either party having seen the other, except for an exchanged photograph. These proxy marriages became a political issue both in California and in Washington's relations with an internationally powerful Japan. They were seen by West Coast legislators and pressmen as evidence of the low moral character of Japanese people, and also as proof of official Japanese government duplicity regarding enforcement of Japanese immigration restrictions known as the Gentleman's Agreement. In March of 1920 the Japanese government accepted U.S. demands not to issue passports to "picture brides."

The Gentlemen's Agreement of 1907–1908 was a joint attempt by the Japanese and U.S. governments to restrict Japanese laborers from entering the United States. With the agreement, Japan was the second Asian nation to be specifically restricted. In 1924, exclusion was extended to all Asian workers and to all Asian wives wishing entry unless their husbands had established residency and were merchants. A quota for non-working-class men and women was set at one hundred.[5] Natsu Ozawa was able to enter the United States in 1924 because of her husband's merchant status.

When I met Natsu Ozawa she began talking about her first experiences in the United States. Several minutes into our meeting, she began to recount experiences of discrimination toward her son and her family's "internment" during World War II.

On December 7, 1941, the Japanese attacked Pearl Harbor. In late February of 1942, a Japanese submarine attacked Goleta, California. During these months, high-ranking civilians and military men, along with such liberal reporters as Walter Lippmann, suggested that the Japanese on the West Coast were a military threat and should be removed.[6]

On February 19, 1942, President Franklin D. Roosevelt signed Executive Order 9066. The order authorized the Secretary of War to select "military areas" and to evacuate "any and all" people from them; specific ethnic groups were not mentioned. The following day Attorney General Francis Biddle, in a memorandum to the president, assured him that the war powers of the president "are broad enough to permit them to exclude any particular individual from military areas. . . . The order is not limited to aliens but includes citizens so that it can be exercised with respect to Japanese, irrespective of their citizenship."[7] Lieutenant General John L. DeWitt of the Western Defense Command placed Executive Order 9066 into operation by directing all those of Japanese ancestry to leave the California coastal area. Between three and four thousand moved inland to California's valleys. In a matter of months all people of Japanese descent on the West Coast were "interned."

People first were rounded up and brought to one of fifteen assembly centers, mostly in California. Within eight months they were moved to more permanent "relocation centers." During the early '40s more than 110,000 people of Japanese descent were moved into ten of these camps in desert areas of six states including California, Arizona, Utah, and Wyoming.[8] The Ozawas were sent to Topaz, Utah. Of those sent, 70,000 were native-born American citizens.[9] No hearings were held. The American left, right, and center did not protest. Families were given identification numbers, once times and places for departure were set; they were forced to sell property for next to nothing or to ask non-Japanese American friends to care for it. Some stored valuables in churches. It is estimated that hundreds of millions of dollars worth of property was lost, stolen, or confiscated.[10]

Many people stayed in camps from 1942 to 1944. Some were forced to stay until the end of the war; others were released in 1942 or 1943. The latter were mostly *Nisei,* native-born Americans of Japanese background who were used to aid the war effort—teaching languages, picking fruit, working in inland plants, and after January of 1943, joining the armed forces. About 33,000 *Nisei* served during World War II, about half from Hawaii and half from the mainland.[11] In three cases during the 1940s, the Supreme Court avoided dealing with the question of the constitutionality of Executive Order 9066, primarily on the grounds of "military necessity."[12] Only a few Italians or Germans or their native-born children were ever rounded up, and these received hearings. Some but not all Japanese Americans in Hawaii were removed to mainland camps.

An effort was made in the mid-'60s to recover damages against Japanese Americans, estimated in 1942 to be $400 million. Only 137 were ever paid anything by the U.S. Department of Justice; these claimants paid out more in litigation than they got back in damages. No compensation was ever made to people like the Ozawas for being unable to recover those years or their previous status.

Only recently has the federal government acknowledged any wrongdoing in these matters. On February 19, 1976, thirty-four years to the day after the original decree, President Gerald Ford publicly apologized and rescinded Executive Order 9066.

My meeting with Natsu Ozawa was brief and intense. It was difficult for both of us. When we finished talking, she turned to me and said, "It is important that the big people should know."

March 11, 1976
The International Institute
Oakland, California

My name is Natsu, means summer, Ozawa and I came here in 1924. My husband was working here and he start a business, export-import company: food, dry goods, all kinds of things. Then he come back to Japan to look around, wants to get married someone. We got married in Japan in the Japanese way. First met my parents, they think he is good for me. Then I saw him. Then got married, that's OK. Wedding day was November 12, I think, 1923. I just reached twenty. Next year I came.

First, that was after immigration law passes so we can't get in, see? I was sent to the Angel Island immigration place.[1] That day is Sunday and all kind of place is closed, so we wait till Monday and we raise a bond. I think $500. Since then, five years we lived in San Francisco.

I had a son, after the marry. Right away I had a baby boy. He had asthma troubles and we moved to Berkeley.

When I come to this country I was young. I was living in Japanese community, so every day I can go to the Japanese store. Talk Japanese. Everything I can buy, do. No trouble. So I didn't think too much. My husband good enough in the wages so nothing to worry about. But we send children to the public school and I could see. Well, sometime people don't show right away speaking, but *feeling*, I can feel, treated like that.

At that time I didn't have any business position myself, just housewife, so every day take care of the house and children. But I always taught my two sons, "Be good boys." Also when we have to learn Japanese culture and American culture, everyone pick on especially. The good things and the bad things both I see. "So have to be very good boy. Study hard. Have to be nice boy." I always told him so they don't get into any trouble.

Then well, just I spend regular housemaker, nothing to worry about

till the war started, and then all troubles start. At that time I was pregnant, but all stress and like that, I miscarriaged. My oldest son was
fifteen. He graduated to go to the high school in Berkeley. The younger
one is ten or so.

That beginning, everything packed away, some of the things we sell,
you know, all kinds of furniture. Some memorable, nice things I want
to keep, put in the church warehouse.

We were sent to the Topaz, Utah, concentrate camp, and spent three
years there. Then I learned how to earn the money. Start working, of
course, beside helping. I work at the mess hall as a waiter, clean up
the table, set the dishes and take care of all the people. Some people
not eat, some have to be chopped, something hard for their teeth. Sixteen dollars a month, huh. [Laughs.]

My sons, they attending Topaz Camp School, we call it. We had an
education system. I learn in the camp too. They have English class,
sewing class, all kinds of class, flower-arrangement class. Of course, I
graduated in Tokyo so I have a foundation in English education. So
I continue. Most of the problem is talking.

After the war, came out, I have to go to start the work because I want
to give an education to our sons. But I have no experience, 'specially
English talking in the country, so naturally I took domestic work. [Her
eyes fill with tears and she pauses.] I work in many houses in Berkeley.

Anyway, that was a good experience. That makes me strong. Oh, so
many small, what's call it, not a happy feeling, you know. Always something hang around. See, I have a handicap in language. Anyway, everybody *quite* nice, even after the war people treated me quite well. So, I
enjoyed it and beside [continues to softly cry] I see the people and
I learn the American what's going to be like.

Right now I am thinking about my older son. Had quite ability working hands and he is quite a bright boy. At that time Oakland Association
of Chamber of Commerce sponsored boys making model airplane
contest and my son make a model airplane. It was very good. At that
time it is 1937 or something, right before the war. He won the first
prize and flew to the Sacramento. That's a very nice prize that time.
When second time contest he was very good. He supposed to win the
first prize but the judge, he didn't give him because they doubt that not
his own hands making that model airplane. Everybody testified that
my son's name Ichiro, Robert Ichiro, that make it by himself. Testified,

but *no*, it is too good for his age, so he couldn't get the first prize. After that I heard about that trouble.

My son, he didn't told me that at that time. *Later* he told. I thought, if it was to happen right now, I *go out* and *speak up*. Treating that way is not good. Have to be fair. [Wipes her eyes.] Especially young children, they are going to become American citizen. He was about nine. At that time I have no courage to go out and speak up, even they told me, but they don't mention that to mother, even they keep it themselves.

Everything past after that, think over that, far away past days not too bad. Small, sad things is just a fade away, because I'm looking forward. America is Christian country and everything is changing.

Enemies quite equal in some ways, but one way we couldn't get citizenship so we couldn't buy a house. After the war we come out from the camp, concentration camp, we can't live. No houses, no furniture, no citizenship and look around all over, nobody wants to sell. They found some reason. Realtor took me all over, but owner, him don't want to sell the Japanese. It is very hard. Son was seventeen after the war. My friend hired my son and then my son got registered right away the papers and we bought it in the son's name. Now, old, senior citizens card, deduct property taxes. We can't have it because it's in my son's name. Of course, we can change but my husband is getting quite old. Now, something happen, after that have to be changed to my son's name again. So my son says, "Oh, that's OK, I'll pay a little of that tax."

That's the way everything for Japanese here. Still sometime very comfortable in this country, but in some other way, it is not comfortable. But America have nice points, of course, so that's all in the past. Still I try to learn how to explain my feeling, write English. I can better read but speaking is very hard. I try to explain my feeling. That is why I talk to you.

I tried always looking on *good* side, so I think America tried best for us so I took the good ways. I learned how to earn the money in camp.

Was your husband able to start a business again?

No. He is quite artistic, so he wants to join getting in the painting. Very artistic idea. Husband finished college education. But he has no citizenship so he couldn't get into the unions, we can't get any place.

He's getting old, retired, and he doesn't complain things, but many people struggle, still struggle, I think.

The law is changed and we can get examination to get citizenship. Right away we studied it, the law and all kind of history and after we tried to buy houses, property, but still has sort of the hard feeling between the owners and the buyers.

Most of my struggle is not physical. Mental. [Crying.] Sometimes struggle makes people strong, you know. I lost my mother and father just before the war in Japan—not too old, they were sick. But I think Japanese in their own country, being there it's a more to struggle. This country's large. They have so many resources of all kinds, rich in many ways, so we are not too bad. In Japan, I think worse maybe.

Because I was not born here, I came from Japan so everything different, especially my language. It was very hard. A couple of years I was really bad homesick. But gradually, now, I can see good sides of America, bad sides of America. It seems understandable, and I can take, but still I try not to think about the bad times. [Wipes her eyes.]

My older son, he can read Japanese. He can speak quite nice Japanese, but the younger one, I tried to teach him at home after school, but you know how hard to keep up the children studying the foreign language at home. Can't read, write, but he speaks nicely.

The first one lives near the San Fernando Valley. Now he is working at the Los Angeles aircraft company. The second one finished medicine and now in Sacramento. Has office there. I have six grandchildren. [Laughs.] There's one that's second year of college. Now, these days, have the trouble with the young boys and girls. They were no trouble at all. I was lucky to raise children at that time. [Laughs.]

There is nothing to talk about so much. Other people struggled more than me. Some people work so hard. Of course, I work so hard after the war. Time has changed. America is growing also. They doesn't want the same wrong road. They want right way to treat people.

First I thought about going back to Japan, but we had two sons and they are pure citizen, see, so we better stay here. I think American try best to do for us. No more always something doing of fright[ening] things or terrible things. I think in many ways very nice the people.

WILLIE BARIENTOS—
Filipino Farmworker

"Some Are Bought, Some Fight"

Willie Barientos was born in April 1908, in Caoayan I Sur, the Philippines. He arrived in Hawaii in 1924 to work on the Hawaiian pineapple plantations. It was a typical route for a Filipino in the 1920s.

In 1898, after the Spanish-American War, the United States took possession of the Philippine Islands. After a three-year Asian guerrilla conflict involving seventy thousand American troops, torture, and concentration camps, an American takeover resulted in United States economic control and a small measure of political autonomy, with independence promised for the future. When the Philippines gained Commonwealth status, Filipinos became American "nationals" free to travel, but did not have the rights of citizens.

After 1900, Filipinos began to fill a role as the new Oriental labor force replacing Chinese and Japanese farm workers, who were dwindling due to immigration policy restrictions. The poor economic conditions on the islands at the turn of the century forced many Filipinos to emigrate to Hawaii and eventually to the mainland. The first large group of Filipino farm workers arrived in Hawaii between 1906 and 1907. They were recruited to work on sugar plantations, adding a new Asian labor force to the Japanese who had been recruited years before. Labor agitation resulted in large-scale strikes in 1909 and 1919 in which Japanese workers protested the use of Filipinos as strikebreakers and demanded the elimination of pay differentials for different nationality groups.

In 1924, the year Willie Barientos arrived in Hawaii, sixteen hundred Filipino workers were in the process of striking twenty-three of the forty-five plantations. After an eight-month strike in which the Honolulu national guard was used, sixteen strikers and four policemen were killed.[1]

Due to the "national" status of Filipinos, they could continue emigrating to the United States even after the Oriental Exclusion Act of 1924 was passed.[2] As a result of this act, more farm workers were needed, especially in Hawaii. The additional threat of a possible cutoff of Mexican labor in the West and Southwest stimulated recruiting of Filipinos for the mainland as well.

The majority of Filipinos arrived between 1924 and 1934. Statistical sources are in conflict; however, it appears that by 1930 there were close to fifty thousand Filipinos on the U.S. mainland, with over three-quarters of these coming to the West Coast. Like the earlier West-Coast farm workers of Asian origin, men vastly outnumbered women, and generally were under thirty years old. At the time Willie arrived in California, Filipino male-female ratio was close to five hundred women to 9,300 men.[3] Intermarriage between Asians and non-Asians was against California law until after World War II.

Filipino farm workers filled the places vacated by Chinese and Japanese, sharing jobs with Mexicans and, by the '30s, with American migrants out of the dust bowl. Earlier anti-Asian prejudice soon caught up with them, however. In Yakima, Washington, in the fall of 1928, anti-Filipino riots occurred. In 1929 and 1930, the riots spread through California to Tulare, Watsonville, Stockton, and the Imperial Valley. Cries for exclusion were heard. As Filipinos got organized and refused wages lower than other workers', they were subjected to increased harassment.[4]

In March 1934 Congress passed an act calling for independence for the Philippines and the "national" status of the Filipino was changed—they now could be legally excluded from emigrating to the United States, along with all others of Asian origin. The Philippines were declared independent in July 1946.

My journey to meet with Willie Barientos took me some 250 miles from Los Angeles, to Delano in California's Central Valley. Nothing prepared me for the Central Valley, stretching for hundreds of miles in every direction, flat, every inch under cultivation. No farmhouses, no people, no cows—only trucks, storage bins, and rows and rows of anything that grows. Much of this area was marshland less than one hundred years ago. With the help of Chinese immigrants and aqueducts, with state and federal subsidies, and in more recent decades, with multi-million-dollar corporate funds, this area is now the richest agricultural land in the world. By 1970, Central Valley agriculture was a $4 billion-plus industry, with this valley alone producing forty-three percent of all the fruits and vegetables in the United States.[5] Mexican farm workers now dominate the region's labor force. The four leaders of California agribusiness are the Southern Pacific Company, Tenneco Incorporated, Tejon Ranch Company, and Standard Oil of California.[6]

Here in the valley I could see how a century of exploitation of Asian and Latin and U.S. farm workers could go unnoticed, isolated from cities. I could also see how John Steinbeck and Carey McWilliams were drawn to write about these people and valleys. Along Route 99, pink almond blossoms appeared occasionally, but this was grape country, and in early March I drove for miles past rows of leafless grape arbors, two to four feet off the ground, four to five feet apart, wires linking the branches in thousands of rows. Driving into Delano, a large welcoming sign read, "GRAPES OUR CLAIM TO FAME."

Leaving the highway and heading out of town about five miles, I parked the car at the Forty Acres, a complex of land and several buildings owned by the United Farm Workers of America. Agbayani Village is part of the Forty Acres. It is a Filipino-styled village completed in 1975 by the UFW and volunteers as a tribute to the work of Paolo Agbayani, a Filipino union member who died of a heart attack on a picket line in 1967. It houses over thirty men, all retired Filipino farm workers.

When I first met Willie Barientos, he wrote his name on a piece of paper and after it printed the word ORGANIZER in large block letters. While telling me about his immigration experience, he also described the role played by Filipino workers in the Coachella Valley during the famous Delano grape strike of September 1965. In the spring of that year, Filipino grape pickers organized with the AFL-CIO Agricultural Workers Organizing Committee (AWOC), refusing to work for less money than imported Mexican labor. That strike resulted in the formation of the United Farm Workers, the first effective multiethnic farmworkers' union in American history.

March 6, 1976
Agbayani Village
Delano, California

When I was young, I was a fighter. I was *born* that way. My mother raised me that way. I left them when I was young. Then my old grandpa said, "Well, young man, I don't have no money in the world, but you're still young. You know how to work."

"Sure I can work. How you live if you don't work?" I said. My grandpa told me, "Your grandpa fight for the freedom of the people, for the freedom of the Philippine. Put that in your head." My own grandpa, he said, "He fight for the freedom of the people in your nation. I raised you more than anybody else. Don't let nobody kid you, because I raise you good. And don't be afraid to nobody so long as you are right. *Nobody*!" That's what he told me. And I fight. I fight until today.

I was about eighteen. They opened immigration just to break the strike in Hawaii, just like they are doing in Mexico now. When they opened immigration in the Philippines, all young kids they came in this country. In 1850, they do that to the Chinese, until 1890. They immigrate the Chinese first. They work and drive them to Chinatown down there in San Francisco. Then came the Japanese, 1924 is Japanese exclusion also, until 1934.[1] Then the Filipinos also came in 1924. Thirty thousand Filipinos came to the United States, 1924. And then in 1952 we got only a chance of quota,[2] fifty to one that means that the quota is only one hundred Filipinos can come in this country, see? That is the historical background I have in my head. I know history! See? Immigrate all these people. Also in the South, the Negro, they are farm workers. They work in the cotton. They know that history. They have sold them for another. They don't take me, I know.

In Hawaii I was stationed in the plantation. We cut sugarcane. We had to have a salary of one dollar a day. Until you had twenty-three days working in land you cannot have no bonus, ten cents bonus. This is terrible.

The big giant corporation opened the plantations. They were the Del Monte, they were Dole.

I was stationed very close to Honolulu, and close to Waikiki in the east part of the Hawaiian Islands. I don't know how to work in the field before. My mother was worried because I was too young and I never do work before. When I went to Hawaii I cut sugarcane, and that is hard work. I confronted the plantation that I could not do this cutting sugarcane. "I don't wanna do this job." They gave me a hoe and let me cut the grass. I said to my brother, "Like hell. I didn't do this all my life."

One time, I went to the main house where we sleep down there in Hawaii. I didn't go inside because I almost cried. I was still young. I don't like to hold that hoe. Hell, I didn't hold no hoe in my life, and I told my brother, "Hey, *Magnon,*[3] is this here work in Hawaii, huh?" I complain. They give me a better job. Guys, they load the cane and put it in the boxcar until it's full. I got to record all those cars.

I went to Hawaii. I saw Hawaii. I saw the people working in the

Willie Barientos

pineapple; I saw the people working in the sugarcane. That's a hard job, a dollar a day. Shit. More than highway robbery. I am poor people. I came from a poor family. I had that in my heart and my mind, to fight for the poor people. I want to see my brother. I want to send him back home [from Hawaii]. I don't want to come to America unless I put my brother to work in the family. I have only one brother, two sisters. We are poor. I stay in Hawaii till 1929, after he left maybe two weeks. I came in this country December 20, 1929. I landed in San Pedro, then I got a job in Stockton.

They wanted me to work in the asparagus. I worked for one week, I guess. They teach me. They got some knife and they cut the asparagus this way. And you *bend* with your back, you know. I said, "I cannot do this job." I told to my cousins and the workers I don't want this kind of work. Then I went to San Francisco.

In San Francisco, I had a friend there. He's working with a family. I go there so someone would hire me and I would go to school. Maybe they got small pay, but they send me to school. I want to learn. I want to see my way better. That's what I got in my head.

So I went up there. I work as a schoolboy.[4] I go to school a little bit, then I change. I got another job. A janitor job. At night time I learn a little bit English.

I got $30 a month as a janitor. That's depression, that's very hard. Well, I heard from some guys that there is work in the field, so I took a bus from San Francisco. Then I met some Filipinos here. I came to Delano in 1946.

They teach me how to plant the grape, how to pick the grape, how to prune, how to thin, how to thick, all the whole operation of the grape. Mostly Filipinos then. Eighty or seventy-five in the camps.

What were the conditions like?

Conditions is not good. That's why I was there. I see them and I watch them very close, what they are doing to the workers. And then I put them in a plan in my head until the union came along.

We started this union September eight, nineteen hundred and sixty-five. I have been waiting for this time, because I want to join the union. And I was one who can stand again to fight the growers.

My boss told me, "Willie," he said, "you've been working for me ten years. But now you are the leaders against me? What's wrong?"

I said, "You don't know? But I'm going to tell you. *Me,* I build you up from your head to your feet, with all my pals, with all my brothers here. Where are you today without my brothers here? Now, I want *my* share. We want *our* share to live as a human being, so we can also send our children to school and be educated like your children. That's what I've been waiting," I told him. And I look him in the eye also. And he think I am scared. "No, I am no scared at you. I build you up, and you think I don't know it, huh? My brothers are here. That's why we had the strike this day, September eight, nineteen hundred and sixty-five, because we want a higher wage, and better conditions. Because we have been *exploited* for centuries and centuries. Here is the time. I have been waiting for this time."

We, the Filipino people, are the one who started this strike, four weeks before César Chávez came out. Don't ever nobody tell you lie, because that is the truth, that we the Filipinos wanted this strike before César Chávez came along. We have identical purposes. He realizes that when the Filipinos and Mexican, Arabian—*all* the farm workers working the field—should unite, they may be stronger to fight them back.

This is not the first time we strike here. No, they tried before but they fail. Why? Because of the divisions, that's the weapon, that's their weapon: divide and control. I know it, even they don't tell me. I saw it with my two eyes.

How did they do that?

Just like this. When you got the Filipino foreman here, Chicano foreman here, they bribe these people and they sell their own people down the river. They do it in Hawaii, and they do it here, and they do it everywhere. It is the historical problem of the union, and it is heartache. Among the workers, they know it. Some are sold, some fight.

Later we march to Sacramento. We started from Delano, and from every city we pick up. And when we reach Sacramento, that was Easter Sunday. You know how many people are there? Maybe around ten thousand there in Sacramento that day. Then it came the investigation when Robert Kennedy came around.[5] We had a meeting down at that auditorium in the high school.

When we started this strike, wages is only $1.10 an hour and now when we have this September 8, 1965, we ask for $1.40. Here in Delano we had $1.20; when we had the strike we ask for $1.40. And gradually we move. Today we come to $2.60. Teamsters, they got $2.54. That's the difference, they are lower all the time. Today we got a contract for

$3.35. We have ten minutes' rest in the morning, ten minutes' rest in the afternoon. We don't have that before in the whole history of the labor movement until we have this United Farm Workers of America, today.

Are you married?

No, because when we came here 1924, the Filipino cannot marry a white. That's the law. This hurt me. We cannot marry. We cannot buy land, until we fight the war. That's all hurt me. That's why I get old in my head and in my heart and in my hand. When I was young, I was strong.

I have seen all those experiences in my life. I saw it. They pass in my hands. I see it with my eyes, that's how I know. I did not go to college and learn this. I know it. I have seen the war in Vietnam. I saw what they are doing in the Philippines right now.

What they are doing in the Philippines? This big giant that they are in Hawaii before, they are moving in the Philippines *now*. They had the pineapple, all kinds. They want to get all the big pieces in there.

Do you live in Agbayani Village?

I don't live here at Agbayani Village yet, but I am gonna live here because I'm the one who is campaigning all over the state to get this village here. We fight very hard for this village. You see, there is discrimination. These associations in Delano, they came to the court and fight that we cannot build this building.

At the court people talk, then they said, "Anymore who want to talk?" "Yes, I want to talk. Your Honor, I want to talk. You tell me you are going to build a building for the old men when they retire? Or would you rather we build a building for them so that they would not sleep on the sidewalk when they cannot walk anymore?" I point them one by one in the court. I point them, all these big shot in here.

"You have a big house, but what about the other side of the road? On the other side of the road, we couldn't get a house there. You mean to tell me we cannot irrigate over here? Why? What reason? You are talking about not supporting Delano. We are the one who build Delano. We buy our shoes, we wear our clothes, come back to the town, put in everything. We are not supporting Delano? The *hell*," I said, "The hell. You are lying." We build them up.

"Who plant the grapes? We plant the grapes. We take care of the grapes like a baby. Like a baby!" I said. "From roots to the top. We made them rich. Where is our share? We want a small one. Small share, so that we could also live like human beings, like anybody else. So that we could also send our children to school, like anybody else. The hell [tears in his eyes]. Who bring all those fruits on your table? But I want my share, that's all I ask."

They've got money; I don't have it. But there are other things: your cause, your *rights,* your dignity as an individual, that's what I'm talking about. That's in me, that's inside, and the only way they are going to stop me is when I die, because I am going to fight until I die.

They make the laws, but they are the one who break the laws. They have the big businessman, they have the banker, the politician. Two hundred and fifty people are running this country. What about us? We elect them. They broke my two legs in the picket line. They tried to kill me. August 23, 1972. They hit me in the picket line, three of us. The sixth rib was broken. Beat my arms. One guy was thrown on the side road, I thought he was dead already. We are lucky. He was still alive.

They tried to get me in Salinas; they tried to get me in Phoenix, Arizona; they tried to get me in Coachella Valley. I'm still alive. They want to break my morale? The hell.

The future of the world is in the younger generation. I might not be here to witness all these things, but I know they will come. We are going to live in a better world.

II. Survivors: 1930-1945

Between 1917 and 1924 the famed Golden Door began to close. From 1930 to 1945 it was virtually shut. On February 5, 1917, a literacy provision excluding all persons over the age of sixteen who could not read some language, was passed over President Woodrow Wilson's veto. This law signaled the increasing difficulty for immigrants who wished to enter the United States. On October 16, 1918, foreign "anarchists" and others who believed in or advocated overthrowing the government also were excluded by law. In May of 1920, an act was passed that allowed for the deporting of foreigners convicted of violating or conspiring to violate acts of war.[1] When the First Quota Law of 1921 was passed, it became the first law in American history to place a numerical ceiling on the number of people who could immigrate to the country annually. This law also demonstrated the power of nativist elements in the country to affect immigration policy in a postwar America which was increasingly letting its racism and parochialism show. It assumed the natural superiority of the Nordic and Anglo-Saxon Protestant heritage to the new, more heterogeneous mixture of peoples from southern and eastern Europe.[2] According to historian John Higham:

> The law of 1921 limited European immigration to 3 per cent of the number of foreign born of each nationality present in the United States at the time of the last available census, that of 1910. This would hold the transatlantic current to a maximum of 350,000 and assign most of that total to northwestern Europe. Ethnic affiliation became the main determinant for admission to the United States.[3]

The law then was revised when

> . . . Congress debated two plans and adopted both. The first plan based national quotas on the foreign-born population of the United States in 1890 instead of 1910 and cut the quotas from 3 to 2 per cent of that base population. By moving back the census base to 1890, the law allowed about 85 per cent of the total quota immigration to northwestern Europe.[4]

The Johnson-Reed Act of 1924 was the result. It became the controlling law of immigrant entry until 1952. If Europeans were restricted in their entry, the Oriental Exclusion Act of 1924 almost ended Asian immigration entirely. As a result of these acts, between 1931 and 1945 fewer than 700,000 immigrants came to the United States. Close to thirteen million had come between 1901 and 1915.[5]

Early immigrants had viewed America as a land of refuge. To what extent was this true after 1930? After 1921 it was difficult for Armenians escaping the Turkish massacres to enter the United States unless they had family there. During the mid-1930s, Spanish Republicans fleeing Franco were generally not admitted, and with illustrious, wealthy, or otherwise lucky exceptions, neither were most European Jews. That the United States during the 1930s was in the midst of a depression of great magnitude cannot be overlooked, but neither can the racial and religious assumptions that were able to close the once-golden door, leaving many of the world's peoples the alternative of mass execution.

During World War II—even after the United States was fighting a war against Nazi Germany—millions of Jews and others trying to escape extermination were kept out by quota laws, anti-Semitic bureaucrats, and by, one must conclude, an American public who did not care. if this were not enough, the story of America's treatment of her own native-born of Japanese origin should give one pause.

But there were those who were able to come and those who were able to survive the psychic and physical tortures inflicted by race hatred, ideological fear, and war. The following are all stories of survivors. "Andrés Aragón" was able to come to the United States due to academic contacts. Because they had relatives who were willing to vouch for them and/or pay their way, Araxi Ayvasian, Anna Yona, and Carl Cohen arrived during the war years. Kyoko Takayanagi's story is included as a second, this time an American, view of the treatment of Japanese and Japanese-Americans in the 1930s and '40s.

ARAXI CHORBAJIAN AYVASIAN—
Escape from Armenia

Araxi Ayvasian's history might have been included with others who escaped from Europe around the time of World War I. She speaks mostly of those years. But since she arrived in the United States in the

1930s, and since, more importantly, her experiences of the Armenian genocide bear similarities to the more familiar holocaust of the '30s, she has been included here. Her story shows the continuities of horror in the first four and a half decades of this century.

Araxi Ayvasian is one survivor of the Armenian genocide. She and what was left of her family settled in Aleppo, Syria, in the early 1920s after having lived through two forced exiles from Turkey. She was graduated from the American College in Beirut in 1924 and worked for many years for the Near East Relief to help care for and resettle Armenian orphans. She arrived in the United States in 1934 with a visa sent by her uncle for his sister, whom she chaperoned to the Boston area. Araxi then lived for twenty years with her family in both Watertown and Medford, Massachusetts. She was and is active in Armenian church activities, the Ladies Auxiliary, and the Armenian Society. She worked for *Hairenik,* an important Armenian newspaper, for twenty years. It was there she met her husband, then the newspaper's manager. "I married the boss. You can put that."

Armenians are an ancient mountain people occupying the plateau that is today in eastern Turkey and the southwestern Soviet Union. They are a people who, bridging the Eurasian continent, have suffered for their geographic location, their proximity to larger, imperial neighbors, and their choice of Christianity in a predominantly Islamic area.

Armenian immigration to the United States began in some earnest following the 1894–1896 massacres of the Armenian people by the Ottoman state. Despite changes in the government during the first twenty years of this century, the Turkish state renewed its attempted genocide against the Armenian people. During those years Armenian villagers were deported, raped, murdered, or starved on a mass march through the deserts of Syria and along the Euphrates River. It is estimated that between one million people and half the existing Armenian population was wiped out by the end of World War I.

I met with Mrs. Ayvasian twice, both times on her porch and both times in the spring. She is a small, gray-haired woman with glasses. Her words are strong and articulate. When I first met her, she spoke mostly in historical terms. She saw herself as part of a panorama of Armenian history. She was often more interested in telling the Armenian story, aware of how little it is known, than in telling her own. As she spoke of her family, one sensed the fusion of her personal world and that of her people.

May 13, 1975, and
June 3, 1976
Arlington, Massachusetts[1]

I was born in Turkey. We used to have an Armenian kingdom there. Of course, after the Turks occupied those places, the Armenian kingdom came to an end.

In the town of Marash there were thirty thousand people where I was born, and we were under the domination of the Turks. Five hundred years since their occupation they have always subdued and massacred and tortured and confiscated property, no matter whose it was, even though we were citizens and we accepted them as our government. The worst came for mass murders starting in 1890—even 1880s—starting in the upper Armenia, and then in the Cilician Armenia 1894, 1895. There was a massacre in 1904 in Marash. In 1907 there was the one in Adana where they killed all the priests and all men of religion and culture—thirty thousand.[2]

I remember the massacre in 1904, I think it was. Even though I was four years old, there were certain events I remember. One thing, my father had closed his fabric shop. As he was coming home they had thrown a bottle of acid on him. Fortunately, it was not to his face. It was his leg that was bad. It was all skinned off. They killed about three thousand people in one day in Marash.

Of course, the worst came in 1915, during the First World War. They just herded the cream, the top—all cultural, professional, and church people. And they said they were going to take them to a certain part of Turkey, but they never got there.

Zeytoun was a village. My hometown was on one side of the mountains and Zeytoun was on the other side. It was a *purely* Armenian village. It was mountainous, it was a summer resort, as well. They had hot springs there. These Zeytoun people had twice fought against the Turks. They lost a lot of men at Zeytoun.

My grandfather, my mother's father, was a representative in the Turkish parliament in Aleppo. He had come to the Aleppo "congress," let's say. He was there two years, I think. In the month of the harvest he was asked, with a clergyman and another layman, to go to Zeytoun and persuade the Zeytounists to give their arms up. He refused. Those three people were the first ones to be deported..

The Zeytoun people were finally disarmed, and they were brought to Marash. After a few weeks they sent them down, to Syria. The first stop was Aleppo. The first station was Meskéné, Razza, Dayr az Zawr,[3] which was the biggest tomb along the Euphrates. People used to walk for days and days and months and months. Of course, we couldn't take much when we left.

I was born at the turn of the century, so I was about fourteen years old then.

In 1915, after the Zeytoun people were banished down toward the Euphrates, then it was our turn. Out of the thirty thousand there were left only a few hundred old people in Marash. The rest of them were all sent out.

Everyone was drafted up to age forty. Later on we found they were building roads, and as they were building roads, they were being shot until every one of them was killed. Nobody came back. You could either give a certain amount of money or go to the army. For that once, it was fifty Turkish pounds. First they drafted; then those who paid were deported six months later. My father paid money and stayed. They took the money, mules, donkeys, our horses; they took them all. Then, six months later, we were deported. My father was drafted.

My family was a hundred people. My father's family was five brothers. We were the least, five children. There were three generations. My mother's family was with us, too, but they were a small family. We had a mule. We had put some food and things like that on it, and we were walking. We couldn't take anything much. We left everything, the homes, the shops, to their mercy. We reached about two miles down. They started killing people already. We found out later one of my cousins was beheaded. It was at night when we went. The group had to rest for a while; you couldn't walk at night.

On the first night, the Turkish gendarmes, they were supposed to protect us—but they were the ones who attacked young girls. They raped them, and some of them were never returned, if they wanted to take them elsewhere.

Every day, every other day the deportations, a group of five hundred, four hundred, three hundred, that way. In a couple of months everybody was out. So we came to Aleppo. It took us about ten days.

Fortunately, my grandfather in the senate had some friends, and instead of deporting them all the way down to Dayr az Zawr, we were taken off a train and to a hideout. When we were deported, my grandfather was already in Aleppo. Through bribery he had found a way to take us into the city. They never let the Armenians go to the city. It would be about three miles out of the proper city, where they'd stay for the night, and the next morning they have to move again.

The night we had reached Aleppo some soldiers came and looked for my father. We didn't know what was happening. They singled us out. My grandfather's family is six daughters, one boy. He was not with us. My grandmother had another member of the family, and us.

These Turkish gendarmes took us from the group. They took us to some interior part of the city. My grandfather was in a hideout, so we went there. We were saved at this first hurdle.

One man, an Arab, also a representative and friend of my grandfather, owned a whole village. He said, "I'll take your family to my own village," because he knew what was going to happen to all the people who were going to Dayr az Zawr. In that village we stayed about six months, safe, sound. We thought we were free. And at the end of six months, an order came that we had to be deported. They had found out where we were.

My grandfather was a lawyer and was an educated man. They really wanted to kill him. So at the end of six months, we were deported again from Maara. My mother was pregnant. It was very difficult. It was *too* hot in the summer. We were still walking. My family, and there were a couple of other families also, whom my grandfather had brought after we had settled there. Most Armenians had already been deported, from Aleppo station down to Meskéné or Razza, Dayr az Zawr. The fact is that these Turkish gendarmes loved Turkish gold pounds. They'll take your money. They'll say they'll save you—one month, two months—and then the final station is Dayr az Zawr. You will finally be sent to Dayr az Zawr no matter what. At Dayr az Zawr they were all put into ditches. They were all shot in groups and thrown into the Euphrates River. How many *thousands*, hundred and thousands of Armenians, were killed in that Euphrates River! They were bound and thrown, all in groups. And some Armenian girls killed themselves there. They were pressured by the gendarmes. Rather than get raped, they threw themselves into the river.

Finally we went to Meskéné. There were a lot of people living in tents with four sticks and a sheet or something. We were held there for a while, and my grandfather had friends in the government who were responsible for organizing from station to station. They had a small

Araxi Chorbajian Ayvasian

house there, and my grandfather did some work for this fellow. He helped us again; we stayed there, but finally the order came for us. He said, "I can't keep you anymore. You have to go."

The next morning, we found my grandfather wasn't moving. He had a shock. He couldn't talk. He couldn't walk. He was in bed. He couldn't get up. We were supposed to leave, but he was paralyzed. They permitted us to stay a few days and find out what the situation was.

By this time my mother had her last child. She was not able to walk. We hired a camel to take care of her. The baby was delivered by itself. There were no doctors, no midwives, nothing. My grandmother helped her. The baby lived, but for worse days.

My grandfather died within the same week. Two gendarmes came and they took him near the river where there were a lot of people. They buried him in a mass grave in the sand, as if it was a cemetery or something. Every day hundreds would die of starvation. They would all take them and *dump* them.

In the time that we were detained there for six months, my father became an army soldier. He had two horse-drawn carts, and he was working for the government. By then we had a visitor, my aunt's husband. He quit the army and he was deported. It was a surprise. He was there—young, strong, a very courageous man. He had seen the world.

Now we are trying to flee because the baby was born, my grandfather dead. We either fled or we would be dead. You can't believe the story, but this is how it happened.. My father gave him one of the carts. He started going back and forth, bringing supplies to the Turkish army. Each time he took one of us with him. One of us would ride under the army supplies, weeds, lanterns, things like that. My mother, myself, and the baby were together. The baby cried. Finally the whole family was transferred to Aleppo, one by one, by this brother-in-law, my aunt's husband. We would ride with him; then about one hour from the city, he would drop us off. He'd give us directions as to where to go. It lasted about two months. Everybody was in Aleppo.

There were so many millions of people there. My uncles died there of diseases; typhus was prevalent. We lost quite a few of the family.

This was 1917 when we came back to Aleppo. After we stayed there, my father was still a soldier, and they transferred him. My mother started working, to make clothing for the army. With the armistice, November 11, 1918, the Allies occupied Aleppo. First the British came, then the French. The French went to occupy Cilicia, where my hometown was. So back and forth letters came. "Marash is beautiful now. The French have occupied. Everybody's free."

We had orange groves, olive orchards, vineyards. So we thought, "All right." We'd been out of the country three years now. We *had* to go back—like fools! This time there were only half the people who were deported that were alive.

We hired a truck, and the whole family rode in the truck. It took us about four days to go back. My father wanted to go back because there wasn't enough for us in Aleppo. We had no home, we had no house, we had no place to be. We were in a rented room, two families—my grandmother's family and my family. We thought if we went there we could at least get the fruits of our land. My father was quite a well-to-do person. With all his brothers they had three clothing stores, and a lot of property. So, we went there.

They vacated the house when we went. Some of them were burned. Most of the houses they had destroyed. Four years was too long a time for anything to stay intact by the Turks. The churches were all ruined. But it was nice. When we went the occupation was by the English. And then somehow there was an agreement between the English and the French. The English withdrew and the French came, and after the French came Armenian legionnaires in the French army.

Everything was beautiful, but the empire was deteriorating. A lot of the territory was taken by the Allies. There was no more Turkish government in Marash. Turkey, it was decimated. They didn't even have twenty-five percent of the old Ottoman Empire. We left again at the end of 1918; this was about a year after we went back, because we had harvested one harvest of rice and vineyards.

The war started between the Turks. This time it was the Kemalists from the north. They had come to fight. Kemal, Ataturk, Mustafa Kemal Pasha, they called them. First the Sultan abdicated, and then the Young Turks took over. During the war the Young Turks were in charge, but when the war was over and they had lost everything, the Young Turks disappeared. And now, Mustafa Kemal, who was against the Young Turks, took over this time.

There were about ten thousand Armenians by this time in Marash. Of the thirty thousand, two-thirds were killed or died, and of the ten thousand, the shooting was going on, the homes were being burned. The Turkish soldiers were coming, advancing every night, one street to the other. When the turn came to our house to be burned, we had to flee.

My father wasn't home on Christmas Day. He had gone to visit his brothers.

We had made holes in the walls of the homes so that we could go from one to the other. Our home was on the street, so it was very easy to get to. There were about five hundred people 'way at the end of the street. They had to move out—all of us.

We ran out of the house. It was a *bleak,* snowy night, in the middle of the night. We left that other child who was born in the desert, in Meskéné. She was left behind. There was one man who took charge of things, and he refused to take any smaller children. We thought that they would not do anything to the children and the old people. There were a lot of old women and other children that were left there. This Armenian–U.S. citizen guided us to the street and told us, "From now on you're on your own. Run!"

A lot of us fell on the street because the Turkish army was shooting from the citadel, from the minarets. It was a very light night on account of the snow and ice, a full moon, beautiful night. We were seeing the people just dropping as the bullets were coming. But we all got to where my father was, a big Jesuit monastery. When we went there it was, oh [sighing], just a mess. There is no room to sit, even leave alone lying or anything. There were about three, four thousand people in that one church.

The French and the Turks fought for three weeks exactly. At the end of twenty-one days there were rumors that the French people were going to withdraw, leave the town to the mercy of the Kemalists. And, of course, it happened. The Armenian fellows were fighting for the French. The Armenians in the church knew that the French were up to something. They said, "You're not going to go unless you take the young people with you." The French refused. There was a skirmish between the French soldiers stationed here in the church and the Armenian young people. Anyway, that night the church was almost emptied of men and young boys. They followed the French army who were withdrawing, whereas they could have won the war if they'd stayed.

It snowed twenty-four hours. They were all frozen on the road to Islahie, where they could get a train. Turkish gendarmes came, two days after the French withdrew. They told us we can go back to our homes. They brought some food and rice. By this time there were some Americans. There was an American girls' college, and there were a lot of orphanages, American orphanages. They went around the city. They collected all these children who were left in the homes and they put them in the orphanages.

We got our child again. She was three or four years old. She suffered from diarrhea because she didn't have enough shelter or the proper food or anything. She was sick for quite a long time, and then I think about six months later, one afternoon, she complained of some pain in her neck. She died in twenty-four hours of the complaints. We couldn't get to a doctor then, you know. No hospital, no medication she got. Those three weeks killed her. She died a natural death, you would call it; but I'm sure if she didn't go through that, she wouldn't die.

Life started again, on rice and olive oil. People were all sick because they were hungry. They all had diarrhea, and it took another couple of years to find themselves, but soon enough they wanted to leave. No matter where, it would be better than Marash.

People in groups left. They were again killed on the road. If five people started, one of them reached Aleppo. Of the ten thousand I don't think two thousand survived.

This time my father didn't go because, well, we were all young people, girls mostly. My brother left with the French. He was only about thirteen years old. My uncle, my cousins, they all left. Some of them perished. The brother-in-law that transferred us from Meskéné from the desert to Aleppo saw my brother on the road there, and he carried my brother all the way to Islahie. His toes were frozen; he couldn't walk. They were later taken care of in Adana, where the French had a government.

My father had some Turkish friends, and those people who had taken care of our lands and property when we were away, they were nice enough to give a truck to my father. We filled in the truck again; my grandfather, my brother, and my uncle were off. The family was *all* women. Nobody. Grandfather died, my uncle had left with the French soldiers, my brother left, my cousins. But we came back to Aleppo our second time; this was our second deportation.

[Some years after I came to the United States] I became a bookkeeper by profession. I was in charge of a small bookstore that we had at the Hairenik Press.

You didn't have any children?

No. I couldn't have children. I was in my fifties when I got married.
He waited twenty years.

*What effect was there on the relationship between men and women as a
result of Armenian persecution?*

The Armenian mother is very different from any other mother. The
man has always been the head of the family. The mother has always
been there for the children; to educate them, to clothe them. "Family
education" is what you give and what the children take with them all
their lives. They learn a lot in school, but we call it the "family education," *vndanegan dataaragoutune,* which is something more than what
any school can give. Mothers have been very, very tender, yet very strict
with their children, both ways.

I'd like to read you something. It's a very short epic poem. "The
Mother's Heart." He says that there is a legend that a boy loved a girl.
And this girl asked to boy to prove that he really loves her. And it says
in order to prove, he should go and bring his mother's heart to her. Kill
the mother and bring the heart. So the boy is sorry and sad, crying,
and the girl was very angry and said, "Don't show your face to me unless you come with your mother's heart!" The boy goes and kills a goat
and brings the goat's heart, and the girl recognizes that it's not the
mother's heart, so she's even angrier. And then the fellow goes again.
He's so sad and he's lost himself. He kills his mother and he's bringing
his mother's heart to the girl. On the way he falls, and he hears the
voice of the mother, even though it's only a heart; the mother's heart
says, "Oh, my boy, did you *hurt* yourself?"

See? This is a legend, but it shows the Armenian mother. Even
though taken out of the physical body, just a heart, the heart speaks to
the boy, in tenderness, and says, "Oh, my boy, did you hurt yourself?"
So the Armenian mother is something very different. It's actually the
truth about every mother.

In the last five hundred years, the Armenian men had a difficult time.
They had to compete to get someplace. While they were doing that, to
provide for the family, the mother was doing everything in the home,
to serve the husband and to serve the children. And mind you, every
Armenian mother, six was the average, six children, at least. My grandmother had eleven, plus two or three that died. My mother had eight.

And she was one of the modernistic ones. If it wasn't for deportations and so on and so forth, maybe she would've had more. We always liked large families. Armenian families lived together. The son would get married and they lived together in one part of the parent's house. There was no such thing as going away. The bride would come right to her in-laws' home and live there, as long as it was possible, as long as they had three, four, five children.

Now, after fifty years, we have the fiftieth anniversary of the deportation, of the genocide. We applied to the House of Representatives. We made a petition that April 24 should be set as a day of men's inhumanity to men. We didn't even *mention* Armenians. But even that was denied to us.

I don't know why the U.S. doesn't sign. Maybe because they have experienced genocide with the Indians and also the blacks. Some Turk may come and say, "Look what you did to your native Indians! Look what you have been doing after Proclamation freeing the Negroes by Lincoln, a hundred years."

We should have learned a lot from the Negroes, you know, what they did. A lot of them were imprisoned, a lot of things happened to them, but they are getting there. The TV screen comes on. What do you see? All blacks. They are getting there, and in business, everywhere. They have better houses. In a short span of life, only a decade and a half. I hope we do something ourselves.

Where is that [pauses] old, beautiful trustworthy U.S.A.? Where is it now? Half the government was indicted, for God's sake. They were all found guilty, even your president, even this president. Four weeks after the country made its president resign, the other one gets up and pardons him. Let him suffer a little bit. Well, they thought, "He might get sick; he might get breakdown." So what? He deserves to get breakdown. He deserved it. Look what *he* did.

No one person is permanent in this world. We all have our ups and downs. But if we are guilty, we should *suffer* [bangs her hand down on the table] the consequences. They should enforce the law, be it on the president, or on the state secretary, or on the community. If parents punish their children for their little mistakes, they will learn to grow better. From children to their parents to the representatives to their government to their president. It starts from top to bottom.

"ANDRÉS ARAGÓN"*—
After the Death of Spain

Andrés Aragón was born into a middle-class family in El Ferrol, a small city in the Spanish region of Galicia. As a young man he became politically active, worked with the Spanish Socialist party, and fought with the Republican side during the Spanish Civil War.

The history of the Republican, or Loyalist, cause can only be traced briefly here. It began politically with the abdication of the Spanish monarch Alfonso XIII and the birth of the Republic through democratic elections in April of 1931. The Church, the military, and the landed aristocracy which ruled Spain for centuries made instant war on the Republic and destroyed it. After a brutal civil war General Francisco Franco took power in early 1939. Spain was the testing ground for both troops and weaponry later used in World War II, and with the aid of Italian Fascist and Nazi troops, Franco was able to establish a dictatorship in Spain that was to outlast Hitler's and Mussolini's by thirty years.

After the death of Republican Spain, the years of civil strife, the thousands who served in the war's International Brigades, the writings of Hemingway, Malraux, Spender—after these came the refugees, children of Catalonia, the Basque country, and all the cities and towns that dotted the Iberian landscape. The Spanish Civil War was a modern war, one with large numbers of civilian casualties. In early 1939 close to half a million people fled across the French border. Some 250,000 were, like Aragón, with the Spanish Republican army fleeing the Nationalists. The rest were civilians.[1]

As the Spanish people were the first Europeans to feel the military might of the oncoming war, they also were among the first to experience massive concentration camps. Aragón remembers the camps along the French border, but was able to escape after a brief stay. By the end of the Civil War, his status as an artist and intellectual gave him options often unavailable to other Spaniards. It was generally true that those Spaniards with means or reputation escaped most easily, while those of the poorer classes were less lucky. The middle- and upper-class nature of Spanish exiles admitted to the United States contrasts sharply with

*"Andrés Aragón" is a pseudonym.

most of the pre-1930s immigrants and has much in common with the phenomenon of refugees from Central Europe of the thirties, like Einstein, Kissinger, Fermi, and Tillich, who were welcomed to the universities of Britain and America.

This, of course, is not to say that to be an exile is ever easy, and to have lost one's cause with one's homeland makes it all the more difficult. Whereas many émigrés from Germany and Italy and even the Communist-bloc countries could return home if they wished, until recently it was not possible for men like Aragón to return to Spain.

It is very difficult to locate Spanish Civil War immigrants in the United States. The quota laws were most effective in keeping them out. The majority of the refugees either stayed in France or tried to emigrate to Latin American countries. Mexico, under the revolutionary government of President Lázaro Cárdenas, offered refuge for many, especially those in artisitic and intellectual fields. Argentina, Cuba, and the Dominican Republic also took a substantial number.[2]

Spanish exiles were also excluded from the United States for political reasons. Some American leftists identified with the Republicans strongly enough to join the Abraham Lincoln Brigade. But the anarchistic and socialistic orientation of Republican Spain was opposed by the United States government. According to Aragón and other sources, pressure from the American Catholic Church tainted official government dealings with the Republican cause and was instrumental in keeping exiles out of the United States.

The history of American fears of radicalism and the linking in certain minds of foreigners and radicals goes back at least as far as the late nineteenth century. Labor unionism was seen by some as a "foreign importation." Violence during the Haymarket bombing on May 14, 1886, was blamed on alien radicals, and resulted in the hanging of four people and the suicide of one. A number of antiforeign and exclusionary societies developed shortly thereafter.[3]

The assassination of President McKinley in 1901 by Leon Czolgosz, an American of east-European origin, led Theodore Roosevelt to press for a restriction of anarchists. Following the Bolshevik Revolution of 1917 and World War I, there was a wave of antiforeignism, political exclusion, and deportation measures. The October 1918 anti-Communist and antianarchist laws and the 1920 provisions to deport alien dissidents were soon put into practice. In November of 1919 and January of 1920, Attorney General A. Mitchell Palmer had Justice Department agents raid public halls and private homes in over thirty cities to round up alleged Communists. About six thousand alien radicals or alleged radicals were detained and hundreds subsequently deported.[4] The antiforeignism and conservatism of the Ku Klux Klan was also well known and popular during the 1920s. Thus there were several historical precedents for the difficulties met by Spanish exiles in the late '30s and early '40s, even after the United States entered the war against fascism. The bizarre experiences of Dr. Aragón during the mid-1940s and into the McCarthy era show the continuities of the antiradical, antiforeign tradition into the postwar world.

Dr. Aragón is a distinguished professor of Spanish language and literature and the author of many books, articles, and essays, both in English and Spanish. When he first spoke with me he looked out of his office window and said, "My case is not likely to help you. It is only for the picturesque aspects of something unusual that happened."

March 4, 1976
Los Angeles, California

As a student I went to the university at seventeen in Granada, in southern Spain, and I became very active. I moved about and I saw such terrible things [in the countryside].[1] I couldn't rationalize these things and I [became] very politically minded.

When the Civil War came about, I was very happy to have a chance to fight. I fought in the fronts of Madrid. At the beginning I was a regular militiaman. Later I got involved with something called *Milicias de la Cultura;*[2] it was to bring political consciousness to the soldiers. I was the editor of a magazine for the front line, also.[3] I was very, very active all through the war, and when the war ended, I felt very bad that I had to cross the border.

I was in Madrid [during the first year of the war]. And after I was called by the government to go to Valencia, where the government was.[4] From Valencia I went to Barcelona and from Barcelona to France at the end of the war.

I was in charge of the war archives of our commercial relations with Russia, and in the last few months of the war, I was [one of] the technical secretar[ies] of the undersecretary of war, department of weapons. In those last months I had to write all the communications to buy weapons and how to pay for the weapons. At the end the head of my office asked me to take the archives out with me to the mountains close to the border in case we lose the war. I went with a group of soldiers to this mountain spot and waited with a radio transmitter to receive orders. Finally one day they told us to burn the whole documentations and to cross the border. The border was closed. This was early February '39. The Pyrenées were completely covered with snow. The people that went with me burned the papers, *but* the Franco troops were very close and began to fire all over when they saw the fires going on at night.

When we decided to go to the border, we were between the French and Franco's forces. People were dying of cold and hunger, thousands of persons. We spent one night in the open there and people would die like flies. The French had the *gendarmerie* at the border. We threatened that if they didn't allow us to enter peacefully, we'd enter forcibly. Finally the French allowed us to enter. Several thousand people were there. There was a small village close by. We started going to the next village without knowing what to do or anything. Before reaching the village we were ordered to wait in a tremendous line. Little by little we were registered and looked over, made to undress, lots of things. Finally we were divided, men one side, women another; and sent to improvised concentration camps. It was snowing.

In my camp, there were [already] probably two thousand, three thousand people. The first day in that camp they threw pieces of cooked horse meat above the wire for people to pick up and eat if they wanted. That was all. No disposition for a place to sleep or anything else. The following morning, they took out of that single camp between two hundred and three hundred bodies that died of cold that night, and that repeated several times in the first days. But this is written in the histories. There were 120,000 in [the Arglés sur Mer] camp and for fifteen days an average of five hundred died.

A few of us escaped. We were protected by an old woman who took pity on us. Finally, after fifteen days of being in hiding, we left the place. I never went back to the concentration camp. I managed to reach Paris. I had a rich uncle in Havana, that's why. He opened me an account in a French bank. Then I decided to rent a castle close to Paris and take with me as many as I could and [hide] there. I took ten or twelve friends.

It was a ruined castle, a big house, only a few rooms with furniture. The rest was in very bad shape. When I signed the contract I didn't know who the owner was, but after the first month the owner appeared and was the head of the police [of a nearby town]. He told me I had to pay double the amount or he'd send [all of us] to a concentration camp.

Then I became a fugitive from the French police. I went to Paris and was given the address of this photographer. This photographer gave me a set of papers that were falsified. Then I took a train to La Rochelle, on the coast south of Le Havre. There I was given an address, and the person at this address hired a boat and took me to the boat that was going to Havana.

The boat was full of refugees. Some were official refugees and others were just people who were afraid of what was going to happen in Europe in a few months. In fact, probably one hundred Jewish people came on that boat and went to Cuba or South America with the hope to come to the United States later on. There were also the remnants of the Cuban batallion that fought in Spain and a few handful of Spaniards. On arrival I was sent to [an immigration] camp for a few days for screening until the Cuban government decided to allow me to stay there.

I was only twenty-one when the war began and twenty-four when the war ended. I came to Cuba when I was twenty-four and stayed there until I was twenty-eight.

Since I had a background as an intellectual professor, although I was very young at the time, they made things easy for me and I was allowed to lecture, to teach, and to direct theater. I never thought of coming to the United States. I knew that it was almost impossible to come, although I knew a handful of friends that one way or the other came to the country. I was thinking if I could not make a living in Havana I would try to do something in Mexico.

I was active politically in Cuba. I was the head of a small group of Spanish Socialists in exile.[5] Spanish socialism was a very old, established political party and was perhaps the best-organized political party in Spain. It had a tremendous importance in the Spanish Republic. It was not Communist inclined; in fact, it was completely different from the Communists. It was a democratic, not an authoritarian, party.

A friend of mine was invited to come to Middlebury College one summer. He came and he paid a visit to a great Spanish scholar that was teaching at Princeton, Professor Américo Castro.[6] My specialization in Spain was Oriental Studies—I was a beginning Arabist. At that time Professor Castro was very interested in the Arabic world. He wrote me a letter saying, "If you want to come to the United States, I could arrange to bring you for a nine-month period with a contract." I decided to accept [and got a temporary visa].

Around August or early September 1943, I arrived in Miami. People were coming off of the plane and a loudspeaker mentioned my name and asked me to wait. I didn't know why this happened. I was on my way to Princeton, but I was detained and interrogated there for four days in relation to my friends and things that happened in the Spanish Civil War. At that time there wasn't a CIA; they were the Navy Intelligence Service or the Army Intelligence Service, or the State Department, I don't know. But the questioning became so silly and so absurd that at one time after four days of asking me not to move from the hotel and to be at the disposal of the authorities, etc., I decided to forget coming to the country.

I phoned Américo Castro. I told him I had unexpected difficulties to enter the country, and that I decided to go back to Havana. I will break my contract. I will not subject the university to anything, but I don't want to continue this type of thing.

Then he asked me to be patient and that he was going to send [to Washington] a colonel who was at Princeton. I didn't know it, but I was going to be used to teach army personnel Spanish, to prepare officers and soldiers in language for foreign invasions. I decided to wait. Then Immigration came to me and said, "Princeton University placed a bond, and you are allowed to go to the university if you want to." I stayed in Princeton teaching Spanish to our [army] personnel and at the same time working with Professor Castro on Oriental background.

In the middle of the program this man asked me to see somebody from the Department of War Information. I went to the New York Office of War Information and talked to the person in charge of the program for Europe. He told me that they had a file on my activities in Cuba. They knew of my democratic ideas, and I could be helpful to the American war effort if I was willing to work for them.

I said, "I don't have any objection to work for democracy and for the Allies against Fascism. If what you want from me is propaganda for Spain, I would gladly accept." They told me they couldn't ask me for anything else, that this was the object of the war, that I would not be forced to do anything that would go against my political principles.

I went to work for the Office of War Information. I became the head of the Spanish News Desk. I was in charge of the news for Spain for eight programs every day, and I became the special technical commentator of the war with a chat I gave for the Spanish underground over shortwave radio once a week. With a name that they gave me I became famous, Andrés Aragón.

I was very happy doing what I was doing. I liked my job. Of course everything had to be submitted to the censors of the office before being allowed to go onto the air. I had eight daily programs of news that I prepared. I had four secretaries working for me at the time, and I had something that I wrote personally as a commentary once a week and that I delivered personally on microphones and spoke directly to Spain from New York. Then I was the official voice of the United States for Spain during that commentary of fifteen minutes or a half an hour, depending on how long it was. I commented on the policy of the American government, with the conduct of the war, what was supposed to happen after the war and to encourage people to resist Fascism, Nazism, and all those doctrines that were present in Europe.

But something happened, and what happened changed my life. I was encouraged by the authorities at the Office of War Information to ask for permanent residency in the United States. They told me that they will be happy to help me get permanent residency, not to worry about my future. I went to a lawyer to prepare my documentation which was sent to Canada to get a visa to enter the country permanently.

After doing this, April 14th of 1944 came about. That was the day that Spain celebrated the proclamation of the second Spanish Republic that was destroyed by Fascism. At that time, some people invited me to talk on radio for Spain with my own name in commemoration of this date, and I agreed to do it. [An agent of] the FBI came to see me and asked me to go to his office. They had an office in the Office of War Information.

I went there and he told me, "We heard that you are going to speak 14th of April for Spain in your own name and advise you not to do it." Then I replied that that was my own time, my own thing, and I didn't feel that I ought to pay any attention to this type of request. He repeated that it wasn't a wise decision on my part. I resented the thing, but anyway I went to this small radio station the appointed night.

Other people spoke that night, too. I don't remember what I said, but at the end of my speech, the man who handled the [program] told me, "I'm sorry, but your speech was not delivered to Spain, it was cut by order of the FBI." I felt bad about it. But that was a small thing, it was not that important and probably would not have any consequence if immediately something else hadn't happened. What happened was that Churchill, in the House of Commons, gave a speech. For the first time during the war, he called that man Franco a "gentlemen" and a "friend of England."

I received this speech over the teletype with instructions to translate it and deliver it to Spain. That was a problem of conscience for me, and I decided not to do it. I went to see the head of my section and I told him, "I am not going to translate this speech. I accepted this job thinking that I would never be forced to say anything in favor of a dictator. That man is not a gentleman and I am not going to call him a gentleman."

The thing had some repercussions. I was called by the authorities. They tried to convince me and I had an altercation with the head of [the European section]. We had some hard words. I said, "You can dispose of my job; I don't want to work here anymore." He threw me out of his office and I left. Then I was officially expelled from the Office of War Information, and I found myself in New York without a job and the thing pending from Canada and what to do.

At this time there was a man in New York who became very famous later on, the famous Spanish movie director, [Luis] Buñuel. He knew about me and I knew about him and he called me and asked me what I was going to do. He offered me a position as director and writer and actor, to work with him in Los Angeles. After some hassling back and forth, I decided to accept.

[I moved to Los Angeles.] Soon I started to work. After three or four months of being here some officers from Immigration came to the door of my apartment and arrested me for illegal entry into the country; I was going to be deported. This was the first news I had that I was running this type of risk. They wanted to deport me to Spain. If I was sent back to Spain I would be shot right there, because I had been writing against Franco and talking against Franco all my life.

I hired a lawyer and they gave me a kind of freedom under surveillance with a second bond I had to put to be able to continue working and doing my things. I decided to fight the case against the government. It took ten years. I also was married then. I had a child. My wife was American. I had not been authorized to leave the country or to stay in the country. If I left the country, I would never be able to come back—I would be a fugitive from American justice. If I stayed, I was not able to move from the city.

That was the period of McCarthy, pre-McCarty, and the period of the Cold War. I saw the loyalty oaths and those things because my job in Hollywood went on for a couple of years. But then that was finished. Buñuel went to Mexico. I couldn't leave the country; I had to stay here, working here and there, giving lessons and things like that. My wife had to go to work. Immigration asked me when I was detained in 1945 if I had some money. I had some money saved. They told me, "You cannot work if you have money." Later when I didn't have a penny, they said, "Now you can start looking to find work."

I decided to come to the university, and I applied for a position here. Since I had some publications and was fairly well known, the university offered me a contract and we did not go into the details of my legal situation. I didn't mention anything, and I started to work here.

My situation was not solved. I was called by Immigration every two or three months and insulted like a common criminal, paying a lawyer all these years. That was very hard, the McCarthy period. I was called by one of the inspectors in Immigration and he told me, "The government has decided to authorize you to go to Canada to get your visa." I felt very happy with this, but before that the Un-American Activities Committee wanted to have an interview with me. I couldn't go. I called Washington. I didn't have any money to spend at that time.

Professor Américo Castro was a prominent man and very, very anti-Communist. He knew me very well, too—he was at Princeton. I asked him if he could take my place and see what these congressmen or senators wanted to find out about me. He went to Washington and was interrogated by these senators and congressmen, and my lawyer here received the deposition showing what he said about me. What my lawyer told me was, it was bad enough that this committee thought I was a dangerous Communist, but to have sent another Communist to Washington to represent me was worse. He was in danger of becoming prosecuted himself for talking in good terms about me.

After those things I went to Canada. I arrived and was received by the American consul there. What this man told me was, "You are never to get a visa from the United States. You know that you are a dangerous man, a Russian spy in my country, and my duty is to send you back to jail. Then you are going to take a plane, without any visa, without anything, and arrive in Seattle and let the authorities take care of you."

I took the plane back and arrived in Seattle. The Immigration officers in Seattle were very kind, nice people and they were very busy. They appointed a taxi driver, a deputy of some kind, to take me to jail. No officer or policeman was there. I told this man to send a telegram to my wife in Los Angeles. I gave him ten dollars. The telegram said, "I am going to be taken to jail. I don't know for how long. Contact our lawyer." I didn't know if the taximan would do it or not. He did that. He sent the telegram.

This is a touch, a literary touch. Since I am a writer, I like this literary touch. Someday I will probably write some of these things. This was 1955, and this country had excellent relations with Franco's Spain, and the Fascist chorale, or Falange [chorale of Spain] , were going from city to city. I had to listen from my *cell* in the Seattle jail, to the chorus singing Spanish songs, the chorus from the Fascist youth of Spain honoring the people in jail. There were common criminals in that jail; nobody political was there except myself, but I went through that experience of being in jail while the Fascist chorale was singing outside.

The second day or the third day I was there, a man came from Washington and I was called to [the warden's] office. My lawyer requested that I was immediately sent to Los Angeles. They arranged some time of release, based on the fact that I owned a house. The fact that I was a property owner was a decisive factor to allow me to come. They sent me here with a letter to the head of Immigration here, giving me fifteen days to sell all my things. Then I arrived here, went downtown, was informed that I was still under a bond and that I would have to arrange my things. The order of deportation was standing. I decided to come to the university, and for the first time explain to the chancellor what happened. I had never said anything about my situation. He didn't believe that this thing could happen in this country.

Then members of the department without exception decided to [sign] a letter of protest to Washington. The head of the department's sister went to college with Mrs. Johnson, the wife of the former President, Lyndon Johnson, at that time the head of the senate majority. [He] called his sister in Texas. Ironically enough, I owe my stay in this country to Lyndon Johnson. He called Immigration and everybody and had the consul in Canada fired. After a few days, I received a notification from Immigration to go back to the office. They told me that I was authorized to go back to Canada to pick up my visa, this time for good, in Vancouver.

I went to Canada. I went to the consulate and the American consul. The following year I became an American citizen and for the first time

I was able to travel freely. I even went to Europe in 1957. My situation became legal after ten years of this type of thing.

I'm surprised you would want to become a citizen after all that.

After so many years of living in the United States I can't judge the authorities on the same level with the American people. I had excellent American friends, I worked in excellent libraries, I was able to do what I wanted to do with my life. I liked American people in general. I felt at ease here, and I think I am now convinced that the only country that I like to live in and die in is the United States, in spite of all these experiences. [Laughs.] If I remember these anecdotes, it is because they were dramatic, but everybody goes in life through bad experiences and bad things and I had my share, probably more than other people. I accepted and I wanted American citizenship, and I feel very comfortable being American. But it's good for other people to know that these things happen in a democracy, too, and [not only under totalitarian rule]. Perhaps other people may think I have a right to be bitter. I am not bitter at all. [Laughs.]

I went back to Spain for the first time after twenty years. I saw my parents one year before they died. I went back several times for short visits. It is hard for me to understand the people.

My family stayed, my brother and sister, and it was hard for me to talk to them. I found that the psychology of the people is very much changed, the character of the people. It is not the people I knew as Spaniards, and it is no wonder. They lived through such terrible times— and human beings, they get accustomed to everything. If you are forced to live like that, it becomes a habit. To change all of a sudden, it is not easy. That country under Franco made me sick. I felt much closer to the American people than that type of life, and I would never go back to live under any type of lack of freedom, lack of dignity.

ANNA FOA YONA—
Leaving Fascist Italy

"Where Could We Go? We Spread the Map"

Anna Foa was raised in the northern-Italian industrial city of Turin. Both she and her husband were Sephardic Jews, their families having been expelled from Spain in 1492. Her family's name was Foa, meaning "faith." They settled in French Provence and later moved to northern Italy. There were two rabbis in the family. One, De Latorre, she called an illustrious but "quite a reactionary person"; the other, her father's father, was rabbi-in-chief of the Turin congregation. Her father was a lawyer who went into the exporting business.

Anna and her two brothers were in their early and middle teens when Mussolini took power. One brother became "an intellectual anarchist" and was arrested during the 1930s. The other "enrolled in the Fascist party" in order to " keep his job" but was later arrested for the political activity of his brother.

The rise of Benito Mussolini to power in Italy in the early 1920s was not, like Hitler's earliest attempts, based on or wedded to anti-Semitic doctrine. Many historians have noted the general antipathy of the Italian people to race doctrines and the separation of Italian Fascism from race dogma until the alliance between Hitler and Mussolini in the '30s, and especially with Hitler's visit to Italy in May of 1938.

After Hitler's visit, racial laws soon came to Italy, and their similarities to the Nuremburg Laws of 1935 could not be ignored. On September 5, those of Jewish birth were excluded from the government-controlled schools, kindergarten through university. Then the Racial Laws of October 7 prohibited Jews from intermarrying, from joining the military, and from working in banks, in insurance, and in many other businesses. As in Nazi Germany, racial definitions of Jews applied to those without religious or ethnic affiliation to the Jewish community. With the increasing weight of the racial laws, Anna, her husband, David, and her two small children attempted to leave Italy. They came to the United States in 1940. Mrs. Yona now teaches at the New England Conservatory of Music.

In late 1943 the Nazi forces occupied much of Italy and began deporting Jews to death camps. There were 57,000 Jews in prewar Italy. At the war's end, eight thousand were dead.[1]

June 22, 1975
Cambridge, Massachusetts

Really the story of my family and my story is based on the Jewish persecution. But quite a bit before the Jewish persecution I had many great troubles because of Mussolini—not because we were Jewish, but because we are anti-Fascist. All my family—my two brothers and my father—were taken into prison, and my brother was sentenced to fifteen years of jail. My older brother, who is here now in Washington, was kept in prison for six months without ever being interrogated, just because he was the brother of my other brother who was politically active. So really, the story of persecution doesn't start with the alliance of Hitler and Mussolini; it started before. This happened in 1935.

My brother at that time was twenty. He was in the anti-Fascist movement for two years, and he was a writer for a clandestine magazine which was published in Paris, *Justice and Liberty*, "Guistizia e Libertà."[1] This magazine was not anarchist or socialist or communist, it was social democratic. There were articles based on the economy, constitutional articles. It was quite highbrow. Those articles were written in Italy, brought to Paris by hand, because mail and telephone were censored. And then they were brought back to Italy in a clandestine way, in order to be distributed to the workers of the Fiat or the Lancia, the industrial bases of Italy. My brother wrote under the pseudonym of "Emiliano." The whole group was taken. Out of 123 several were sent to the special tribunal "for the protection of the State." My brother was kept *incomunicado* for nine months, and finally he was brought to trial in Rome. It was very difficult to find any lawyer who would defend him. Finally my father found this schoolmate of his who agreed to be the lawyer for my brother. They sentenced him to fifteen years in jail, just because he had written articles. This is what happened a few years before Mussolini had the alliance.

In the meantime, every year Mussolini put into prison some people, but they always left out someone on purpose. The group started to work with other people, so the secret police would follow them. More and more people went into prison. This was their policy.

My husband was a Zionist, and he was head of the Zionistic organization in Turin. At that time I was also a Zionist, and so I met him. To be a Zionist at that time meant to be an anti-Fascist. I was active in a passive way because I was always eager to hear and to read, but we really couldn't do anything. His idea was to be a collaborator with this newspaper. For instance, when the war in Spain started, we tried to collect some money for people who went to Spain to fight against Franco. My sister-in-law's brother died in Spain fighting against Franco. But very few dared to give money, even if they were very wealthy, because they were afraid that the government would come to know.

Just to tell you a little example how the Fascist regime was—when the

Ethiopian War started, Mussolini asked all the women to give their wedding rings to the country because the country needed gold. So many women, many stupid women, gave it. Many other women took a yellow curtain rod [ring] and they kept their wedding ring. My mother gave a curtain rod, and she was given an iron wedding ring, but she kept her wedding ring in the drawer. I refused to give it, and I wore it on my right hand and you know that I lost many friends? Because I *openly* said, "I don't want to yield to such a silly request." And so there was a real atmosphere of *fear* before the Jewish persecution.[2]

When Mussolini became an ally of Hitler, the Anti-Semitic Law came—in July 1938. Some laws were enacted in July, some of the laws were enacted in September, so that we never knew what was going to happen next. We always considered ourselves Jewish and we always considered ourselved Italian, without making any distinction between the two. What is *first*? Are you first a Jew or are you first an Italian? Then, when this thing happened, we decided we have to leave because my husband lost a job.

My children were very small. They were going to nursery school. They were forbidden to go to the nursery school. I couldn't go to the library, I couldn't go to the movie, couldn't go the theater. We couldn't have any help. So everything is by us, and without any machine or gadget. We had a very nice girl as a maid. She used to come from seven o'clock in the night and stay until two or three o'clock in the morning, and go away so that the secret police wouldn't see that she was doing some work with the house.

After 1935 there had been other arrests that had been exclusively political. After the Jewish Law came it was absolutely incredible. They published in the paper that the Jews were third-class citizens. They said that Jews had been cheaters, the moneylender—you know, the usual things. So not only the law was very, very depressing, but also the attitide of the press.

On my honeymoon I went for a little trip, on a little cruise to Denmark. We went on a boat, and there was a German Jew who had just escaped from Germany. At that time I knew German fluently. We became quite good friends, and he told us, "What happens now in Germany will happen in Italy. Why don't you get out? Why don't you get out!"

At that time my husband and I were considering it slightly, the idea to move. But then our family ties were very strong. We decided that we couldn't stand it anymore when the Racial Law came, when they said we don't have a job, when we don't have the possibility to educate our children. We cannot have communications with our friends because by then they were quite scared to have anything to do with us, and we had our children we had to think about, and so we decided we wanted to move.

In 1939 we tried desperately to emigrate, *anywhere*. The last place was America. I don't know why, we wanted to get to South America. To go to Brazil we had to convert to Catholicism—and even if this was some water over our head, my husband and I decided we couldn't do it. We took the map of the world. Another place we wanted to go was Patagonia, the tip of South America. I met a lady who lived in Patagonia and she said it was very beautiful so I said, "Let's go there!" At the end of 1938 we thought to move to France. It was not yet the war. But then in 1939 the war came, so it was impossible. Then in 1940 the Pétain regime came.

We looked at the map and really we didn't know where to go. So we tried Patagonia, we tried Brazil, we tried Paraguay. They told us that there was a great depression, no jobs. England was out. Australia, they wouldn't take any Jews at that time.

How did they say that?

They say it very clearly. We went to the consulate to see how was the immigration law. At that time I remember the Australian consulate said that the "*quota*" for Jewish immigrants was closed. You see, in 1940, German Jews, Polish Jews, had tried to emigrate all over the world. We tried to go to Australia, New Zealand, to Paraguay. It was impossible. All the doors were closed.

Then we decided, let's try the United States. We had some relatives who had come here in 1939. Very wealthy, Italian also. And they offered to give us an affidavit—you must promise not to be a dependent of the state. So they put five thousand dollars in escrow for each of us, in the bank. We never touched this money. I have an eternal gratitude for them, because naturally these twenty thousand dollars they couldn't touch. We were four of us. Especially in 1940, today it would be like 100,000 dollars. These cousins sent us a telegram in which they said they would give us four cantaloupe. A cantaloupe was a code name for five thousand dollars they would put in the bank. So we wired back that we would accept their offer. That was it.

When we tried to come to America, we tried to get a visa through the American consulate, which was in Naples at the time, and they refused us—I don't know why. They told us that the American consulate in Zurich was much more lenient. My husband went. At that time my children were both sick and I couldn't go with him. He went to get the visa, although only for himself. They wouldn't give the visa unless one goes personally. His visa was given in January 1940. So he came back and said, "Listen, you have to go now with the children."

It was in January. It was very cold. At that time, the Jews could not cross the frontier. We were told that there was a law officer of the Fascist party who would give us the visa with some bribe, and they said the bribe would be about two thousand lire. So we got the money. We learned his address and where to see him. I remember we went up five flights of stairs. He was a very low-paid officer. We banged and banged and a woman came in a very dark apartment. The man came and David said, "I understand that maybe you would be able to give the visa to my wife and children". He said, "Yes." My husband took out the envelope from his pocket and handed it to the man. The man opened the envelope. There were four bills of five hundred lires. And he took out one and returned the three to my husband. He said, "Five hundred lire is enough."

So I got the visa with my children and I went on the train from Turin to Zurich. The train was unheated, and I was the only passanger for the whole trip. I stayed in Zurich for a week in a little pension, because we had so little money; I was afraid that we wouldn't have any money. I remember we didn't have *diapers*, so it was impossible. [Laughs.] The situation was very terrible.

Every morning we would go to the consulate and wait there, I with those two small children. We were terribly lucky, because after eight days the consul gave it to us. This woman had been there for nine months and didn't get a visa. It was just an oppressive action.

We came with the boat *Exorcorda*. I left from Genoa. We came here, really, the last ship before the war.

A great difference between the Italian and the Nazi government was the Italian Fascists didn't allow us to bring any money out of the country, but we had very nice furniture and we were allowed to bring it. So under this point of view the Italians were not as cruel. When we arrived here, we didn't have any money, we didn't have a place to stay, I didn't know one word of English. We started selling furniture. Every month we sold some. For about thirteen months we sold furniture. For instance, I had a German Steinway. I sold it for $100. Can you imagine? But I didn't know the value of it, and I needed the money. I sold things for nothing, absolutely. I don't regret it now. We would not be here now. We didn't have to ask for any money. We brought our bed and our mattresses, all of those European things that when they are here some of the people said, "Oh, how beautiful!" But the majority of those things were not in use and Americans did not know what they were for.

We arrived in New York. Eight times we moved in two years. Then my husband found a job here with an engineering firm. So we moved in a little apartment.

I did all kinds of jobs. Also my husband was on a farm. In New Jersey, there were three or four very benevolent Jewish organizations which had tried to enroll all those people who were engineers, doctors, lawyers, and so forth, to become farmers. [Laughs.] My husband's father had a big farm in Italy. This was a chicken farm. So he went to New Jersey for a month. I lived with my sister-in-law, brother-in-law, and his wife. After one month was *Rosh Hashanah*. He decided he would come home. We prepared some chicken. When he arrived he said, "Ah, this chicken is delicious. This month I had three times a day chicken."

But anyway, he said he couldn't stand the farm. These organizations—maybe *someone* liked them. They were kind of paternalistic, and this was one thing we didn't like at all.

[In Boston] I worked for Bonwit Teller. I was selling lingerie, I was making gloves for a very elegant store—all things that I never did before. I was also a salesgirl in the North End. It was very funny because I was hired because I speak Italian. In the North End at that time was half-Italian and half-Jewish. The Italians were against the Jews and the Jews were against the Italians. Being both, I got along with both groups.

I had some experience of anti-Semitism here too. When I went to look for an apartment here in Cambridge they told me point-blank, they wouldn't rent it to a Jewish family. They asked me, "What are you?" "I'm Italian." "Hum, I see." Then I say, "I am Jewish." "I see. I am sorry."

In the meantime, the life here, I would say, although it was very difficult, although I found people quite conservative, terribly scared of communism, terribly scared of any change, I really found, I tell you, real friends here.

I found some jobs. I started really to live the American life, although

I kept very close with my family. I tried to adapt myself and see what was good here.

In Italy, especially among the middle-class Jews, you had to have the friends that your mother had, that your grandmother had—there is very much a class feeling. While here, probably there is, but I don't feel it. So I felt much freer, in one way.

I was on the radio for a while. In 1943 I was a commentator in Boston. I was very strongly anti-Fascist, naturally, and I was telling my audience how I felt about Mussolini. Many of the Italian-Americans were Fascist. I started to receive some threatening letters.

My mother and father had remained in Italy, because my brother was in prison and they wouldn't leave him. I think they were very heroic to stay. My parents were hiding. Since they were Jewish, they would be taken away, and so they changed identification cards every three or four months. My mother was telling me after the war, she never knew what her name was; every three months she changed it. From 1941 up to 1943, we didn't know whether they were dead or alive. And then in 1943, when Mussolini was overthrown, my brother was freed, because all the political prisoners were set free by Badoglio.[3] But that was for a very short time. When Italy signed the armistice with the Allies, Italy was signed over to Germany, the Nazis took over Italy. The Allies had Italy up to Rome, not further. My brother went into the underground.

These were the worst years because the Nazis took over Italy completely, and these were the times when more than two-thirds of the Jews were taken to concentration camps. Twelve of my closest relatives just disappeared. Concentration camps. This was in 1943. Up to 1943 it was a terrible moment, but there was never this open anti-Semitic persecution as my mother told me afterward. After 1943 it was just like in Germany.

Many Jews were allowed to go in convents, because they didn't have any belongings. This cousin of mine, one family, all five of them were living in a convent. Mother and daughter who was like my sister, and son who was a very brilliant archaeologist, with a wife and baby. They had all been there three or four months, never going out. That famous October 16, 1943, they were looking out the window. In Italy a tobacco store is a monopoly of the state, and the state store was open only certain times. My cousin, the archaeologist, he always liked to smoke; he hadn't been smoking for about three months. So he said, "I'm going down to get a package of cigarettes."

They looked through the window. There was a long line of people waiting for the store to be opened. He was about to enter the store, but two Nazis took him and put him on a truck. He starts screaming and looking toward the window. The Nazis came up and took the mother, the sister, and the baby. And we never heard from them. [Her eyes fill with tears. She pauses.] I knew all these things after 1945.

When I went back to Italy, I found most of my closest friends had been brought to concentration camps and not returned, or they had returned and they were completely broken. Some were fantastically strong and completely regenerated by this experience.

In Turin there were about three thousand Jews when I left; now I think there are about five hundred. Maybe fifteen hundred have emigrated and a thousand were taken to Auschwitz.

CARL COHEN—
A German Jewish Survivor

The first time I saw Carl Cohen he was addressing a large group of high-school students at a program in memory of the Holocaust. He was in a gray wool suit, and with his white hair framing his face, looked remarkably like Albert Einstein.

Carl Cohen came to the United States in November of 1940. One of the students asked him why he did not come to the United States during the '30s. He replied, "I couldn't come to this country because it had a quota system—28,000—and a few hundred people born in Germany were admitted every year.[1] This country did not change its law in our favor. Nor did President Roosevelt dispatch one bomber to destroy the railroad to the murder camps. He was told about it. He had maps. . . . He did not have one bomber to save maybe two or three million lives."

The Nazi plan, or "Final Solution to the Jewish Problem," as it was euphemistically called, operated in two phases.[2] The prewar phase lasted from January 30, 1933, when Hitler came to power, until the invasion of Poland on September 1, 1939. This phase was a period of increasing harassments for the Jewish population of Germany, and of the passing of anti-Jewish legislation. It culminated with the events of November 7 through 10 of 1938. On November 7, the assassination of Ernst vom Rath was attempted at the German embassy in Paris, where vom Rath was a third secretary. A young Polish Jewish student was responsible, and when the secretary then died, the incident was used as a pretext first to kindle the flames of what became known in the annals of Jewish history as the *Kristallnacht,* and then to arrest and intern thousands of German Jews. Inspired by the S.A. (Nazi storm troops) and the press, mob action put the torch to Jewish synagogues, businesses, and homes. The worst destruction took place on the night of November 9. The name *Kristallnacht,* or "Night of Glass," derives from the broken glass that littered the streets of cities and towns throughout Germany. Estimates are that one hundred Jews were killed and close to thirty thousand Jewish men and boys, including Carl Cohen, were placed in concentration camps at Dachau, Buchenwald, and Sachsenhausen.[3]

During the second phase of the Final Solution, from the invasion of Poland until Germany's defeat, concentration camps were replaced by the extermination camps of Poland.[4] Carl and his wife escaped this phase; his parents and 125,000 other German Jews did not.[5]

Carl Cohen was born in Essen, Germany, at the beginning of this century. Following World War I, he studied in Bonn, Munich, and Frankfurt, and received close to a Ph.D. equivalency in mathematics. He also became a self-taught scholar in Judaic studies, and is the author of numerous articles in that field. Once in the Boston area, he was able to approach the late Dr. Harry Wolfson of Harvard University and through him receive a scholarship to attend Harvard's graduate program in mathematics. Mr. Cohen subsequently became a teaching fellow at Harvard, and he later taught at the School of Engineering. During World War II he worked for the U.S. Navy Air Force as a research mathematician.

In recent years, Professor Cohen has taught at Cambridge Junior College and Tufts University. In June of 1977 he retired from his position as an associate professor of mathematics at the University of Massachusetts in Boston. He has lived in the same wood-frame house in a quiet Cambridge neighborhood for over twenty years. His first wife is now dead and he recently married a woman from the Munich area.

"On my own ledger," he said, "everything is positive. I am in good health, I am still very young in spite of my old age, my wife loves me— at least she says so. . . . Unless one of the two of us dies, I will be happy, I think."

April 10 and May 4, 1975
Cambridge, Massachusetts[1]

Thirtieth January 1933, twenty minutes after eleven o'clock in the morning, central European time, Hitler came to power. I learned about it two hours later and started the underground immediately. I started in Frankfurt with leaflets, acts of sabotage. We did other things later. When Hitler came to power, we led double lives, my wife and I. It was day by day.

I started to publish in Jewish periodicals to hide the fact that I was doing underground work against the Nazis, and after my first publications I liked it and I published more and more on all kinds of Judaic subjects. I lived on private lessons. Of course, I lost my position at school, being a Jew and an anti-Nazi. Before Hitler I was teaching in the high school, and Jews lost jobs in '33.

I was arrested fifteen times, but only once I was in jail and later six weeks in the concentration camp. Eventually when they arrested all the Jews, they arrested me, too.

I had to turn all my money over to them. I got it back, no worry. First I went to a police station, where they booked me under the charge of being a Jew, then to the Jewish school, then to the largest hall in the city. Our number grew all the time. And then at dark they took us in buses to the railroad station. We were on a train which was locked from the outside, eight people to a compartment. There are small compartments on German trains. We distributed whatever sandwiches we had. Then, it was the concentration camp.

We were all Jews, but not just by religion—priests, monks, among us, whose parents had been Jewish. One honest-to-God non-Jew was there. He was a physical-education teacher teaching in a Jewish school. If the Nazis had known he was not Jewish, they would have killed him. It was better for him to pretend to be a Jew; as a Jew, you see, he had a chance to get out.

We were called "November Jews." We were arrested for being Jews in November in '38. Most of us got out, the so-called November Jews. I counted six hundred corpses in the six weeks I was there.

The Nazis wanted money! The American and English Jews would send money to get us out. German Jews were fined one billion marks, which in those days was only $250 million, but in those days, much more than it is today. And why? Because the Polish Jew had killed a

German diplomat, Ernst vom Rath, in Paris. They arrested absolutely all they could lay their hands upon, except in the capital, Berlin, where there were so many correspondents of foreign papers and diplomatic corps. There they behaved a bit differently. But besides that, practically every male Jew from sixteen to sixty, sometimes youngsters under sixteen and quite often old men above sixty, were taken to three different concentration camps and herded there into the most narrow living conditions.

My living condition was about that broad—one foot, two feet—as long as I am, a bit longer, maybe, and as high, two or three feet high. I could lie on my back or on my stomach, and had to crawl in every time. There were five tiers. One barracks broke down with about twelve hundred people. I'm not sure about numbers. At any rate there were five tiers—I was in the third.

The first two weeks were the hardest. When we arrived at 2:00 A.M. it was dark and they had placed obstacles on the ground. Very clever. Many people fell. Nobody who fell ever got up alive.

Food was very poor, about five, six hundred calories per day, not excellent, either. They put detergents in our food, which unmanned the men there. We had no men there, which depressed many people very much because they did not know what it was. For three solid weeks I did not see water, let alone wash my hands or drink water. We got a cup of brown liquid every morning. Nobody knows why it's called "coffee," maybe because it was brown.

One night they gave us rotten meat and many people had to go to the bathroom. It was not a bathroom. It was neither a bath nor a room, a latrine. They broke out of the barracks, and dogs bit them.

Some people got crazy. A man next to me yelled, "Fire! Get out of here!" And I said to everybody that I could reach, "Do *not* get out of here!" There were dangerous dogs outside led by the Nazi and they really would bite these people. They got money for prisoners who were shot. They would shoot for almost anything.

Some people gave up—stopped to eat and stopped to get as warm as possible. It was awfully cold and at best we had one thin blanket, no heat. For a few nights it was as cold there as it is here on the coldest nights in winter. Then we had an epidemic of the flu, and the death rate was pretty high. At least six hundred in six weeks. You needed a strong will to survive, which I had, and my friends had it, too. All of us sur-

Carl Cohen

vived. A friend from the underground was in the camp. He gave me a sweater. Maybe the sweater saved my life.

We helped each other in every possible way. We talked about things far away from the concentration camp—about chemistry, astronomy—rather than the situation. Mathematics played a great role for me. I found another mathematics teacher there. He recognized me. I didn't recognize him, because the heads were shaved and the beards grew and we were awfully dirty. We had no chance of washing, even our hands, even after following the call of nature. It was impossible. Then I said to him, "Good that we meet here. We can do mathematics."

He said to me, "Are you crazy!"

So I made fast a mathematical statement; on purpose I knew it was wrong. Then he said, "How can you say such an idiotic thing!" Then I said, "Then prove that I am wrong." Then he set off to do that, and every day we did some mathematics inside the camp.

We had some of the finest scholars there. Suddenly we were standing together, a group of twenty or fifty or a hundred, and somebody started to say something about social life in China, the distance of the stars. It was good. Also helped were corny jokes. The corniest joke is better than no joke. We laughed a lot, imitated the Nazis—they spoke a funny dialect. We talked about the sociology of the camp, and all these things that kept us alive. We never debated the question whether we would get any food. While the other fifty percent debated, number one, "Will we get something to eat today?" and number two, "Will they let anyone free today, and if so, how many?", we didn't take part in these debates. Not at all.

And there was an Orthodox Jew who cried on my shoulder. So I said to him he should be ashamed of himself. He believed in God, didn't he? He dried his eyes. You see, this was another way of surviving. You could help people. That is a wonderful thing in such a situation. Help people and you forget your own troubles. Not out of altruism, out of selfishness.

When I came to the concentration camp, my first question that I asked myself was whether resistance was possible. I came to the result, no. In the best case we would have killed one Nazi. They had machine guns in towers everywhere, barbed wire and coils of barbed wire in front of the electrified barbed wire. So it was simply physically impossible to escape unless you killed the Nazi, and you couldn't even reach them. There was a rule. When a Nazi came to you, you had to go back—the distance always had to be the same.

We from Frankfurt had no money. Other Jews had loads of money, so we asked for it. We got money. Hardly ever got a chance to return it, because you couldn't write names and addresses there. I remember one or two addresses. To those I returned the money. But such things, they really meant a lot.

There was a small Bible printed on cigarette paper somebody smuggled into the camp. Out of that I taught a number of rabbis who were in the camp. They heard that I was there. They knew me from periodicals for which I wrote. So they came and asked me to teach them. We spent time together, lying on our stomachs. That was also wonderful. Four or five people and one Bible. All these things helped.

In those days I was an atheist. I knew Hebrew and always was interested in Jewish culture and history. I have some faith now. I returned to God, but I do not go through the mechanics of being an Orthodox Jew. I eat what the doctor permits me. But I think I'm a Jew, religiously speaking. Judaism is not a manual for engineers, as far as I am concerned, or a cookbook. They call a pious Jew a Jew who eats Kosher. I have my own belief in God. I got it through mathematics. Everybody has to find their own way to God. I'm not a missionary—I don't try to win you to my way. But I've always had a deep interest in the Jewish past.

They released people either when they had served Germany during the First World War or could emigrate fast. In order to speed up immigration, it was hoped that American and English Jews would give money. I don't think they did. They were very bad to us. German Jews had been bad to the eastern-European Jews and then the chickens came home to roost: the European Jews in this country were bad to us. Of course, I generalize. I was in the underground, and therefore didn't want to leave Germany before '38. I got offers in '33 from three universities: one in America, the Sorbonne, and the Hebrew University in Jerusalem. I left Germany in March '39. I was released from the concentration camp 21 December '38 and I was very ill.

I was living in Frankfurt in an apartment with my wife and my mother-in-law. The apartment had been demolished by the Nazis. My typewriter and desk had been thrown from the second floor to the street. My documents were lost.

I had to report to police twice a week. I couldn't, since I was ill; the

Nazi doctor gave me a statement about that. After I could walk out again with a cane, I went through all the necessary formalities to leave Germany. I think I had to visit seven offices three times each to go through all the formalities. A friend of mine went with me. Her husband had been murdered in the concentration camp. So she concentrated all her efforts on me, to get me out of the camp on the strength of a fake visa to a Latin-American country. Then they told me that I had to leave Germany very fast. Relatives in England were contacted. One of them was a very high nonpolitical official, and he sponsored me.

Then about 6th February 1939, I think I had finished all my necessary things. I went to Gestapo and asked them to give me more time to travel through Germany to say good-bye to parents, relatives, and friends. And they said the 15th of March is the last day of my stay in Germany, and actually I left Germany on the 16th of March '39, to Holland. Stayed eight days in Holland and then I went to England, where I stayed with a cousin of my wife's. They were very helpful. But still, I was very hungry.

Then my concentration was on two things: number one, to learn English, and number two, to help other people to get out of Germany, especially my wife and parents.

I left Germany on the 16th of March and my wife, on the 31st of August, just one day before the war broke out. If she'd waited twenty-four more hours, she wouldn't have been able to go out. She had got the last plane from Germany to England.

My wife was a paraplegic from the age of thirteen on. Her spine was paralyzed and she couldn't be cured. Her parents hired me to teach her mathematics. That's the way I met her and then nature took its course. We got married when she was sixteen and four days, and lived happily together in Germany. When Hitler came to power, we were together in the underground. After they'd taken me to a concentration camp and released me only under the condition that I emigrated, only then we made up our minds to leave.

Before that we had applied to the United States consulate and gotten a waiting number, and we were told that our number might be called around 1941 or '42. That was in 1938.

We were lucky to find a refuge in England, to wait it out there. It was an almost insurmountable difficulty to get my wife into England, because we were allowed into England only if the English authorities thought that we would leave soon. Therefore she needed some promise she could go to America.

We were allowed to take the equivalent of $2.50 with us out of Hitler's Germany. I had some money in England smuggled there by my father, but I wanted to keep it for my parents, who were still in Germany. To touch that I could do only after a long soul-searching, and of course for my wife's life, I did it.

I was not allowed to take any job in England unless I could prove that no Englishman could take it. I [taught mathematics privately] during the week and made, I think, ten shillings, half a pound, and I lived chiefly on dog food, which was sold very cheaply. And of course I was invited quite often when some of my friends were able to cook a regular dinner; but generally I was extremely hungry. I was one year and a half in England.

At any rate, I had a sponsor in New York, a very distant relative. I think his grandmother had been a second cousin of my step-great-grandmother. He simply declared me a cousin. And he was a wealthy man, a lawyer, and he gave me the affidavits when I was in the concentration camp, first one for myself and then one for my wife. On the strength of this affidavit, my wife got the permit to come to England.

Because of all the delay, we arrived at the place where I lived at midnight and the telephone was ringing furiously. My father was calling from Germany. He was very angry with me that I hadn't called him, and I tried to explain to him that I could not have, and he didn't listen. [Softly.] That was the last time I heard my parents' voice, so that is, in a way, a bitter memory.

My paralyzed wife got the map of the German oil storage when she came to England, which she gave to me. The next day I gave it to a member of the British Parliament. They bombed the oil storage at the beginning of the war. It did damage to the German war machinery. This was the only big thing which came out of our work with the underground, a little map. Germany had no oil. They bought a lot of oil in Rumania and stored it somewhere. A close friend of mine slept with a person very high in the Nazi air ministry, and gave this information to my wife.

We couldn't live together in England, only for a few weeks, then she went to her sponsor on the latter's insistence. For about a year I could visit her, as much as I could pay the fares. She was close to Gloucester, and I was in London.

But France fell and we were afraid the Nazi—I always say the Nazi, not the Germans—might invade England and start to kill people there. My wife didn't want to endanger her non-Jewish hostesses, two teachers. She left them. They were very angry, but got reconciled later. Then we stayed together, with no money at all. But somehow we managed.

The house in which we were was bombed a few times, and I contracted pneumonia and was taken to a hospital. No doctor available, telephone service was often out, in London. The Nazi preferred to bomb churches and hospitals. They called them military targets.

I left the hospital against the wish of the doctors because I wanted to catch the boat. The American consulate in London had given us a visa before my illness. My wife couldn't come to the medical examination. She was on the street in an ambulance. The doctor said I had to see the consul. American consuls are almighty. They say "yes" or "no"—you cannot do anything about it. We had excellent letters of recommendation, and he offered me a cigarette, to my great surprise. I am not a cigarette smoker, but I had learned and read in a German Western story, that Americans are offended if you refuse what they offer you. By the way, I'm American, I am offended if you refuse. [He offers cookies, wine, potato chips.] So I smoked a cigarette for my wife's sake and managed right through. After about thirty minutes of conversation he said to me, "I grant you the visa. I see you are an independent person, but watch out that somebody is on the shore when you arrive, because you will have troubles with the Immigration authorities."

The visa of the American consul is no guarantee that you are let in; it is a suggestion, and the last word is with the Immigration authorities. In 999 out of a thousand cases, it's all right. November 1940, we sailed for America.

Because of the war situation the boat didn't go to New York. Our sponsors were in New York. We arrived in Boston. Here everybody was admitted to land except for us. We had to stay on the boat as prisoners. Next morning we were taken to the East Boston Immigration Station, where we had a hearing and they sentenced us to deportation, back to England. In England I had been told, "Should you come back now, we send you back to Germany." In Germany they had made it very clear to me that should I ever come back to Nazi Germany, I would be in a concentration camp for a lifetime. So we had to fight it, and we did fight it.

Because my wife was paralyzed it was against the law to admit her. Paralyzed people, blind people, anarchists, prostitutes, inmates of lunatic asylums, and people who say "yes" to the question, "Would you kill the president of the United States?" I never heard of anybody answering "yes." Because of this they would not allow my wife to come in, and not me either, because they thought I would abandon my wife. Some such thing had happened before. People got married on paper, without consummating marriage, just to save somebody's life, and I'm not above it. I would have done it, too, but it so happens that I was in love with my wife.

I was there for five weeks. Then I got tired and sick of it and announced a hunger strike and sent a letter to Mrs. Roosevelt, the wife of the president. I lied—that I had a personal relationship to her, an introduction—that I was going to write to her on the basis of this introduction, asking her whether it was a crime in this country to be married to a paralyzed person. Mr. Roosevelt was also paralyzed, but I didn't say that. I said all this with tongue in cheek. That evening they got a telegram from Washington, D.C., that they should parole me. I said, "How about my wife?"

"Nothing about her. We'll still keep her."

So I didn't know what to do.[2]

They sent a telegram as a result of this letter?

I don't know. "I tell you only what I know"—I quote Mark Anthony.

I got a job, which was floor-sweeping and toilet-bowl-cleaning in South Boston. As the floor-sweeper there I went through the whole establishment and asked everyone to tell me their stories, so I learned American society from the bottom, first the foreign prisoners, then with the very fine workers in the factory, later on other people.

I got my first teaching job on my own—Hebrew-teaching in Roxbury, which was then rather Jewish. This job also paid very, very little—about half of what we needed, $ 950 the year. This was in '41. During the war I tried to inform Jewish groups about Germany. They didn't listen. One of the reasons was because I was a Hebrew teacher and Hebrew teachers are regarded as very low-class.

German Jews were desperate, and the American Jews did not react. They could have given affidavits. This *might* have helped. They should have lied, "This man is my cousin," as the man in New York did for me. After all, when his grandmother was the second cousin of my step-great-grandmother, he was *not* my cousin. With this affidavit I got in. Why didn't a hundred thousand American Jews do it? Look, in the Bible there is the sentence, "A new king came up over Egypt who didn't know Joseph." You know what Joseph did for Egypt? The Talmud says, "He didn't want to know about Joseph." And that is the story of the American Jews.

And when I talked in Christian circles, it was unpleasant, too. Almost always someone came to me immediately after my talk with a friendly smile and said, "Aren't you happy you're in America!" And that cut me off.

During the war, when I taught soldiers, sailors, and civilians at Harvard, that was very gratifying. In my opinion, I contributed something: number one to victory and number two I told the students that Germans are like all other people. Germany is the country which gave me culture. My mother's family lived in the same city from 1470 on. When my friends and comrades in the underground were suffering in concentration camps, I could not forsake them. I made many enemies this way.

I want to tell you that my late wife and I were not permitted to send food. They wanted to starve the Germans, which was just what the Nazis did. Nazis wanted to kill the Jews, and they wanted to kill the Germans, so I told them, "You are Nazis." I get still angry when I think of it. So we made up our minds and we had very little money, maybe a thousand dollars, and we spent it on food packages. This was in '46, '47, when they were starving the Germans. Eventually it spread, other people did it too, but again we made enemies.

Well, all right, I was used to suffer for being a Jew and I didn't mind to suffer for being a German. I want to be with the underdog and suffer with him, and I have led a very happy life this way. I have got my satisfaction. Not in material ways, but I got it. And looking back now on a long, long life, I must say it was blessed.

In 1970 I treated myself to a trip to Germany. First I was in Israel in '70 for thirteen days. Since I was expelled in 1939, I am not a refugee. I did not *flee* from Germany; I got expelled by order of the Gestapo. I went back to every street which I had remembered had been there, both in Frankfurt and in Essen. And I was treated like a prince by everybody.

My parents died. I say they were killed, starved to death in Theresienstadt, a concentration camp for old Jews. Leo Baeck[3] was the head, and I got him together with my father. My father could practice medicine there. My father was a doctor. In Czechoslovakia. Theresienstadt.[4] Yah, there both of them died. [Softly.] They could have gotten out. They could have come to England. They wanted to go to Chile. The problem was how to pay for their fare from England to Chile. Moreover, the British climate was not good for my mother, [faintly] so they stayed in Germany where the climate was better.

KYOKO OSHIMA TAKAYANAGI—
Nisei Daughter Remembers the Camps

All of the people in this section are somehow survivors of twentieth-century hatreds and fanaticism. The others were not born in the United States.

Kyoko Takayanagi was born in Oakland, California, in 1924. She is the mother of a former student. In a telephone conversation I asked her if she could help me contact an *Issei,* a first-generation Japanese who spoke English. Hours after I hung up, I realized that by speaking with her I might understand a good deal more about the Japanese-American experience. She had spent time in a camp during World War II.

During the evacuation of the West Coast in 1942, an American born of Japanese parents, a *Nisei* like Kyoko, was treated as a foreign enemy. That most *Nisei* were very young or teenage children was not taken into account. Approximately 70,000 *Nisei* were evacuated and kept in camps with 40,000 other people of Japanese birth. Key officials would only say, "A Jap is a Jap."

After several other conversations, Mrs. Takayanagi invited me to her home. During our talk she laughed a great deal, as if to say, "Things weren't so bad." She would also digress if uncertain about what or how much to say. When we were nearly finished, she spoke of the experiences of her children as *Sansei,* the third generation. Her college-age son had to learn karate while in high school in order to defend himself. When she spoke in her daughter's junior high-school class about her own internment, her daughter almost cried when hearing her friends say "the most prejudicial things." She said her daughter had a "terrible time, but she said it was better that these things were said and up front and you can speak to people and tell them how bad they sound."

We left the house and talked awhile at my car. She said it was good to talk of these things and concluded, "I guess we had a good deal of self-hate."

August 12, 1975
Newton, Massachusetts

May isn't my legal name. It's on all my school records. My name is really Kyoko because I'm named after Kyoto. My teacher said, "Well, your birthday's in May; I'll call you May." This happened a lot. So people have names that aren't their own. My older brother's name is Isao. His name ended up as East. And my brother whose name is Hayao, his name ended up as John. The "Ky" combination was a difficult one for people. I used to write it, Kyoko. Then people said, "Coconut," "Cocomalt," all those other things. [Laughs.]

The outskirts of Oakland, California, was country then. There were creeks and fields and wild flowers. We didn't have a lot of money, but we lived in rural areas where there were wild plants, wild fields. We moved around a great deal 'cause my father never went into business himself. I never knew we were poor until someone mentioned it. But the fact that we moved around so much really drove me up the wall. I think I got shyer and shyer and just sort of withdrew, because every time we had to go to a new school. You'd be standing there during recess and there would be all these kids standing around saying, "Chink, Chink, Chinaman!"—that kind of chant. I just died every time we made another move. By high school I had gone to ten different schools.

In this one farm area in California there were more Japanese, and the kids would talk Japanese to one another. I was embarrassed because they were speaking Japanese. I should have realized, even if I tried to be Caucasian, I looked Oriental. But it just embarrassed me to have somebody speak to me in Japanese. When our mother met friends in the street, they would bow and go through the amenities they're used to going through. I would look to see if people were looking. I would think, "They look kind of foolish."

Growing up in all these different schools, I used to envy kids whose parents came to the PTA. My father never had time and my mother, she didn't speak English. She was just too shy to go. When you got older, that seemed so dumb, but it was *so* important to me then.

My parents sent us to the nearest church. I've gone to everything from a Seventh-Day Adventist. 'Course both their families were Buddhist to start with. My mother became Christian when she was in Tokyo because she liked the music. My father also became Christian.

We played with neighborhood kids, so there was a mixed group. But as we got older, it was a little different. We were very friendly with them at school, but your social life was separate. I remember in high school there was a Hi—Y—it's like a teenage senior-high club. It was segregated, all Japanese-American, *Nisei*. They had athletic clubs that weren't necessarily connected with the Y. There was a *Nisei* segregated basketball league and baseball league, and there was a girl's basketball league. They'd have different segregated dances. I remember this one fellow who was just completely this blond, blue-eyed kid. They were older than I, but I remember the girl he was interested in was a *Nisei* girl that we didn't think was very pretty. We used to think that she looked, we used this expression, "She looks so Japanesey." We wanted to look more like the accepted looks, with being more Occidental-looking than you could possibly be. So that's how we described people. "Oh, so and so's so Japanesey." The lighter you were and the taller you were, these were things that were nicer if you could be long-legged and tall.

I must have been fourteen when I went to live with a family. The Chinese girls did that, but they did work after school and then went home. Their parents never let them live with them. I'd have one day off a week. I would get my clothes or whatever I'd have to get for school, because it was only like $20 a month. But they were *terrible* people, when I think about it. First I went to just work in the summer. The man was an ornithologist. My sister was a year and a half older than I was; between the two of us we took care of the child, who was about seven years old. We took care of the house, too. I had a bedroom in the basement. She had no business putting me there. And I felt so superior to them.

I left suddenly in the middle of the night because the mother was in the hospital and I woke up and there's Mr. [Jones] sittin' in my bed. I just told him to get out. I was scared to death. It was two or three in the morning. I have no idea how far it was to my sister's. I walked over there at that hour and never went back—I must have gone back to get my things.

We were living in rural areas in California when the war broke out. The summer of '42—that was my summer. [Laughs.] That was the year I graduated. But we went to camp in April. Graduation was supposed to be the following June. Pearl Harbor was 1941, and we were evacuated the spring of '42. We didn't finish up the end there.

Living on the coast you'd have blackout curtains on your windows and all of this stuff. And the Japanese had curfews. We had to be in off the streets by nine o'clock, in our houses. The Chinese wore pins, "I am Chinese."

It was like a Sunday morning, and it must have been eleven o'clock when we heard the news. I just dreaded going back to school that Monday. Of course, it was worst the first day, the Monday after Pearl Harbor, 'cause every class you went to discussed it and kids acted just like it was your fault. It wasn't inferred. It was, "Those damn Japs!" It was all of this, and you were part of it. There were those who included you, that you were responsible, too, because you're of Japanese descent, was the feeling we got. It was, "Oh God, I'm going through the floor." And there were those that said, "I'm not speaking to you anymore." You know, I began to feel so guilty—that I had to take the blame too because it was Japan and my parents are from Japan. But there was a tension in the house about Japan, too; there was an embargo placed on Japan and there were things happening there politically.

My parents didn't know what was going to hit. Then my father, as an alien, had to get permits to go, I forget what the distance was. He was having trouble making money. My brothers were commuting to this high school and junior high school. Absolute strangers would yell, "Get the hell to Yokohama!" "Get the hell off the streets!"

My father had the worst experience. I don't know where he had been, but he was walking. I don't know how far he was from home. A group of people started following him and yelling epithets at him. I don't know what provoked it. He just didn't say a thing and just ignored that mob. I'm sure if he had started yelling at them or said something, they would have attacked him. Maybe it was just some kids, I don't know. So at that time, it was kind of a relief to be sent to camp.

My family didn't sell. They just gave things away. Certain things we stored with the next-door neighbor—this black family. My mother had two big *kotos*, the Japanese instrument that's six feet long. She used to play that very well. She taught us to play it. It's the only thing she wanted, and we never got it back.

The Japanese associations were basically like merchants' associations.

They disseminated information about leaving. First, you had to report to get your typhoid shots and all your other shots. And then families were assigned numbers, and we all wore the tag with the family number, and our luggage would have the tag on. Then they'd tell us we had to report to a certain place at a certain time. That's when we left. We caught the buses that took you to Tanforan Race Track. They called it an "assembly area." That was the first camp they put you into, and that was at the race track. People were at race tracks and fairgrounds in different parts of California. That was the spring, April of '42.

When you first arrived, you were assigned your barracks. The barracks, the horse stalls, are in rows and they're given numbers. They're in blocks. You have a block number, then a number for a particular barracks. Then they gave letters to the apartments, like we'd have "A" and "B" or "C" and "D" or whatever. You'd have people who were block managers and council members.

They had the metal army cots. You all had to report to a certain place where they gave you muslinlike mattress covers and you filled it with straw, for your bed. Since we had a large family, we had two stalls. And the stalls were divided because the horse stayed in the back, and there was a front area. So what they did was whitewash the walls and put the linoleum on the floor. My father, mother, and the younger ones were on one side, and my older sister and I and the two older boys on the other.

They were able to build more permanent camps away from the coast, and those of us in that particular area were sent to Utah.

I remember leaving in January. We went to the more permanent camp in Topaz, Utah. That was on a desert. The dust storms were *awful*. There was nothing you could do except get inside, because all that sand would be swirling around and it would filter through the windows. Everything was just covered. And then the winters were cold. I worked in Utah as a nurse's aid.

You had to have a job to leave the camp. People worked as domestics or worked at defense plants, so I took a job as a domestic in St. Paul. You got FBI clearance. I wasn't old enough to have been involved with political groups. People who were very active with Japanese associations, who either sent things to Japan or whatever, might have had some difficulties, but I just filled out the form and got it automatically.

There was more trouble in that camp after I left. There were spies from the FBI to report people. I don't know all the facts and what was done, but there were certain problems when I was there. I wasn't involved. There was always animosity and conflict there. There would be conflict between parents and the kids.

My youngest brother was two. He stayed in till he must have been five or six, when he came to Minneapolis. He spoke with all the *Isseis,* who spoke Japanese all the time, so he spoke English with a Japanese accent.

The whole idea of wanting to be put in a camp—it's like running away. For the while, you're not as exposed someplace like that. If all through the war they didn't put us in the camp, I don't know how things would have been in terms of jobs and so on.

So you were relieved.

At that time, yes. But when I think of how the whole thing was done—I guess it could happen again, with an Executive Order, and never mind about taking any rights. There are many people in different parts of the country who were not aware of that whole evacuation, and those who were aware, they thought we were just like our parents who were born in Japan.

One of the things that really bothered me after the war happened to me in the Twin Cities, and it happened to me in Chicago and various places. Somebody would just try to pick you up on the street and then tell you, "The girls from Yokohama or Osaka were nicer to me"—like the conquering hero can do anything, pick up anybody. I just don't like that. I was dumb, just taken aback; I'd just stand there instead of telling him to bug off.

III. New Generations:
1946 Through the 1970s

Walt Whitman called the United States "a nation of nations." At the beginning of the twentieth century millions of people from around the world came here to build their lives. They were part of a tradition of refugees and seekers who brought their ideals, inspirations, and prejudices to an expanding land. With the late 1920s it was predicted, and among some circles hoped, that the age of immigration would soon fade into history like the age of the Western frontier. In fact, postwar America has experienced a surge of immigration. Again the mixture of peoples is diverse; again the newest immigrants most often find their way into America's cities. But the United States of the last quarter of the twentieth century is obviously not the nation it was in 1900. Politically it is more powerful and, in a nuclear and post-Vietnam world, more cautious and less expansive than the nation of Teddy Roosevelt. Economically and geographically there is also a new sense of limits. Socially, the American experiment of democracy and a pluralistic society has not succeeded without racial strife and poverty.

But who are the American immigrants of the postwar world and what have been the policies determining their immigration? How is the American public receiving them? How are the immigrants included in this section similar to or different from those presented earlier, both in terms of experiences in and their feelings about the United States?

The major groups entering into postwar American society can be divided roughly into three often overlapping categories: political refugees, economic and technical immigrants, and immigrants with families residing in the United States.

The political immigrants came as a result of a government commitment to help settle refugees from World War II, especially those from either socialist or Soviet-dominated regimes. Displaced persons were accepted in 1948; Hungarians, Cubans, and some Hong Kong Chinese came in the 1950s and early '60s; Soviets and Vietnamese in the early and mid-'70s.

The economic immigrants have come, as in the past, in search of jobs and a greater share of the world's wealth. They include refugees, but are mostly those who already have family in the United States. Often economic immigrants are from less industrialized areas of the world, and from areas where legislation rigidly excluded them until 1965. These immigrants include highly trained technical and scientific people. Economic immigrants also include "illegals," undocumented or improperly documented migrants who come as visitors or students and fail to update their papers, or who cross the Canadian or Mexican borders in search of work.

Differences between the postwar immigrants and their earlier counterparts show up in the statistics. Geographic origin, sex ratio, and the occupational status of incoming immigrants all have shifted. While the great wave of the early part of this century was predominantly from southern and eastern Europe, the newest immigrants are from Asia and the Western Hemisphere as well. In 1970 Europeans contributed approximately thirty percent to those immigrating; Asians, twenty-five percent; West Indians, close to seventeen percent (nearly half of the North American total). South Americans contributed nearly six percent.[1] Of course, total immigration for the year 1970 was only 373,000, and not all immigrants remain, so the final numbers are quite small when compared with the more than one million who came in years like 1907. The point here is that a new mix of immigrants has arrived.

The other major statistical differences are in terms of the sex and occupational status of immigrants entering. While the pre-World War I immigrants were overwhelmingly male, after 1930 women, in the case of legal immigration, have outnumbered men.[2] There is a striking difference between earlier and present immigration patterns in terms of occupation. Twenty-six percent of the immigrants who arrived between 1901 and 1910 were laborers. From 1961 to 1970 fewer than four percent were. From 1901 to 1910 only one percent of incoming immigrants were professional or technical people. In the 1961 to 1970 period, professionals accounted for ten percent of the immigrants.[3] Most of these statistical changes are a reflection of the new U.S. immigration laws.

The Displaced Persons Act of 1948 was the first major piece of immigration legislation passed since the mid-'20s. Initiated during the Cold War era, it enabled the entry of refugees from socialist and Communist-bloc countries.

The continual influence of racism, and the growing fear of subversives from without and within, motivated a review of policy in the early

McCarthy years. In 1952, Senator Patrick A. McCarran of Nevada chaired a Senate subcommittee whose findings stated: "We have in the United States today hard-core, indigestible blocks which have not been integrated into the American way of life but which, on the contrary, are our deadly enemies." The result was the McCarran-Walter Immigration Act of 1952. Besides keeping the national origins system of the 1920s intact, and providing a quota of 100 for nations still without quotas, it also added several "security" provisions against admitting and in favor of deporting those the Immigration Service deemed dangerous to the nation. An important addition was that this act issued the first set of preference categories for skilled workers and for relatives of U.S. citizens wishing to immigrate.[4]

In 1965, due largely to the work of the then late President John F. Kennedy, a new Immigration and Nationality Act was signed by President Lyndon Johnson. This act greatly revised American immigration procedures. Passed in 1965 and in effect by 1968, it ostensibly eliminated race and nationality as barriers to immigration. Under the new law, although national quotas were abolished, numerical ones remained. Prior to 1965 there were no restrictions on immigration from within the Western Hemisphere; a quota of 120,000 now exists. The non-Western Hemispheric quota is 170,000 people annually. No country may have more than 20,000 enter in one year. The 1965 law keeps the 1952 provisions for the use of preference categories for uniting families, and for people with special skills. The 20,000-person restriction and the system of preference categories was extended to Western Hemispheric countries as of January 1, 1977.[5]

It should be noted that the present immigration laws, including the Immigration and Nationality Act of 1965 and its recent amendments, have their own restrictions and priorities. First, while political refugees from socialist and Soviet-bloc regimes have been welcomed, Haitians, Chileans, Filipinos, and others trying to escape from right-wing dictatorships have not.[6] Second, the technically trained may come legally, and in many cases, easily. The poor and working class are excluded unless they have relatives here; they often come illegally. Third, new 1976 restrictions on Western Hemispheric immigration, although presented as a way to give eastern Europeans and Asians entry status equal to those from the Western Hemisphere, are based on anxieties about the growing number of black and Spanish-speaking immigrants. Perhaps the restriction is a more subtle form of hostility than was the Johnson-Reed Act to southern and eastern Europeans or the Oriental Exclusion Act to Asiatics of the 1920s, but it expresses fears of new "hard-core, indigestible blocs" nonetheless.

So much for policies. How have Americans received the newest immigrants? In the 1940s, Gunnar Myrdal's study on American blacks noted that although American ideals proposed to uphold black freedom and equality, its practices did not.[7] A similar observation can be made about most immigrants. The Statue of Liberty's torch symbolizes America as a land of refuge and opportunity. But as in the past, racism, legal restrictions, and social and economic discrimination all indicate a deep ambivalence toward the new arrivals.

The state of the nation has often been the determining factor behind what kind of reception new immigrants receive. New immigrants from Latin America, the West Indies, and Vietnam, in the context of the inflation-ridden and stagnating economy of the 1970s, are often accused of causing the social and economic ills of the country. Some are called criminals, prostitutes, scabs; they are accused of taking away jobs, of going on welfare, of "ruining the neighborhood"—the same slurs used earlier against Italians, Irish, Jews, Chinese, and Poles. Illegal aliens come in for special attack although, according to a *Wall Street Journal* study, undocumented immigrants provide more to the federal government in the form of social security payments and taxes than what they get back in the form of public services, and that despite notions to the contrary, few ever go on welfare.[8]

The problems of immigration are international. They exist in England, Canada, Australia, and western Europe. The difficulties often arise when immigrants, especially poor ones, are called upon to meet the needs of industrial countries for certain types of manual labor, at the lowest levels of those societies and for less pay, less security, and fewer benefits than would be accepted by workers within those countries. While a population of low-paid garment workers, farm workers, and domestics are welcomed by some segments within industrial capitalist societies, the problems resulting from their employment are not.

Another postwar cause of immigration has been the collapse of colonial and semicolonial regimes. In the cases of Holland, Britain, and France, many former colonials immigrated to the mother country, creating, as James Baldwin says, "European Harlems." The national and socialist revolutions of the postwar years have also created their share of immigrants.

Since the world's economy is an unequal one—with certain nations having more wealth than others, with some nations having more political and creative freedom than others, with war a common phenomenon, with some nations discriminating on the basis of race, religion, or language—one can expect immigration to continue being of international significance.

The stories of fourteen members of the postwar first generation follow. The people here differ from the immigrants in earlier sections in several ways. The oldest person is in his forties, most are in their twenties or teens. Unlike the earlier people, the majority of those in this section who are married have married native-born Americans and people outside their ethnic background. Their attitudes toward their stay in the United States are often different from those of the earlier immigrants, although in many cases they had similar reasons for coming.

Whereas the earlier first generations look backward to experiences from thirty to seventy years before, most of the new immigrants still are in the process of integrating themselves into American society. Several are uncertain whether or not they want to spend their lives here. The ease and accessibility of air travel makes it possible for them to visit their original homelands, and for many a continual comparison goes on.

A general ambivalence about being American marks many of these stories. The United States is seen as a good place to make money, but, it is questioned, what is sacrificed? "I am always missing my family," said one woman; "How can you turn your back on what you are?" asked another. Neither wished to reject a vital part of her own identity. The pace of life, the treatment of old people, and the loss, among refugees, of former economic and social status—these are the themes discussed in many of the histories. But there were those who said, "I like this country—it's a beautiful country."

The stories of these postwar immigrants depict the lives of people from a wide variety of political, economic, and cultural backgrounds. They portray another first generation who have already contributed and will continue to contribute to American society, and whose children and grandchildren will make up new generations of Americans.

"ANTON TAMSAARE"*—
From Displaced Person to Distinguished Person

Anton Tamsaare was born in 1939 in a small Estonian town, "an only child, a very sheltered, protected child." At the beginning of World War II the Soviet Union annexed Estonia. Later, Germany occupied the country. The Soviets began to reoccupy in 1944.[1] At this point Anton and his family left Estonia for Germany. After the war they lived in camps for displaced persons until being allowed entry into the United States under the Displaced Persons Act. Private agencies were responsible for placement. The Tamsaares were sent by a Norwegian Lutheran Church agency into Moorhead, North Dakota, in February of 1949.

During the war years it is estimated that thirty million European people were driven from their homes. The task of caring for displaced persons was organized by forty-four Allied nations in late 1943 under the aegis of UNRRA, the United Nations Relief and Rehabilitation Agency. At the close of the war more than a million people were stranded in Germany, Austria, and Italy, the largest numbers having come from countries on the eastern front, from the Baltic countries through Poland, from the Ukraine to Yugoslavia. UNRRA and the IRO, the International Relief Organization, attempted to repatriate displaced persons, but huge numbers of these people resisted their efforts, not wanting to return to Soviet-dominated countries in the east, or if of Jewish origin, fleeing the ashes of the Holocaust. In late 1945 new refugees left eastern Europe for similar reasons, and in May of 1946 the figure for displaced persons was close to one million.[2]

In the middle and late 1940s, a major political squabble ensued as to the status of displaced persons. Soviet-bloc nations argued that repatriation was the only solution and that most people not wanting to return were war criminals fearing prosecution. One study claims that the Allied Expeditionary Forces in Europe forcibly repatriated two million displaced persons to the Soviet Union between 1944 and 1947.[3] Another dubious aspect of the refugee resettlement occurred when member IRO nations tried to pick off the most highly skilled of the group, often refusing to keep families together.[4]

Between 1948 and 1953 a series of Displaced Persons laws was passed, enabling close to 400,000 people to enter the United States. In 1947

---

*"Anton Tamsaare" is a pseudonym.

about half the Baltic refugees came to the United States. There was a large percentage of Poles, (Polish) Ukrainians, Germans, and people from the Soviet Union as well. Close to 10,500 Estonians came to the United States under these acts between 1948 and 1952.[5] The Displaced Persons laws were the first refugee acts of their kind in the annals of American legislation, and it signaled a commitment to settle refugees, especially those from Communist regimes. This return to the policy of the golden door was, however, not altogether removed from the politics of the Cold War. As a condition of entry there was to be an emphasis placed on the weeding out of politically undesirable elements. Recent studies show that "undesirable" was defined as "Communist" and that several important Nazis entered as ardent anti-Communists.[6]

Dr. Tamsaare is a physicist. As we sat in his office he mused over the impact of the course of history on his life. He wryly noted, "I've had the distinction of living in Nazi Germany and also in Stalinist Russia." He suggested his pseudonym, Tamsaare, the name of an Estonian writer. In Estonian, "Tamsaare" means "oak island."

June 26, 1975
A Boston area university

We left Estonia late in '44. I was five, and that's about the time I start to remember details. Before that, one day was just like the next; you play with your dog and so on. But at that time it was the German occupation. We were in this little forested area some miles from the capital city. We got on a wagon and traveled about a hundred miles for several days; and that was new, that was different, and I remember every bit of that. I remember where we stayed every night.

We left really quite late. We left when the fighting was proceeding up to where we were, from the capital city of Estonia, Tallinn. We went on a ship which was evacuating Germans from Estonia. My godfather was an official in the German-sponsored government, and he arranged for us to get on this ship. I remember a lot of people were sort of living on the deck, and somehow my father gave an officer a case of whiskey or something, and we got a cabin that was relatively comfortable. As we were sailing away, we could see the city being bombarded.

My father had been in the interior ministry, and at one time had a job equivalent to secretary of the interior in the United States. During this interim period [of German occupation] he was basically in charge of forests in a certain region—which was not a particularly important job. That's what he was doing from the years '40 to '44.

When we got to Germany, we went to Berlin. My father went to the government officials there and presented himself as being a refugee from the German-dominated country of Estonia and essentially asked for a job working with forests. He received a job as an assistant forester somewhere in Bavaria.

We lived in a small town, Everdorf. I was five then, and I started to go to school. My first year of school I spent in a German school, in Nazi Germany. This was '44; the war was over in '45.

There was never any question of starvation. We just felt dislocated. It's hard to say when I got a political awareness of what was happening. I guess even with adults, when you're in that sort of situation, I don't think the political factor is that important. You're just eager to survive and stay alive. My primary political motivation that I received from my parents was one of anticommunism and anti-Russian. That was always talked about; that was the consuming orientation of our whole life. My parents had lost everything. They lost their position, their home, and after the war there was a great paranoia about war breaking out again and Russia overrunning the rest of Germany.

We stayed in this little German town about a year after the war ended. By that time the Allies were organizing displaced persons' camps and encouraging people who were scattered throughout the country to settle in these. Sometime in 1946, we entered this particular camp run under U.N. auspices. About a thousand Estonian people were living in what were formerly German Army barracks. It was not an uncomforable life. Our family had one room in this building, which was something like a dormitory, and there was a bathroom down the hall. Actually, we moved from one camp to the other, but the basic idea is essentially the same. We had our own schools. I attended these schools in second, third, and part of fourth grade. They were conducted in Estonian. English was taught as a foreign language. We were not confined to the camp. You could always leave and walk around town. This was a benign kind of camp, not a concentration camp. We lived in a camp for about two and a half years: '47 and '48, until we left in January of 1949.

Again, what people were talking about all the time was possibilities of war breaking out again, and fear of Russia. Occasionally a Russian officer would come to the camp, trying to encourage people to go back to Estonia. This was a formality that the Allies had to respect. In order to get into the camp, we had to claim that we were forcibly taken from Estonia by the wicked Germans. Then it would follow that we'd all be eager to go back now that Estonia had been "liberated" by the Allied Russians. I suppose some very old people did eventually go back to Estonia, but the ones who were there were there for a good reason. They were the professional classes, the bourgeoisie. They had no interest in Estonia anymore.

Late '48, early '49, apparently some new immigration bill was passed in the United States which superseded the quota for displaced persons and allowed for immigration, whereas I think the Estonian quota had been a hundred people per year. We were eager to leave.

Before anyone came, he was assigned to a place to go. In the United States some organization had to sponsor him, had to guarantee a job. But the match-up was made arbitrarily. One day we learned that we were to go to North Dakota. That brought in a new stereotype, namely that North Dakota was an arctic region, which it is, really, but we overdid that—in the summertime it's very hot. We thought we should take along everything we had because they wouldn't have anything— they would be underdeveloped, they would be moving by dogsled. So we took along a great deal of stuff, including our mattresses and bedding and furniture.

We came by boat. I remember it sailing into New York. [Laughs.] My father woke me and showed me the Statue of Liberty. It was kind of nice! And then we took a train across the country. We were met in Fargo by some people from the Lutheran agency. We were taken to a little place with a population of one hundred or so—Arthur, North Dakota—where they had an old-folks' home. My father's job was to be a caretaker there, and that's where we ended up for a little while. We were placed in a situation that was fairly unchangeable and somewhat paternalistic.

Estonians were scattered all over, but the place we went to we were the only ones. We stayed there just for a few months. It was so isolated. We did want to get to a somewhat larger place, and within six months we moved to Fargo-Moorhead. Fargo, North Dakota, and Moorhead, Minnesota.

This being a little bigger town, people began to congregate there. At the high point, which was in about 1950 or '51, there were perhaps seventy-five Estonians there. But then after that, I guess the general trend seemed to be that everyone kept going to larger and larger cities, so eventually there were maybe only two or three families left. We stayed, and I went to school there, sixth grade through high school.

There's a college in Moorhead—Concordia College. My father took a job there as janitor. We lived there for the greater period of my adolescence, from age ten to twenty-two, because I went to college there.

I had a relatively conventional kind of midwestern American upbringing insofar as school life was concerned. At home, it was still quite foreign. We spoke Estonian, still do when I go home, but it's not a place noted for any kind of immigrant culture. There are no ghettos. People kind of forget that you've come recently. You live just like everyone else.

There are many Scandinavians, and that helped somewhat. I guess that's why we ended up there originally, because of this church's sponsorship. Lutheranism is the state religion of Estonia also, so you have that kind of cultural tie-up. It's basically the same kind of Nordic people. We associated with Norwegian people and went to a church that was Norwegian Lutheran. I was very happy there.

No one ever made fun of me for being different. I suppose that was helped a little bit because I was a very good student.

There was another interesting factor. My parents were very eager for me to succeed. This is not uncommon, I'm sure, with immigrant families, but there was an understanding that I was supposed to be number one in what I chose to do. I did manage to succeed there. I was valedictorian of the high school and of the college and straight A's all the way through. I took a great deal of pleasure in this. This was the way I made my identity.

It got to be quite a thing. It's almost embarrassing to talk about this, but I'm, as they say, a legend in my own time in this town. Everyone who knows me almost reveres me. I had by far the strongest acedemic record in this college in its whole history. I was accepted to all of the Ivy League schools for graduate study, and got a Danforth and a Marshall Fellowship and went to Oxford when I was through. This added an entirely new dimension.

And so we come to a tremendous transition here. By this time I'd completely forgotten this whole immigrant thing. Actually, at one of my graduation banquets at this college, the president was speaking about me and saying something about how a displaced person had become a distinguished person. I was sort of shocked. It had never really occurred to me for years that I was a displaced person. I found it curious that he should remark on that thing, because this didn't seem to form any part of my heritage anymore. And, once I left Moorhead at the age of twenty-two, I don't think in a conscious way that being an immigrant plays any role anymore. In a way the story kind of ends there, or maybe it ended when I was fifteen.

Let me say just a couple of other things which occur to me as being important. One is this dislocation that occurred, which is so strong with my parents. Going from being upper middle class to lower middle class, this hurt them a great deal. They've dealt with this now. But this is an absolutely overpowering sort of theme. This change of status and then an attempt to gain respectability and wealth in some limited way. That is why they were very careful and very eager to have me do as well as I possibly could, and I'm sure it's also been in the back of my mind.

I've adopted some sort of Anglophile way of life. When I went to England, I enjoyed that. So if I see any cultural orientation, it's become that. Someone might say, "Well, you should adhere to the Estonian subculture." You have to have a somewhat smaller unit to identify with. In the case of immigrants—especially earlier ones—it was their own community that provided the focus. Well, I haven't had it, so I'm simply trying to explain what I have adopted for that subculture.

Did your parents expect you to marry an Estonian girl?

No, not at all. There weren't that many Estonian girls around. [Laughs.] Well, there was talk about it, but it was never serious. Or maybe it was.

Sometimes I wonder about a different question. If the little country of Estonia had just continued as it had been when I had grown up there, what would my life be like now? I don't know.

THOMAS BLATT—
Remembering Hungary

The Hungarian Revolt of the fall of 1956 shocked the world by the force and brutality of the Soviet Union against an indigenous and apparently socialist uprising. Estimates are that 200,000 left Hungary.[1] Arthur Koestler notes, "I do not think there has been a migration of scholars and artists on a similar scale since the fall of Byzantium."[2]

In January of 1957, three months after the Hungarian Revolt, President Eisenhower asked the 85th Congress to revise the Immigration and Nationality Act of 1952. The revised act provided for the "parole" of refugees from Communist nations into the United States, with a provision for their permanent residency. The Act of July 25, 1968, granted permanent residence to those Hungarians admitted to the United States following the October 1956 revolution.[3] Approximately 200,800 Hungarians escaped, about two percent of the population; 38,000 were admitted to the United States.[4]

The Hungarian refugees were not the first major wave of Hungarians to enter the United States. Because Hungary was part of the Austro-Hungarian Empire prior to World War I, it is hard to get precise figures, but it is estimated that between 1870 and 1920 close to two million Hungarians entered American ports. This large and early migration settled primarily in the cities of the Midwest: Cleveland, Detroit, Columbus, Indianapolis, St. Louis, but also in New York and Los Angeles. Like the majority of turn-of-the-century immigrants, they were generally of peasant or working-class origin and set up their own churches and ethnic organizations around tightly knit urban neighborhoods. Politically, the older group has been characterized as leftist in orientation. In contrast, the post-1956 middle- and upper-middle-class immigrants tended to be strongly anti-Communist. They also were highly educated and technically trained. Many became economically successful shortly after their arrival because of their educational status and because the economy of the 1950s was a growing one, especially in the areas of scientific and technological development. The post-1956 immigrants, therefore, did not have a great deal in common with their earlier-arriving countrymen.[5]

Thomas Blatt was born in Budapest in 1933. His family was from the upper middle class, his father a doctor and his mother a librarian. "My father's family was Jewish; my mother's family was Lutheran. I was brought up as a Catholic. Not really, but I was registered as a Catholic, so I had to go to Catholic religious classes in the school." Mr. Blatt was ten years old when his father died in a military hospital in the Soviet Union of wounds sustained while fighting with the Hungarian (Fascist) forces. "Everyone fought on the wrong side during that war."

Mr. Blatt's father's side of the family had been watchmakers for generations. His mother's family was blessed with a towering intellectual and moral force—his grandmother, who was a leader of the Hungarian feminist movement, raised six children, and wrote three books, dying at ninety-three in the middle of a fourth.

Mr. Blatt studied at the University of Budapest, but left during the Hungarian Revolution of 1956. He was graduated from the Massachusetts Institute of Technology with a master's in engineering and received a master's in business administration from Boston University by attending night classes. He has been working for over sixteen years at a Boston-area technical company, where he is a manager and a vice-president of a new subsidiary heavily involved with international operations.

Through my acquaintance with Mr. Blatt's American wife I was introduced to him and invited out to their home. The Blatts have two children. It was a winter evening, and their large old elegant home had a fire going as I entered. I found Mr. Blatt charming, relaxed, and friendly.

January 28, 1976
Weston, Massachusetts

I was twenty-three when I left; I had just finished college. I was reasonably adult so I remember everything in detail; in fact, the whole thing started at our university. The uprising was a completely spontaneous matter. If it hadn't been, it would have never happened at all because they would have stopped it.

It was very interesting the way it started. Even the day it started there was no indication. What happened was that Hungary became a Communist country more or less in 1949. Until about 1954, when Stalin died, it was total repression. And then when Stalin died it became a little bit lighter. The intellectuals, the writers, and what have you became more and more open, and by 1956 it became pretty open with criticism of certain aspects of the system.

In 1848 there was a big revolution everywhere in Europe—the longest one was in Hungary, which lasted into 1849. There was a very famous Polish general who fought on the side of the Hungarians. In 1956 there was an uprising in Poland that was beaten down. The university students, as a gesture, marched on October 23rd, 22nd, to the statue of this

General Bem. They put some flowers there to protest the beating down of the youth movement in Poland.

The entire Hungarian government was outside the country—they visited Tito in Yugoslavia as a peace gesture. Suddenly about 100,000 people collected in front of the Parliament. That's the way the whole thing started. I wasn't there at the statue, but I was at the Parliament— it was a few blocks from where I lived.

Nobody got organized. We just saw a lot of people walking, and we started walking with them. The architects, in fact, started to put together some demands to the government. In 1848 the greatest poet in Hungary's history put together a list of fourteen points, what the people wanted, and the architecture students put a letter of fourteen points. I wasn't there, but then the fourteen points were read into the radio because the crowd occupied the radio station. But again, it was just a crowd, no leaders, nothing. And in fact the leader whom the crowd wanted was a Communist, who was a previous prime minister of Hungary, a moderate—Imre Nagy.

Then on October 23rd they started the shooting. It was very disorganized. The real fighting was outside the city, mostly by the armies. There were some individual groups who took it upon themselves to occupy a church or something. Anyway, it was pretty serious because the Russians had to regroup November 4th, which was ten days or two weeks later. On that day the tanks and everybody came in with two hundred thousand soldiers. It was just ridiculous at that point. On November 9th, we realized it's all over, and on November 13th we left.

I didn't have to get out of there. I always wanted to get out of there, but it was hopeless. There was no serious possibility because the border was mined. Hungary was completely surrounded by Communist countries: Czechoslovakia in the north, Yugoslavia in the south, and of course Russia in the east and Romania in the southeast. There is a very small border with Austria and that was completely mined, so there was no way to go through. They picked up the mines in the summer of '56 and that made it possible to go out. The Hungarian army did it because the tension relaxed.

The decision [to leave] was a spontaneous one. We were thinking about it before, but we never really materialized it in our mind. For a few days, after October 23rd, we thought the uprising might succeed, but even that was mixed euphoria, not quite complete euphoria. In

Hungary there is a famous joke: "If you meet one Hungarian, that's a Hungarian; two Hungarians mean sex, three Hungarians mean four political parties." We had about twenty-five political parties there and nobody knew who wanted what. It was difficult to establish whether what is coming would be worse, better, or even different. There was no leadership. In fact, the new leaders were also members of the Communist party, so it was not quite sure at that point what was going to happen.

Saying good-bye wasn't so easy. I was an only child, and I lived with my mother and my grandmother. Two of my friends and I decided one evening to leave the next morning. I spoke to my mother. She was a very enlightened person, sort of an ideal woman, in many ways. My friends used to come to talk to her because they felt that my mother was a better mother to them than their mothers. The relationship between us was a very interesting one, a very intellectual relationship, in a way. She was very wise.

I used my sarcastic sense of humor before leaving. When she said, "What are you taking with you?" I said, "I am taking with me my school papers, a bathing suit, and a deck of cards." I still have those cards. I was a great cardplayer all my life. When I was fourteen years old I was playing cards till three in the morning, making more money than my mother did at her job.

If you want to hear how I got captured and came out of Hungary, that is a long story. I have to drink when I talk about that one.

One of the three friends left earlier and he went through. I had a girl friend whom I wanted to marry at that point, but she didn't want to come. It was difficult to leave her. It had a long-lasting effect on my life—but anyway, the remaining two of us left. He lives here now.

There was a general strike, there was no transportation. We carried our suitcases. Each of us had four bottles of apricot brandy and our bathing suits. You have to carry all this, because Hungarian apricot brandy is something with which you can bribe anybody any time.

So we waved down a military truck which was going in the correct direction. They stopped and we waved a bottle of brandy and they took us on the truck halfway to the Austrian border. We got blank permits and forged our name on them because there was a limit beyond which you couldn't go west. So we left. We hired a car. There is a city called Győr, which is halfway between Budapest and Vienna. We slept there at night. The next morning we rented this car and were taken to a canal. We had to go across that which was rather difficult and we started to build a raft. We went to a farmer and bought nails and what have you. We knew that to the right is Czechoslovakia and to the left is Austria. There is a bridge and Russians were there so we had to be careful. At night they were shooting right away, so we had to go during the day, at which point the worst that can happen is that they capture us, but they won't shoot us, so it was complicated.

Suddenly a third guy showed up, an older guy. He said he would like to join us. Well, fine. The problem was that this raft that we built would take only one man. So we decided that we would make a rope out of scarves. One guy goes over and pulls the scarves. Then we can pull the raft back with the scarf, and the next guy goes over and whoever is left can pull it back, and the third guy goes over. This third guy fell off the raft and into the water and started to yell; it was very cold water. At this point, for the first time in my life I got drunk.

Finally they captured us; they put us in a camp. We were there for six hours at the border. Then they put us on a truck, and they started to take us east. We didn't know whether they would stop in Hungary or take us to Siberia. By that time it was around midnight and we were back in the city of Györ. We came in this truck which was full of all the people they had captured. There was this guy who was driving the truck in front and there was a guy with a gun who was beside him, but he could not see us. The truck was going about thirty-five or forty kilometers per hour, not too fast. So we decided we are going to escape.

I was the one who jumped off first and my friend threw down the two small suitcases. Then he jumped down and then the third guy jumped down, who broke his leg. We picked him up, we took him to a house, and we left him there.

Next day we tried to escape again, which was a much more difficult situation because it started to snow. Then my friend said, "Let's go home, because there is the snow; they will capture us right away."

I said, "All right, let's try one more time and let's start walking." Then we walked down to the city. It's a city of about eighty thousand or one hundred thousand people. Suddenly we saw a big truck with all kinds of people on it. "Where are you going?"

They said, "Well, we are all truck drivers. We are going to the border because a lot of truck drivers escaped from Hungary to Austria and there are all the empty trucks we have to pick up there."

So they took us and they drove us much further west than the previous time. There is a city called Sopron, which is right on the border. They dropped us maybe five miles from the border. It was all covered with snow. We didn't know what to do. We didn't know where we were and we asked somebody.

Imagine this. Suddenly you see railroad tracks. It is like a groove in the land which is dug out for the train, and there are the tracks. This guy says, "Well, the best thing is to go down there, because they won't see you, because the Russians are all over at the top." So I started to go and suddenly there is a guy with a machine gun, a border guard.

He says, "Where are you going?" and my friend says, "We are going to the movie." [Laughs.]

He says, "Seriously, where are you going?" and we told him, "We want to go out." What can you tell him? We tell the guy the truth, "We want to get the hell out of here."

The guy started to go into a philosophical discussion. "You know that this is a nice country. Why do you want to leave?"

We said, "We really want to come back, but we just really want to go out to study. We are students." Finally I said, "Look, I give you all the money we have. We don't need it, anyway. Take it."

So the guy said, "All right. It is five miles to the border. It is five miles to go and you have forty-five minutes. You have forty-five minutes because in about forty-five minutes the train will come," which is the Orient Express. "When the train comes you have two things to do, you either climb up there, in which case you would be captured, or you let the train run over you."

So we started to run. We passed about one hundred and fifty people. Apparently he let everybody through. We passed these people and we ran like crazy. I was in tremendous physical condition. So we were going like crazy and we were totally dead, and finally fell down onto the Austrian side of the border. Three more people came, then came the train. Then nobody came. We barely made it. That's the way I got out.

What happened after that? I didn't have a clue what I wanted to do. Twenty-three years old, highly educated, highly intelligent, totally immature, and totally lost.

We were in Austria for a while and then we went to Paris, where my friend had relatives. I was in Paris for a while, which I loved. I thought,

"I don't want to stay in Europe, I want to go to America for a while." So I decided to go to Canada.

I flew from Vienna in one of those really old airplanes which had to stop at every big tree, so it stopped in Belgium and Scotland and Iceland and had to stop in Gander and finally Montreal. My first experience you should write a book about. I arrived in Gander, Newfoundland. Yes, forty-three below zero, six feet of snow and the Salvation Army playing music for the refugees who arrived. Then you go into the inside of the airport and you see on the television wrestling—four guys are killing each other. I said, "Jesus, what a place we came to!"

There were agencies. There was the whole International, God knows what. They processed everybody—where you wanted to go—and got visas.

I decided I'd go to a place where I don't know anybody because I have relatives everywhere: Australia, South America, Sweden. I went to Canada because I didn't want to become dependent on anyone. I went to Montreal for awhile. I hated it, but looking back it's not such a bad place.

As to English I didn't know a damn thing. I started to learn it in Paris already—I didn't speak very well, but anyway, I got a job. Not so bad, actually. I didn't even have such a bad salary, in fact. And I rented a room in the best part of the city. That's the Hungarian philosophy, live in the cheapest room in the best hotel.

In Montreal there were seventy thousand Hungarians. Montreal is a fantastic Hungarian center. [But] I was too lonely. I was missing my girl friend and everything else, but anyway. I couldn't stand the cold winter, the hot summer. After three months I decided that I wanted to go back to school.

I chose M.I.T. very happily later, because that was on the East Coast and I didn't want to go far west. I thought, "The East is still closer to Europe"—there is still this attraction. So in September I came down. I saved $1,100 in six months, which was a lot of money since my salary was only $360 a month. I worked a lot of overtime. I also played cards. [Laughs.]

What were your first impressions of the United States?

What is the impression of a civilized people going into a jungle? This is not a different country, this is a different world. The difference between even western Europe and the United States is great. It's much, much bigger than even a Communist country and a non-Communist country, in my opinion. Number one, the whole place seemed like a nonpermanent residence.

It was a big shock walking in Central Square, Cambridge. You expected that you have to go to Africa to find a place like Central Square in Cambridge. Central Square in Cambridge is so primitive even today. You don't believe that people live permanently in tiny little wooden houses one beside the other, and then combined with the great ethnic and racial mixture: blacks, whites, Arabs! It was a big shock walking in Central Square in Cambridge and the downtown area of Boston, Washington Street. Compared with the Champs Elysees in Paris, it was a very depressing feeling.

My first impressions were negative. First, I remember there was the total lack of quality in municipal government. Second was the way they treat the old. Third was the lack of health care, and fourth was that I thought the people were so uptight sexually. At the time I felt that people had a wall; they were closed. My impressions were not all bad. These were cultural shocks, which were very difficult.

Of course there was much that was positive. You can go anywhere you want, any time you want. I was a student at M.I.T., had no background, nothing. And credit. They sold me a $1,500 car in 1958 and I didn't put down a penny. Nobody asked me questions. That was incomprehensible. That is fantastic!

I fould people extremely generous here, much more involved, sometimes too much involved, in other people's affairs. People were friendly to me. I found that it might have been because I was an Hungarian.

You said you were in Hungary last year?

Last year I went to Europe. I went to Germany and Austria and Italy. So for the first time I decided to go back to Hungary.

All the people who had left Hungary had dreams—like you went back and they don't let you out again, all these things. I had that dream for a long time. But I was always feeling funny going back there. Finally I flew in. As soon as I got there, I didn't have any fears anymore. I had lots of relatives there, cousins and uncles and aunts. Several of them visited me here. My mother's family is extremely close.[1]

The first major surprise was that I had no feelings about that place. I felt like a tourist except that I knew the streets and I knew the houses.

I met people. I met everybody in the family: cousins who were two years old when I left. I met my old girl friend, whose marriage I screwed up once, and interestingly enough I showed up from nowhere and it turned out that I arrived five days before she was to get married again. I had a wonderful time. I think if you like to eat and have fun, nowhere in the world can you eat like that.

The Hungarian immigration was different because it was the top of the society. It was the cream of the crop of the college population. Do you know that I went there, that layer is missing, the people who are forty to forty-five years now, of top executives, scientists, writers. Two hundred thousand people left; two percent of the population. It's a fantastic number.

I felt nostalgic about the reasonably easygoing life that those people have there. People see each other much more. They are much more socially outgoing than we are. People are poor, I'm sure, even in western European standards, certainly by American standards. The major value of my visit, I felt, was that what I remember was reality. That was the best thing I found out over there. You know, after twenty years you glorify certain things or make it look worse, and I think that my memory about Hungary and the life there and the people there was extremely realistic.

RODOLFO DE LEÓN—
Leaving Cuba

Rodolfo de León is one of more than 700,000 refugees who have left Cuba since the revolution in 1959.[1] Unlike many of these, who came from Havana, Rodolfo was born in the rural province of Camagüey. His family remained in Cuba through the first few years of the revolution. They owned some storehouses in Camagüey, which were nationalized by the revolutionary government. In 1962, at age eleven, Rodolfo, his brother, and his mother left for Miami. His father followed a year later, and his maternal grandparents, two aunts, and an uncle came in the late '60s.

The waves of Cuban immigration to the United States roughly follow a class pattern. Those who left with Batista or immediately after the Castro takeover were from the wealthiest classes and the military and were closely tied to the Batista regime. In the early '60s, as the government became more socialistic, some Cubans lost their livelihoods, and what they saw as the betrayal of the revolution forced them out. Many members of the middle and lower middle class left in the early and middle '60s. Inasmuch as one of the primary aims of the revolution was to improve the life of the *guajiro,* or peasant, fewer poor or rural Cubans found their way to this country.[2]

Cuba, after the revolution, was the only nation in this hemisphere given no restrictions on immigration to the United States. A Cuban refugee program, which was set up and administered by the federal government, provided at least some aid for most of the Cubans leaving Cuba after 1959.[3] Even so, Mr. de León, his brother, and his mother had to wait a year and a half before they could leave Cuba. His father left later, and only after much difficulty. His aunt and uncle tried to leave for five years before meeting with success.

In the 1960s, Cuban refugees were often pawns in Cold War games. Some were used by the U.S. government as secret invasion and espionage forces against the new Cuba. The American media hailed them as valiant fighters against communism while Castro called them "worms" and betrayers of their country. Castro also claimed that if American Immigration had been as generous in its invitation to Cubans during the Batista years there would have been a mass exodus then.[4] The American press responded that if Castro's Cuba was heaven, why were so many people leaving?

At the time of the de Leóns' settlement in Miami, tensions were growing between the Cuban and "Anglo" communities; gangs often formed, usually along ethnic lines. Today, Dade County has a large Cuban population, and disputes over jobs and the use of Spanish in the schools are frequently reported in the national press.

I met Rodolfo de León in the fall of 1972. When I began taping some conversations with him I was not working on a book. Later he consented to the use of most of those early tapes. Mr de León has attended the Museum School of Fine Arts in Boston and has exhibited his paintings in regional shows. He was graduated from Boston College in 1976 with a degree in economics, and he is presently the director of a Cambridge recycling program. Since our first tapings, many years have passed and some of the attitudes he then expressed have changed. He no longer wishes to return permanently to Cuba. In January of 1976 he became a United States citizen.

Fall 1973 January 7 and 8, 1974
Cambridge, Massachusetts

I remember the last two weeks of '58. In la Sierra[1] they had a radio station. I remember hearing every night all this static. You would hear what's happening. Everybody was pro-Castro—not everybody, but a lot of people. I remember, so that nobody would catch us, we would close the windows and try to get the radio.

Those two weeks were really the most exciting weeks because Castro was moving. Che Guevara over here, Camilo over here.[2] They were going to cut the island in half and establish a government on one side.

The day that we knew Batista fell, I was woken up very early. Everybody was out on the streets. I remember my aunt made three or four 26th of July flags[3] and we went around in cars, BEEP-BEEP, and people were drinking. Plus it's New Years's—perfect timing. [Laughs.] And there was a strike all over the island.

I remember I saw Castro once, and that's it. Never saw him again. On January first, Batista leaves, right? At four in the morning. And so, Castro is in Santiago. And there was this looting in Havana and tearing down of parking meters. Somebody said that they were going to take a Viscount plane and take Castro from Santiago to Havana. Meanwhile, he had declared Santiago de Cuba the capital of Cuba, because he didn't think Batista was going to leave—the island was going to be divided for a while. So Batista leaves. Castro got into Havana the 6th, I believe.[4] He said he wasn't going to take a plane, he was going to march to Havana. That's how I got to see him. Our street, General Gomez, [led to] the center of Camaguey. He was coming in a tank. He came through Camagüey, the second or third day. He was as near me as fifty feet, and he was on top of a tank. And there were people on the sides of the tanks, and people marching. We were all standing there.

But his face seemed very white. That's the impression I had that day, and I didn't get his features very well, since he was so far. He seemed very angelic, like Jesus Christ. He just went by.

The first few days, they started collecting people, the Batistianos. Not because of Castro, just popular demand. It was kind of brutal. I witnessed the whole thing. They came in a truck. I remember running after it. They had already four or five people inside the truck, tied up. They searched for Pataganzo.[5] Pataganzo was this *gusano*[6] henchman. He lived about two blocks away. That's what they called him because of his leg. He had a defect. They dragged him out of the house. I think they tied him by one leg and just dragged him across the street. They tied him to the truck by the leg and pulled him. They didn't kill him then.

Who did this, the army?

Not the army, just people. He was very well known. Everyone was afraid of him. You couldn't look at him the wrong way. He was an informer. Batista paid people all over the island. He paid them $33.33 a month. They were *chivatos.*[7] You had to watch what you said around him. We used to close the windows whenever he came by. He was really ruthless. I remember hearing of people disappearing, being taken in the middle of the night because of him. They killed him later on, they shot him.

In the summer of '59 we moved to Doble Vía. We rented a house there. About a year later we moved to Calle Siete. My father bought this big house, really nice. It cost something like $19,000. He made better money after the revolution till the business got confiscated.

From where we lived, two or three blocks away, there was a small community, marginal type of people, very poor. They came with signs and all, against us, *"Gusano."* I don't know what these signs read. I forgot. They kept going around our house. They were chanting things. They did that for about a half an hour. My brother came out with a jar of cold water and glasses. It was hot, so he started giving them water. From then on they call my brother the diplomat. After that they left.

What do you remember about the Bay of Pigs invasion?

The Bay of Pigs—the only thing I remember was that they captured a lot of people; the militia, the government, the regime. They captured a lot of people who were believed to be counterrevolutionaries. Just for national safety they captured them, rounded them up, you know. I don't know if it was the night before, or the same time that the Bay of Pigs was on.[8]

There was a seminary, a Catholic seminary, about two blocks from my house, and they turned that into sort of like a concentration camp. Not a concentration camp—not that connotation—just a place where they put them. A friend of ours was one of the people captured. I remember they let him go.

I went near there. There were people standing inside a wall. There was a wall there. Just men. They were standing around. Families brought them food. There was a sense of thrill, because there were these people captured there. Going over there and sneaking and looking through.

In that seminary they put up a megaphone and about three times a day they used to sing the "International" [sings] : "*Qué Viva los pueblos del mundo.*"[9] It went on a lot, maybe three or four times a day. It was a middle-class neighborhood so they figured they'd bother us playing it early in the morning, waking us up with it, going to sleep with it.

I remember once they started the day-care centers thing—everywhere for mothers to bring their children to the centers. The *gusanos' bola*—means rumor, *bola* means ball, which gets bigger and bigger, and it was rumored around that they were going to take the kids away from you and teach them Marxism-Leninism, but in a very naive counterrevolutionary *gusano* way, "Here's an apple; God didn't give it to you, Castro did." Those were the examples they gave us, and that we should hide. And we did. We did hide. We didn't go anywhere; we were inside. Any time trucks or anything came by, the paranoia was so much, we hid under beds and things like that. So we didn't go to school for a while.

We left Maristas, the school we were going to. We went to this private school which was all *gusanos*.

Often there [was a troop of about twelve people marching] up and down the street, the militia, I guess, I don't know where the hell they came from, and we sort of heard or guessed that they especially sent them to that street.

Did you realize something profound was happening?

During the first years of the revolution I had good experiences. My father was doing well. We went to Havana for the first time. We went to Varadero.

After the revolution, the changes began to be noticeable. In Havana there was this Yuri Gagarin Restaurant. It was self-serving. This was a new thing for Cuba. The Ten Cent Building in Havana had an escalator; they served all types of sandwiches. I remember once going to a militia camp about two miles from our house. They built all these apartments near my house, near Puerto Príncipe. They took *campesinos*[10] and put them in these houses, even in '61.

A special trip I remember was with my father. We went fishing. It was in the river, and it was really fun, you know, catching fish. They were men, and it was very nice under different shades of trees. Just cooking. I remember looking when my uncle opened up a fish and took out the insides and fried it and ate it, everybody drinking beer and rowdy and playing dominoes, in the middle of the country.

In Santa Lucia, when my father bought a house—those were really nice times. I enjoyed that. I remember going swimming there three times a day. In the afternoon the tide went very high, so it was dangerous. I remember we went to the beach swimming, getting hot, and my skin was getting dark, going back to the house, and there was a shower outside the house so you could clean yourself up, to get all the sand off. The water felt cool and so nice. The water felt good. I would stay in the hammock in the afternoon and just relax.

We were at the beach, and my father called us. We waited for him at the entrance of Santa Lucia. We waited a lot that day, and he didn't come. Finally, he came with the news that his business had been confiscated. They had offered him the job of administering it. He refused. Immediately he brought the lawyer with him to make up papers and passports for us to leave.

From then on everything was downhill. I felt there was something bad going on, that we were going to leave the country. I didn't know what the hell that *meant*! I didn't know. I didn't know what that meant that I was going to go somewhere else; I didn't have any ideas of sociological orders, economic ideas, whatever. I wasn't aware of a lot of things.

I remember crying when he told us that. I was really upset.

But then we did a lot of traveling. My father was trying to get passports. I think that's the first time we spent a lot of time with him. We went different places, to Varadero, Havana. My father was spending a lot of money to get a suite in the Lincoln Hotel. It was kind of nice. I was feeling like a type of millionaire.

In August or July we got a telegram in the middle of the night saying that we were authorized to go. I remember being excited at first, then I *really* felt bad. I remember crying. I remember looking back. I said to myself, "This is the last time you're going to look back." I remember I kept on looking back at my house and feeling very bad, very sad, and then going to Havana and going to the plane. I don't remember how many days we stayed in Havana. My father was in a nervous state.

They looked through our baggage. They took my brother's watch, a

Rodolfo de León

couple of things of value. We got on the plane and took off. I kept looking at the coastline as far as I could, as long as I could. It was just maybe five minutes when we landed. It didn't take that long. So we landed in Miami.

The people who were waiting for us—they were opportunistic, *stupid, low-down rats!* They were the worst kind of people you can imagine. My father had sent money over here for us. The dollar was going very high on the black market. So my father had to pay I don't know how many Cuban *pesos* for a dollar. [He had sent] about $400 in different installments many times. We only got $200. These people were *stealing* it. They didn't give us any money. This was the only reference we had here. They were friends of [a friend]. They had done that before. They had "taken care of" people, sons who came.

We stayed at their house, two weeks, three weeks. My mother couldn't stand it, we couldn't stand it. We went to bed hungry.

Why didn't your father come with your family?

Why couldn't he come? Well, I'm not quite sure why he couldn't come, but he felt he had some business to take care of. He felt that he wanted us to be secure in this country before he left Cuba.

The second or third week we were here we started receiving help from the government. We collected some food, and we got $100 a month. We rented one place first. The rent was fuckin' way too high. The rent was $95. We had five dollars left for the month.

After a month or something like that we found this other place, which was $72. We were renting the apartment for $72, and so we had $28 for the month. That meant a dollar a day. We lived on that for I think about a year and a half. Aside from my mother baby-sitting for about two dollars for six hours, that was the only income we had.

I remember in that place we had only one pillow. One day my brother and I started fighting for the pillow. We really got into a brawl about it. I started chasing him. My mother was chasing us. Then my mother broke down crying. We stopped. I really felt bad. We were fighting for this fucking pillow.

And we were eating really bad food. It was not only bad, but we were eating it constant' anned government meat. A whole year. Breakfast. Lunch. Dinner. And beans. My mother would soak them overnight, and then she would spend the whole next day cooking. We sort of had this pot that we found. She spent cooking all day, and I remember we sat down to eat and it was very solemn, we sat down and started eating. Somebody made a remark about the beans, and we started laughing and then crying. Between all that a bean got stuck. It got stuck right in my nostril, and I couldn't breathe through my nose for about two weeks. I remember one morning I went to school. Here I was, they put me in the fourth grade. In Cuba I was in the eighth. It was early in the morning. I went *ah ah choo!* [Laughs.] Thing was *green,* starting to get some moss. They were still *hard,* you know?

So it was a kind of bad time. I remember I wanted to drink a Coca-Cola. My mother had probably thirty cents in her pocket and I felt really bad that I wanted one. Really bad.

There are a lot of experiences like that. You know, going to school and being kind of odd. I was much bigger and older. And I would bring my Spam meat sandwiches, which smelled. Everybody around just dispersed every time I sat, every place I sat.

We used to have dancing classes. It was part of gym; it was compulsory. All the boys would line up this way, and all the girls would line up next to them. I was interested in girls, but not American. It was funny, but it really hurt me that they did this. The girls would count, the first one in line, to see who got me. She would count, and she was trying to move back or front or somewhere so she wouldn't dance with me. So usually, after all this rearrangement of all the girls moving from one place to another, there was this very fat girl, who was completely unaware of anything, what was going on, who landed in that place and with me. And it got to my turn and it got to her turn and we danced. I don't know what the hell else. I was embarrassed to death. *My soul felt stale* through those years, through many years afterwards.

The first [two months] we were here my brother heard of this place where you could pick up doughnuts and sell them—make a couple of dollars. The first day they left us the doughnuts and a metal case to carry them. We went out with this stuff and walked around. Finally we found this guy out mowing his lawn. He thought we were just kids selling stuff so he called us over. He said he wanted one. We gave him the bag. As he gave us the money, he must have realized we were Cubans, not American kids. He took the package he'd bought and threw it in the garbage. My brother was really upset. He was upset like hell. He wanted to go home. At that time I didn't understand what that meant. I didn't understand what Ricardo was doing. I said I'd do it. He was upset and shy. He was hurt. He was very hurt. I wasn't so much hurt but I figured—what were we going to do with all those doughnuts? Later on my mother wound up paying for the rest of the doughnuts. We didn't try to sell the rest. My mother had to pay six dollars for them. We ate stale doughnuts for weeks.

We went trick-or-treating. They told us you could get a lot of candy that way. So we did that. We ate candy for a long time.

We used to file down pennies and use them for cigarettes. Then we heard that the telephone people and different people were complaining about it—high rate of filed pennies being poured into machines. [Laughs.] At night we'd just file pennies. We'd file about a hundred pennies [Laughs.] We only had *one* dime so we filed it to that point. We bought a file that cost thirty-two cents. We got a lot out of that file! My brother used to go to the cigarette machines. He used three pennies. We'd get thirty packages and sell them for fifteen cents, so we were making twelve cents a pack. We used it for food, candy, telephones. After we did that for a while, we thought they were checking. We took it easy. We went to different areas. Can you imagine a guy opening up a machine and all those pennies come out? Not even good pennies? Struck a copper mine.

Let me tell you, necessity is the mother of invention. When we moved to the $67 place, we didn't use it as much. It took us all night filing pennies. Our hands were shaking. We filed pennies in the dark. I think we used a candle.

What did you miss most?

I missed the whole thing. I can't say I missed this particular thing. Everything was misplaced at once. Bang. A whole new picture. Everything was misplaced. Everything that I knew, everything that I felt good with, that I felt secure. I felt aggressive. I now became insecure, passive. I was in front of this thing I just didn't know how to deal with. Especially where I hadn't been born here. Also the bigness of it.

Seeing my mother was depressing. She was trying to get work. I remember she finally found work before my father came, for maybe four, five, or six months. She was working in a *camaronera,* shrimp-packing, to get the thing out of the shrimp to be packed.Her fingers, a piece of her hand is wasted, you can see it—take a look at her hand. It's from peeling shrimps. She probably came home with $30 after about forty, forty-five hours. She came home at five, maybe six o'clock.

When we were in Miami in '62–'63 we used to look for my father many times. After the Missile Crisis, there were no more planes coming in. We didn't know when he'd get here.

We were visiting some friends in Tampa when we got word that my father was coming from Cuba. We drove back the next day to Miami. I remember I was very anxious to see my father. I remember, before, we kept waiting for him. We kept going to meet all the incoming people. They used to bring them all to the stadium in northwest Miami. At that time they were trading medicine.

He came over on the *Máximo,* on a boat, a big boat. I'll explain. You know the Bay of Pigs thing? People that were captured, somehow they struck a deal with Cuba, where they were sent ships of medicine in exchange for troops, these people: prisoners, mercenaries. So that on the way back a lot of other people came, too. Most of them were well off. So my father left the car there. And he didn't know he was coming. He couldn't send us a telegram or anything. He'd been trying to come. And we had heard that he was feeling bad. He was doing all these weird things. He was praying. At home he would fall down on his knees.

It was very hard, first time I saw him. He looked very different, and I just didn't react the way I used to. And ever since then I haven't reacted the same way. Before we left Cuba, it was more like Daddy, Daddy—you know, father. It was more he represented something else before, and now he didn't. Something had been taken away. He didn't have the power he had before, the image that I had of him.

Even when we were together, my father couldn't work, couldn't find work. When he did, he found it in Boca Raton, sixty miles away from Miami. He picked tomatoes. And that was sixty miles away. They had a car pool, and some guy took him. So he had to pay, I don't know how much. He went about five o'clock in the morning and came back about ten o'clock at night. He got paid six dollars a day. Two dollars for the car, something like that.

My biggest impression came when we were driving from Tampa to Boston. We stayed in Miami, then we went to Tampa. Here I was, *guiding my father* a *guajiro* from Camagüey. My mother, you can imagine! We were driving up to Boston in a Chevrolet '54. And you know that time was in '64. And my father drives *slow.* You can imagine what hassle, to New York and all that. We got lost once and went the wrong way in the Lincoln Tunnel.

I remember something the second night, or the first night. I remember my lips were bitten, you know, blood was coming out of my mouth, from nerves. I was riding with my chin on the dashboard. We got lost because of the traffic. We couldn't take a left and the traffic just took us along with it.

Do you think you want to go back to your country?

I would like to go back to my country. But I've been here such a long time! I'd like to be able to drive around the place where I was born, once in a blue moon, you know. And I like to be with my own people and say, that's where my father used to own his business, and that's where I lived, and this is where I played when I was a kid, and these are my people. When I get in trouble I don't have to give excuses, where I'm from and when I came here. Maybe I will, maybe I'll spend the rest of my life in this country, but I hope I don't have to do that.

Do I think my parents are happy here? No. But they have to keep their myth up. They belong to another generation—old Cuba.

I'd like to go back. Coming to this country, it's just like my whole life turned on me. I can't express myself. The whole thing is just changed, my new life, a new person. Everything turned worse the day I got off the fuckin' plane. From that day on everything, everything went bad. I wish I could go back.

"ELANA CHRISTOPOULOUS"*—
A Mother and Daughter from Greece

Elana Christopoulous arrived and settled in the United States during her elementary-school years. She was born in a small mountain village in Greece, about seven hours' drive from Athens.

Elana and Pasqualina, whose story follows, share several experiences: both are from southern Europe, both came to the United States at a young age, and both were able to enter the country because relatives had already settled in the United States.

Like Philip Bonacorsi and Mose and Joe Cerasoli, these young women, although technically of the first generation, are very similar to native-born children of immigrant parents. They speak English with Boston accents and are externally indistinguishable from other American teenagers. But they are from abroad and live in homes where the language

---

*"Elana Christopoulous" is a pseudonym.

and culture are Greek and Italian. Like second-generation children, they move between two cultures.[1]

On arrival in the Boston area, both Elana and Pasqualina moved into the homes of aunts and uncles. In terms of the 1965 immigration laws people with relatives have favored status; the closer the family tie the easier the entry. In 1975 over 65 percent of European immigrants have entered the United States under this "relative preference" category.[2] Of the close to 123,000 Greeks arriving between 1966 and 1975, a majority used family connections to facilitate entry.[3]

Elana is now in a college work-study program and plans to return to Greece to work in the field of immigration. "I think I can understand too how the people feel, since I have gone through it. The hassles and everything. I think it's really what I want to do."

June 10, 1976
The Boston area

I was nine when I came. My mother's brother was here so we came here. I used to live in a little village in Greece. It was very primitive. We didn't even have a high school. Everybody was a farmer—that was the only thing to do there. If I stayed there, I wouldn't have been able to go to a high school unless I moved to a city. It would have been really hard, so mostly I came over here to get an education.

I left with my mother. I didn't have any brothers and sisters. My father died when I was really small—I never really knew him. It was really hard gettin' out of the place, and it was hard coming here. You come and it's not just the language, it's a whole different system.

I've been here almost nine years. When I first came here we lived with my aunt and uncle.

I came here, and the first time that I saw a person who was black or a person who was Chinese or a person who was different than I was, their skin, I was really scared because I had never seen them before. That took just a little while of gettin' used to. Now I'm plenty used to it. But you see foreigners that come over, and they're older—like they're in their forties or fifties—they're pretty much prejudiced, and they stay that way. Living in the United States won't really change them. They don't change at all, their values. They're living here in the United States—actually, they're living in their old culture, with the same rules and the same morals and the same everything. They try to bring their kids up that way, too. Even though you're still living in the United States, you're still really living in Greece or wherever you came from. That was the hardest thing [laughs], trying to tell my mother that this was a different place we're living in and people act differently, they live differently. It's *not* Greece. And that took a very, very long time. Last year I used to break down a lot.

One of the other problems was that I was living with my aunt and uncle. My uncle was born in Greece. When you're living with relatives, you're really not living in your own home. You're supposed to be perfect and proper, and you can't yell and scream even if you feel like it. When I was small, it didn't really bother me, but when I started gettin' older and I wanted to have friends and choose my own friends, especially when it came to guys—it was just really bad. They wouldn't allow me to have anyone call or anybody come over or see me or anything like that. I was constantly fighting with my uncle and my mother, from the time I was about fourteen to the time I was about seventeen.

I started sneaking out, at first. They caught me.

What did they do?

When I think about that—well, when I was fourteen, I started doing it 'cause that's when I met the first guy I wanted to go out with. We were in this car one time, riding by. I had been going out with him for like a month or something, and they didn't know about it. And my uncle caught me, and when I got home, he beat me. I had black and blue bruises all over me. He was really wild.

After that they wouldn't let me out of the house, even with my girl friends. But then as I got older, it still went on, up until the time I was seventeen. He just didn't want me to go out with guys, that's all. Why were they objecting to it? Because it would make me look *cheap,* and it would make me look like a tramp and maybe I'd get pregnant, and he would be so *ashamed.* I think mostly that. Or that "good, proper" girls didn't go out with guys. And he figured that when it's time for me to get married, that they would *find* somebody for me. They'd say, "Hey now, you can go out when you're thirty or something, twenty-five."

Then I went to Greece in the summer I was fifteen, and I met somebody else. He was, like—this is a complicated story—my aunt's husband's nephew. See, my aunt is my mother's sister, and it was her husband's nephew. He was an older guy, twenty-two, and I was only fifteen at that time, and he was out of college.

When I went down there, I had a really terrible time. They wouldn't let me go out again, unless I went out with him. So I said, "Damn it! It's better than sittin' home." I went out with him once, and I didn't like him. But I said, "Well, I'll go out with him 'cause I don't want to stay home by myself. I did go out with him, and finally we did get along and I thought I really loved him. We were planning that I was going to come back and we were going to get married, later on. He was the college type. So it was OK to go out with him, and when I came back here, I wasn't supposed to see anybody because I was supposedly being faithful. [Laughs.] It wasn't that I wanted to say that to him. It was that they sort of made me say it.

Who's they?

Well, my aunt, because that would keep me from going out with other guys and causing all the trouble. [Laughs.] And also, here I would have a guy to marry when I was twenty or whatever.

The thing was he was twenty-two, and he knew what he wanted. And I was only fifteen and, you know, when you're a teenager, you change your mind about fifty million times. You do! [Laughs.] Anyway, I came back and that's why I didn't go out for the next two years.

Then I met somebody else at a dance. I did go out with him, despite my uncle's disapproval. Then he started beatin' me. I liked the guy. I didn't know whether I wanted to be with him forever, but I liked him for the time being and I didn't want to give him up. So I asked my mother to move out. We couldn't move out at that time. I just went out with him anyways. I said, "If you don't like it, it's too damn bad for ya. If you beat me, I'm taking you to court. And don't think I can't do it, 'cause I'm gonna do it!" He would come up to me and everything. But I'd just say, "Hey, keep away from me." He never did touch me because if he did, and believe me, I would have taken him.

Now we moved, and I live with my mother, and its different. I don't live with them anymore.

My uncle paid for us to come here, but she worked for so many years, I'm sure she repaid him. My mother's the type of person that—she's very patient and she's very docile.

She works in a factory now. They make some kind of computer

equipment, putting together parts and stuff. She's learned to speak English, because she didn't know a lot then. She didn't know anything then. She's been learning, and she speaks pretty well, too. I think she rather likes havin' our own place now, being away. We still have fights. I still yell at her and stuff to get my own way, but there really aren't that many problems.

My mother doesn't really have very much time for a social life 'cause she works. She's at her job until 4:30 and it takes her another hour, hour and a half, to get home. She's not home until about 5:30 or 6:00. She takes the bus. She's usually very close to her family, even though I have hassles with them and can't stand most of them. She still keeps in touch. She goes to their houses.

She never goes out to an American restaurant; and Greek ones—there's very few—and she never really wants to go. She doesn't like the theater or anything, clubs—she get's scared. She went one time and she saw a belly dancer. She was so ashamed, she wanted to leave. She won't wear any makeup. She doesn't let me paint her nails and she doesn't want me to wear lipstick or anything. She's very plain. That's because she's from the village. She's typical. In Athens, they wear makeup.

The only reason she stays here, to tell the truth, is so I'll finish school, so she can help me through school. She decided she wants to go back. She doesn't really like it here because all her friends are down there, and there's really a difference between living here and living in Greece.

I will be going back as soon as I get through school. I'll have some experience doing immigration work and I'll be gettin' American pay. I'll definitely get married there. Men down there are more outspoken than they are here. You know how they *feel*.

When I go out with somebody, I make it clear to them from the very beginning that if they don't treat me right, if they don't do what I want—well, you know, sort of like I'm the boss in my relationships, which is not very good, but that's the only way to keep a man in line. If we're seriously dating and he's going out with somebody else, I'll just say, "If you don't stop it, I'm leaving you." I will do it. And they know that I won't take it 'cause first of all, I'm heading towards the education that I won't need them. My mother would be so content to stay home; she'll clean up the house twice a day, cook for him, wait up. If she had a husband who had a job, she wouldn't mind being just a housewife and stayin' in there.

She wishes she had gone to school. It wasn't possible for her to go. She's not even interested in meeting anybody—don't even speak of it! [Laughs.] My mother—she's a typical nun. That's what I say to her. In a convent. She really is. She has to do everything according to what's "right" and what society's going to think. She'll never do anything because *she* wants to do it. I'm the opposite, totally the opposite.

PASQUA LINA—
Growing Up Italian and American

"It Wasn't Like We Were the First People to Come Here"

Pasqualina was born in 1958 in Catanzaro, Calabria, on the boot of southern Italy. She settled in the Boston area when she was five.

I first met Patsy in the fall of 1974 when she entered Newton North High School and was assigned to my homeroom. She was later one of my students. In the winter of her junior year we taped her memories of leaving Italy and becoming an American. In June of 1977 she looked over a draft of our conversation. She was readying herself for graduation and college.

December 16, 1975
Newton North High School
Newton, Massachusetts

I left Italy when I was four, and I had my birthday on the boat, so actually when I arrived, I was five. It was a real change.

I remember quite a bit. It was like something that no one could ever take away because it was something so deep in my mind, though I was small. I remember my feelings, and what things looked like. I knew people pretty well. I was always secure and always felt loved, and sometimes here I don't get the same feelings. I didn't have everything, but there were a lot of things I don't think I'll ever have again.

The most vivid thing I remember was when we were all gathered there, ready to go to the port. It was like a hurting feeling. I knew something was happening, but I didn't exactly know what. I was leaving and it really hurt because it was really precious what I had, this family connection. Then when we got on the boat, I think it was in Naples. I remember I got attention from people. The attention was still there during the whole trip. I didn't feel a loss of anything, because even though it wasn't from the immediate family, I still felt the closeness. It was really nice and it was like a good time: the boats, the pool, the tennis courts. It took quite a while, though, to get there.

Then I remember the first words when I got to New York. I was upset with my father because here we were and I was really like a sharp little kid. I used to talk and I used to say, "Well, Daddy, you brought us to this new country and no one's gonna pick us up. Are we stranded here? Daddy, what are you gonna do? Are any of your relatives coming to pick us up?" It was like, what are we going to do now? I didn't know where things were heading to. I really wanted to know what was happening.

That night we drove from New York to Waltham. His uncle picked us up and brought us to his sister's house. It was a new experience because I'd never seen these faces before. My cousins couldn't speak Italian because my aunt had gotten away from it. It was something out of the past, and they didn't start learning it until we actually got there. The surroundings were different. I don't think I was impressed by the way they lived because I sensed something was missing.

Then, within a short time, two months, we moved into an apartment, three families.

My father used to work all the time. The only time I saw him was on Sunday afternoons. I always looked up to him because he worked so hard. He's the type of person who has a hard time showing feelings, but you really know the way he goes about caring for his family. He was working in gardening. He worked for many years and saved money, then he bought a house. My mother was very worried because she didn't think we could pay for it. We managed, and my father got a car. Things started happening. You could see the change. We were able to get more things. But still I don't know, getting everything, being the type of person that I am, doesn't mean that much to me.

It's quite an experience; it's been good and bad. As a human being I've grown from it because I've seen two cultures, two different ways of looking at life and death, the whole process of living. I've been able to pick out a philosophy of my own about certain things, and it's been good in that sense. But if I had to go through it now, I really don't know if I could have done it. When you're younger, it's so much easier.

It was really an experience as far as school went because I didn't have anyone to help me out and it was frustrating. Sometimes I really accomplished something. The effort that had to be put into it—sometimes I wanted to give up. I never did, and that's why maybe sometimes I'm so caught up at school because of the fact that that's the thing that started me off and got my interest. I wanted to learn things. I've been given a chance that many people don't have—I couldn't see letting it go to waste, I had to get something out of it.

Going back there, I saw all those young kids my age. Their way of thinking about life was very simple, like life and death, and I couldn't see myself living that way even if I was back there. Just seeing them I thought, "You have to make something of yourself." Sometimes that makes me sit down and I say, "Well, you're so worried about getting ahead and back to materialistic things." And it's true, in a way. But then I sort of stop myself and I say, "You've also gained a lot as a person."

My mother and I, we helped each other along. I remember having to call the telephone company and connect the phone when we were moving, and they were asking questions like was I married or single. I mean, here was a little kid like nine or ten and doing all these things, and I helped her with the things she couldn't do, and she helped me. She always took the time to talk to me. She gave me a lot of things, but I don't feel spoiled because I'm aware of what she did and I appreciate it. I really respect her for what she's gone through, and she's coming out of it really well considering all the sufferings.

Doing things, my mother and father are pretty open-minded, and they trust me and I appreciate it and I don't take advantage of it. You always think of the father as being head of the family. Well, he is a head in a sense, but my parents can discuss things and come to a decision. I don't really fight with them a lot. They were just waiting for the right time to give me my freedom. So there has never been that real conflict. Sometimes I see things differently, but it's not like we totally disagree.

We speak Italian at home, because it's something that's awful to forget. It's really nice to be able to speak two languages. My mother was shocked when we came here that my cousins couldn't speak it. It was like they wanted to get away from it. I don't know why. How can you turn your back on what you are?

ANTONIO CARDOSO—
Boy from the Azores

"I Like This Country"

Antonio Cardoso was born in the São Pedro section of the city of Ponta Delgada, on the island of São Miguel in the Portuguese Azores. His father had been a mechanic in the Azores, but decided to emigrate with his family to join other relatives in the United States. Antonio's grandfather had come to America with the great immigrant wave in the early 1900s, taking a job in a shoe factory in Cambridge. When Antonio and his family arrived, they moved into their grandparents' home in Somerville, Massachusetts.

Between 1901 and 1965 over 230,500 Portuguese immigrated to the United States.[1] Azoreans provided a large percentage of their number, due mainly to the islands' geographical proximity to America.[2] Large numbers of the early immigrants settled in Massachusetts, forming Portuguese communities in Cambridge, Somerville, Fall River, New Bedford, and the Lawrence-Lowell area. Their transition into American society was cushioned by their membership in the Catholic Church. By 1920 many "National" parishes were founded in southern New England cities and towns. In these churches, aside from the Mass, the Portuguese language was spoken, and the church served as a community center.[3] New Portuguese did not replenish these first settlements inasmuch as the quota laws of the 1920s had the effect of cutting Portugal's visas to 440 a year.

The second wave of Portuguese immigration began in the late 1950s, when a volcano struck one of the Azorean islands and the Azorean Refugee Acts of 1958 and 1960 granted close to 5,000 Azoreans immigrant visas to the United States.[4] With the 1965 immigration law it became much easier for people with relatives living in the United States to emigrate. Between 1965 and 1974 approximately 110,000 Portuguese left Portugal for this country. Of the 11,302 Portuguese who arrived in 1974, 3,655 settled in Massachusetts.[5]

Like the earlier wave at the beginning of the century, a large number of these arrivals are from the eastern Azorean islands like São Miguel, where Antonio was born.[6]

One Saturday evening I was dining with friends at a local Italian restaurant. I was amused when I discovered our waiter to be a Portuguese immigrant, and I asked if I could talk with him about his experiences. Later that week we sat down with the tape recorder.

When I first spoke with Antonio he was sixteen years old. Since that time, he has married. He has a baby daughter. I asked him if the family attends a Portuguese Catholic church. He said they all used to attend Saint Anthony's in East Cambridge. "Now," he continued, "I go to the American church. My wife's American. You gotta go where they wanna go."

June 26, 1975
An Italian Restaurant
Cambridge, Massachusetts

We came by plane. My grandmother—from my father—she had some money over there. She gave my father about $5,000. Over there is a lotta money. After we got here, we all working part-time job to repay my grandmother. Then after nine months my father's sick.

I came here in the summer. That summer I didn't work. I didn't even know how to speak English. My father never worked. He was too sick. They made a bad operation on his stomach. He was always painting the house. When he first came here, he went to the hospital for three months, then he came out. Then, was Christmas again. He went another two months. The welfare paid because we had a big family and nobody working for us. My older brother used to work for us. Then he got married.

My father died. Nine months after we were in the United States he died. That's why he came to bring us here. He wanted to leave us here first before he died. I was eleven.

When we moved from my grandfather's house, we moved to my cousin's house, but the house was too small. We bought one in Somerville near Glen Park. We bought a big house there. We had some trouble with some American kids over there. They burned six garages that were part of the house. In that neighborhood, these American kids, they see strangers, they don't like 'em. I don't think they like foreign people. They see foreign people, start in to call us names and everything.

I was coming from school with my brother and they were asking me for money. I told 'em I didn't have any money. If I had it, I wouldn't give it to them. This kid slapped me. They slapped me, spit at me. So

Antonio Cardoso

I had a hockey stick. I took the hockey stick and spinned it around, hit a lot of the kids. The next day they came with knives to school and they try to stab me. My grandfather's a butcher, so my grandfather uses big knives, so I took one. Got the kid right on the knee. I knew they were going to take them because they said they were going to kill me the next day. So I took a knife. If they say that, I don't think that's right. So I took this knife, too.

Next day there was about, I'd say, seven kids. They were all surrounding me with knives. What to do? They were talking to me. I had a big knife near my shoulder. One kid just start running. Well, the kid was bleeding, you know, a lot. So the police came, they took me right up on the wall. I said, "He tried to kill me." So the police took the kid to the hospital.

They all start blaming me at home for all that stuff. I said, "Wasn't my fault, what can *I* do?" I'm not gonna' let nobody kill me. Defend yourself as much as you can.

Then we moved. We bought another house. This was in another part of Somerville. It's a good neighborhood. We moved right away. I was about fourteen. I switched schools. They switched me to a Greek church which had Portuguese bilingual. They put me in the sixth grade. I was fourteen.

Now, I'm at Somerville High. I quit for this year because I had this accident. These kids they came to revenge on me again. I was comin' from work, was about one o'clock in the morning. I was coming with my bicycle. There was a red Mustang. When they saw me going down the hill, they followed me with the red Mustang. I fell all the way down the hill. I had a broken skull, broken leg, broken back. I was in the hospital a month.

I still, I don't know if it was those kids or not. It should have been them because I don't know nobody around here that hates me. I got hurt very bad.

My brother was coming with me. He was on a bike, but he went down the hill faster than I did. He was home already. I was right on my street, and he looks back and I was right in the middle of blood. I was in concussion for three days. The police picked me up and I punched the police in the month. I thought it was the kids. Some kids! That's what my brother told me. They took me to the hospital. They gave me X-rays and a lot of that stuff. I don't know whether I had surgery. I'm still going to the hospital.

I'm gonna try and get those kids. I know who they are and where they live and everything. I wanna make sure. I'll find out from friends. I have a lot of friends. Once I find out who they are, they in trouble. I got a lotta brothers, got a lotta friends.

They're Americans. I don't think a foreign kid would do this. Just like a foreign kid, he don't call me "Portuguese," call me names. I don't mind when they call me names. But when it comes to attacking me, when it comes to the nerves, they got hot already. They saying that every day. You feel like going to them and slap 'em on the face. But there are too many of them. You can't do it alone.

Somerville High School is almost half Portuguese. We have the soccer team. I'm in the soccer team and all these Portuguese here, they're also on the team. We were goin' to win this year. That's when I had the accident.

Do you find the teachers at school helpful?

The teachers are not very helpful. I don't think they care. That's my opinion. One of my teachers, I told her I had problems in reading English. So she told me to come after school. I go after school and she has more students over there and she lets me read by myself. Read by myself I can do it at home if I want to. The bilingual program is below the level that I'm at. What they want is to let you learn how to speak English first, and that's it—you're on your own.

Hopefully, I want to go to school next year again. At least I want my high-school diploma. I don't want the college. I don't think I'm smart enough to go to college. If I finish high school, I'm happy already.

I have three brothers. Two are married and one is gonna get married. There's three of us workin'. My mother doesn't want all our money we make. I'd say I make $200 a week. I give money to my mother for the food, for making wash the clothes and everything. She doesn't want all the money. She says, "Keep it for yourself, one day you're gonna need it."

I used to work in a Japanese restaurant, wait, make Japanese food. I was eleven. I told them I was fourteen. They believed it. I came to work [here] as a dishwasher. Then "chef." I used to help the chef cook. You learn to know what each job is, how hard they are. I work every night plus Saturday.

I enjoy working. I'd rather be working than be at school. School is kind of boring; you sleep. If working all the time, you moving. Like I know a lot of people. They don't like work. Maybe they don't need money. They sit around studying problems or stuff.

It's not hard for us. Portuguese kids are really hard-working. I don't say Portuguese. In my house everybody's hard-working. We work hard, work for the family and everything. We have no bills to pay. That's the way it goes.

I like this country. I like it as much—the other one was good. Here is better living. The other one I think was more beautiful than this, was a nice island. We had a lot of fun there. Here, if you look around, you'll find a lot of good things too.

My mother and my grandmother are thinking of going back. We said to my mother, "If you wanna go, you can, but we don't want to." None of my brothers wants to go back. We don't have nobody there. Who do we have there? Just my father's mother that's there. Once in a while we'll go visit. Otherwise, what are we gonna do over there? For vacation, that's a very small island. You go, I mean, I know the island from bottom to top already. You go there on vacation, whatta you gonna see?

GRACIELA MENDOZA PEÑA VALENCIA— Mexican Farm Worker

"I Want to Have Something"

Graciela Mendoza Peña Valencia was born in 1944, the oldest of five children, in Ciudad Juárez, a Mexican border town. By the age of twelve she was working a seven-day week in a local bakery. At fourteen, her maternal uncle sent for her to come to Los Angeles. After some family problems forced her return to Mexico, she commuted to work from Ciudad Juárez to an American canning company in El Paso. All of the money Graciela earned went to her family. When laid off by the cannery, she became a housekeeper in the homes of "Anglos" in El Paso.

The history of migration in the Southwest predates the national formation of either the United States or Mexico, when the Southwest was the exclusive province of a variety of Indian groupings. In the 1500s and 1600s came the Spanish conquest and the gradual intermingling of the native and invading populations. The rise of an independence movement and the subsequent end of Spanish rule in 1821 led to the creation of Mexico out of New Spain. But in the following decades Texas became a part of the struggle in the South's crusade to extend slavery. As white and black population moved into Mexican territory the United States and Mexico moved toward war. The defeat and humiliation of Mexico was sealed in 1846 with the Treaty of Guadalupe Hidalgo, annexing Texas into the United States and throwing in what is now New Mexico, Arizona, California, Nevada, Utah, and southern Colorado in exchange for $15 million. Besides losing their land, money, and pride, Mexicans in the Southwest became "strangers in their own land."[1]

It is estimated that there are seven million people of Mexican origin in the United States. Next to American blacks they are the largest minority in the country.[2] Migration across the Mexican border has been continual since the Mexican War, rising and falling with the Mexican economy. In 1975 over 100 million legal aliens crossed the Mexican border, some entering daily.[3] Legal entry is encouraged by the use of border-crossing cards, keeping cheap labor available in the border towns for agricultural work, household help, unskilled labor, and occasionally for strikebreaking.[4]

The Mexican worker is valued as a cheap source of labor in the Southwest. To assure easy entry, legislation like the Bracero program was passed in 1942.[5] The program ended in December of 1964 and new restrictions on immigration from this hemisphere went into effect. Since 1976, Mexico, like other Western Hemispheric nations, is restricted to a maximum of 20,000 immigrants within the 120,000 hemisphere total.

Recently much media attention has focused on *mojados,* or "wetbacks," and other undocumented Mexicans. In the years 1974 and '75 the number of Mexican deportable aliens found by the Immigration service was close to 700,000.[6] The true illegal number in unknown.

At the age of twenty-one, Graciela's commuting ended when her parents acceded to her wishes to come to the United States as a farm worker. She met her Yucatán-born husband in the strawberry fields on her fifteenth day as a field hand. He was her foreman. He married her and moved her from a barracks to a two-room house. They had their first child within the year.

Mr. Valencia is a Teamster member. In February of 1976 tensions around the Teamster–United Farm Worker struggle for recognition as the major farm union in California continued to run high; neither Graciela nor her husband was eager to discuss it.

Over the past several years the family has had to move to Los Angeles for half the year to pick celery while moving back to Salinas the other half to pick lettuce. "When you move, the child they don't learn nothing," she said. Graciela, her husband, and their three children live in a small, comfortable ranch-type house in the Salinas Valley. Her youngest child, a girl, is named America.

February 27, 1976
Salinas, California

My uncle wrote to my parents they have money for me to stay with them in Los Angeles. Is my mother's brother. I was fourteen. That first day I come from Mexico, I come on the bus. The first time I take my valise he said, "OK, first you take bath because I don't want dirt from Mexico." He take me to meet inspection. I don't say nothing. I feel something gonna happen to me after that but I don't say nothing. Sometimes I go to the bathroom and cry because I feel I want to stay in Mexico, not in United States.

I work in the house, but she promised I in school at nights. And this why my mother send me, to study more some English. But when I come here, he not put me in the school or nothing. He said, "I give you money to buy clothes," and he don't give me nothing. I remember the first time the old pants they buy me. Next he give me clothes from my aunt. They don't fit. Old clothes. Sometimes I feel something because I don't have nothing to eat.

Did you write to your mother?

No, because she keep the letters. Once I go to send letter, she opened my letter and read it out. I said, "Mother, I don't want to stay here because they make me this," and she throw the letter. She said, "Oh, your mother don't like you, because you not going to be nothing."

My neighbor, in the backyard she hanging clothes and I saw her and I said, "Maybe I go tell my problems and maybe she gonna help me go back to Mexico." And I go and she help me. She said I could move in and stay with her. I don't have to work in the house, nothing. The first time I go there she give me clean blankets and she give me food. I feel so good, and she take me to the school.

Both my uncle and my aunt found me there in the school. They call the police and the Immigration and they go for me. I was scared because I don't do nothing. Only they take me like this [putting her hands around her wrists]. They put handcuffs on me in the schoolroom. The principal come and speak to them and they take me to the Immigration office in Los Angeles. My uncle said I leave all the kids alone. I say, "No, she went to the store. When she come back I leave the house." I go and tell the neighbor everything. It's the same I tell police. That's why Immigration make my uncle take me to Mexico.

He drive me to Mexico. He not speak to me nothing. She, nothing. At my house they speak to my parents and I don't know what because I in another room. My father protect me. He say, "If she don't want to stay there, it's OK for me. Why they treat not like his family?" And he is mad because it is the brother. My mother feel sorry about, she told me, "You not helped your family."

I say this because I don't want other people to try the family way and friends that they turn bad.

Soon I start to work in Mountain Pass Company. I was sixteen. About three hundred or four hundred work there. Really two or three months we work hard. They need more people. I would cross the border every day. I had to pay a dollar for a day for the two rides from Ciudad Juárez every day to Saint Anthony. Sometimes I leave about 4:30 or 5:00 in the morning. Sometimes I come 10:00 in the night. If I work three or four hours I come back early, or sometimes late. One time I come to my home at 12:00 in the night because I don't have a ride.

We can chilis and tomatoes. The tomato comes with the skin; you cut all tomatoes up. You take all the skin and put in a little can. They put the tomatoes in hot water so I can take off the skin. You have a plastic apron. All your hair back with something. But sometimes the tomato is still soft and spill at your face and clothes. They pay the hour, $1.25. Sometimes I get $150 a week. It is more to clean the chili than the tomatoes. You have to do the same thing, skin the chili. They make the little chilis with four chilis in the can. I do this about two years. Then they said, "Wait for the next year."

I worked in houses in El Paso for four dollar a day. I worked about two years. Sometimes they pay me four dollars, but you need to pay for the trip. Two buses in Mexico and two buses in El Paso. Sometimes is a dollar because is cheap down there. About sixteen cents the trip in Mexico.

I want to come to United States. My parents say, "Wait, you are too young." I wait. Then I am twenty. I saw they needed people to pick strawberries. I went with my friend to contractor in El Paso. The contractor said, "You have never picked strawberries?"

"No."

"Oh! That's easy. Have big trees. You just pick the fruit off the trees."

I come here and I see those strawberries on the floor, oh! It's more hard. I came with my friend. When I come here the first day, I saw the big rooms. I feel like I'm going in jail. Only the little beds, no chair, no nothing, only the bed. For a bedspread you got a gray color. I was in a room with twelve people. But you know the big man who rents the camp? They give us a little room for the three, for my two friends and me, because he say, all the three are good people.

It was hot in the fields. First, I never worked in the sun all day, the second because is too hard. First day I take a break at 12:00 for eat. I want to stay, lay down on the ground because I feel tired. The sun make you all red in the face and everything. That time I don't have no hat or nothing.

I don't work now. Last year I work at celery, in the shed packing. Now, there's more good places to work. If you come here alone first, it's more complicated. When I know the place and everything, I bring my brothers and my mother and my sister. She marry a good man, they got a big house. My brother's got a new car. I was the first one to do farm work in this country. Second, my sisters; next, my brothers. Because if you here first you don't know nothing. When they come here, my husband have a good job and he help my brothers. It's more good to come like that than alone.

I like it here. I am happy with my kids, my husband, the house. My uncle could see it! He say I never do nothing.

ALMA MEJIA UMINSKY—
Guatemalan Girl, American Boy

Since 1951 Canada has accounted for the largest number of immigrants to the United States. Mexico has followed Canada, with close to two million legal immigrants. Central America has fallen into last place in the hemisphere, behind Canada, Mexico, the West Indies, and South America. Between 1951 and 1975 there were a little over 260,000 legal immigrants from Central America. Between 1966 and 1975 fewer than

20,000 of these immigrants came to the United States from Guatemala.[1]

Alma Mejia was born and brought up in Guatemala City, Guatemala. Her father owns a print shop and her mother is a nurse. She was brought to the United States after her high-school graduation by a suburban Boston businesswoman to work in the woman's home. While in her late teens, she met and married a native-born American.

With the exception of the Cerasolis, all the people in this collection who immigrated before 1945 and married, married someone from their native country or a second-generation person of their own ethnic group. But among the eight post-1945 married immigrants with whom I spoke, five had married native-born Americans whose ethnic background had no relation to theirs; only three had wives or husbands from their native country. Although too scanty a sample upon which to base generalizations, I found it an interesting point. Romantic and socioeconomic factors appear to have determined these marriages more than ethnic ones.

Almost all the pre-1945 immigrants with whom I spoke have become United States citizens. In the postwar group many have not. Alma Uminsky is a permanent resident, wishing to retain her Guatemalan citizenship.

An attractive young woman with dark hair and dark, expressive eyes, Ms. Uminsky works as a marketing and sales coordinator for hospital products at a corporate subsidiary. She attends night school at a local university.

We sat in my livingroom on a Sunday afternoon. Her husband, an optometrist, remained in the dining room reading the newspaper, while their small dog, Cha Cha, jumped up and down on the couch, trying to control the conversation. As we finished, she paused. "I came when I was seventeen and I had seventeen years of Guatemalan background. . . . My parents put me on a good road, so to speak. I can see now many things went wrong because my parents always thought they were right, but I am glad I was brought up in that background. They were strict with me. . . . I think I have to say I am very proud of what I said. I feel very strongly about it and I want other people to see what it's all about."

January 25, 1976
Cambridge, Massachusetts

Barry and I met at a wedding that neither one of us were invited. [Laughs.] Barry's parents own a flower shop, and his parents were doing the flowers for the wedding. The family I was living with in Needham—they needed a baby-sitter for all the kids, so they asked me if I wanted to come to the wedding to baby-sit. I had nothing better to do, so I said, "Sure, I'll go." So I was waiting for all the kids to come to me so that they would sit with me. Barry came to help his parents to set the flowers and he saw me in the background. He says he didn't talk to me in the beginning because he thought maybe I was waiting for a guy to come and get me. But he says he waited and nothing happened, so he approached me. We started talking and I got excited because he said he spoke Spanish. So immediately I go on speaking Spanish, and he didn't quite understand what I was saying. The day after I met Barry, I never expected him to call me back.

How did your family react to your marrying an American?

It's funny, but underneath, my parents were very happy I was getting married, and even happier that I was marrying an American fellow and not a Guatemalan fellow, because my father was always very protective. He always was very concerned about his daughters. He wanted nothing but the best for his daughters, right? And Guatemalan people, like many Latin American people, have been brainwashed that this country, it's a beautiful country, and this is nothing but the best and American men are so wonderful. People have been brainwashed. I know my parents are. I can see even more now, now that I have been back here for five years and really have become part of the American way of life.

Their idea is you come here, you become rich—everybody in this country is a millionaire. As far as my family is concerned, I am very rich. I have this nice home. But they don't know that you have to work harder than they have to work to make a living here. And they don't want to realize that, either. They don't realize that. All they want to think is that, "This is the country to come and make money." That's why it happens that you see so many people from different Latin American countries coming into this country and never going back. That's why there are so many millions of illegal Latin Americans living in this country. Many of them stay just to make the money, and then they can go back home with a lot of money. Then they go back with a different attitude. They are no longer the poor Joe. Now they are rich because they have maybe $300 in their pocket. They had to work very *hard* doing it, but they never tell people what they had to do to earn that money. To this point, as I said, my own parents, my father, must have thought, "Boy, she's marrying an American, a *gringo*!" They never said it to me face to face, but I knew what was going on.

We got married here in July of '71. My parents came up for the wedding. Barry is from a Jewish background. I am a convert. That's one of the things I had to say I'll never regret in my life. When I was a Catholic by name, I went every Sunday to school, but I never understood what I was doing. When I met Barry, we both decided *this* is what I want to do. He never forced me. His family never put any pressure. It was my own decision. I am very happy. My parents accepted it. It was hard for them, but they kept thinking of marrying a *gringo,* and that, God, "That's very important. She's going to be rich." It's terrible, it's so materialistic, but as I said, they have been brainwashed.

It sounds like part of you would like to go back there.

Yes, as the time goes by and I get older and more mature, I miss my family, because my family is getting larger and I have a lot of nephews now from my two sisters who are married. When I have gone back home, they are so beautiful, and it's so wonderful to see all the family together and growing, seeing those things, and seeing that this is not such a wonderful country like it was pictured to me when I came, this is not really the end of the world. It's a big country with much more problems than you have at home. I said to myself, what's here, really, to keep me? Barry and I are married; he has his practice here, so this is my home; but if he had a choice to go *home* I would definitely be the one for pushing it.

There are so many things you would like to have your mother to talk to or a sister, and I just don't have that. And although I have a good relationship with my parents-in-law, I still don't feel that I can speak to my mother-in-law the way I could speak to a sister or my own mother. I would like to have somebody really close to me that I could talk to, someone to discuss problems, but I don't, and I miss that.

The families here are *not* like the families at home. People may see each other once a year and they don't communicate, they don't make any effort to keep that family together. I think many factors cause that. One, you have to commute for such a long time. You waste a whole hour just going one way or coming the other way—spending eight hours in an office every single day. Then when Saturday comes you have to do your cleaning because you didn't have time to do it during the week, and you have to do the food shopping. There is no time to say, "But gee, let's go visit such and such." And I still don't like that. I don't get used to it. I don't like this rushing all the time.

Are you thinking of having children?

I am going to have a family for sure. We are having a good time right now. We both are working, putting money aside so that we can get a home and then do some traveling. Once the children come, you can't do any of those things. You can't just pack your things and go. In Guatemala it is different. If you have an emergency you don't have to worry, "Is my baby-sitter going to come?"

I have my own cultural background and I am living in a different culture. Many of my ideas are not American ideas, are not Guatemalan ideas, they are my own. One example is as far as children are concerned. To me, this has become very important and is a priority that if I'm going to have a family I am going to have to stay home, and I would not even think of going out to work. Another thing I feel very strongly, when I bring up *my* kids they are going to be brought up the way I was brought up. I would not let my kids manage like the kids do in this country with the parents. The kids in this country, what I have seen, they *yell* at their parents. They slam the door in the parent's face. They just take off and they do as they please. They have no respect for the elderly people, for their own parents. My gosh, I can see so much of it—it's incredible. I want to bring up my kids, not as strict as I was brought up, but I want them to respect and be concerned for other people, not just themselves.

I don't want my kids to expect things from me all the time, because it's not going to be possible unless you're in a position where money doesn't mean anything. But there are not that many people in this country like that. Most people work, and whatever they have they have worked for it. It's not like they have millions and millions. Hopefully I would like to bring up my kids not like Americans, not like Guatemalans, but something unusual [laughs]—something of my own.

Maybe I am old-fashioned, but I would prefer to be in a small country than a big one with so many problems. Honestly, I would prefer ten times to go back to Guatemala, and I know, I'm fully aware that when I got back to Guatemala or if I ever go to live in Guatemala, I cannot expect to live at the same standard as I live here. It's going to be an adjustment because here, God, you have a dishwasher, you have a washing machine, and a dryer. But I can live without those things, but you're spoiled here.

No matter how much money I am making, no matter what kind of position I have in my company, having a nice home, living comforable, it still does not make up for what I am really missing, which is my family. When I first came here I was so excited about coming to this wonderful country that I said, "Oh, my God, it's going to be so different and some day I'm going to be making so much money"—that's all I could think. I was like anybody else, brainwashed. But now that I have learned the language and I can communicate and I can pick up books and read in all these subjects and I see what goes on, I say, it's not such a wonderful country, it's just a big country, that's all, where everybody's a number. You are no longer a person.

"DR. A.L. SARKAR"*—
Indian Researcher

Dr. A.L. Sarkar was raised in Allahabad, India. In 1969 he came to the United States with his wife and child to work on a doctoral degree in electrical engineering. The increased migration of Asians and of highly trained scientific, technical, and professional people are two important post-mid-'60s phenomena in American immigration patterns. Due to discriminatory quotas between 1951 and 1960 fewer than 2,000 Indians came to the United States. Over 24,000 Indians arrived between 1966 and 1970, after national quotas were dropped. From 1971 to 1975 the annual rate ranged between eleven and slightly over sixteen thousand. One-third of those entering were classified as "professional, technical or kindred workers" and close to half, their wives and children.[1] These families, along with similar ones from the Philippines, South America, and Europe, and to a lesser extent Africa and the Middle East, are part of a current population movement known as the "brain drain."[2] Their skills give them preferred status over other less-skilled immigrants.

---

*"Dr. A.L. Sarkar" is a pseudonym.

Dr. Sarkar received his master's degree in science and technology at an Indian university and did development work in India for eight years in the area of radio and television. After completing his degree in 1974, he accepted a job in a multinational corporation on Route 128, west of Boston—an area considered to be a national center for corporate scientific research. Dr. Sarkar, his Indian wife, and two children live in a Boston suburb.

Thousands of people from the developing nations come to the United States, Canada, and other western countries to advance their training in science, medicine, agriculture, and education. Whether they remain or return home after their stay is always a critical personal decision. Often the economic effects of these decisions have national and international ramifications. In many developing nations, the home country pays for the skilled worker's entire education, through college and postgraduate work. There is an enormous financial investment in this process which is lost, at least in the direct sense, if the trained individual remains abroad. This personnel migration or "brain drain" is the subject of much international debate and is often seen as a robbery of the developing nations by a few wealthy, highly technically developed nations, predominantly the United States and Canada. It has even been suggested that developing nations seal their borders to scientific émigrés or require them to pay some of their salaries to their native country as reimbursement. Another suggestion is that the receiving nation pay the sending nation, as if an art object had been purchased or a part of the national treasure lost.[3]

Some professionals with whom I spoke appeared defensive when I mentioned the "brain drain." One Indian radiologist admitted that "the job" was the main reason she and her husband, also a physician, had left India. "Whatever you learn around here, you can't practice in India." She then added, "There are so many doctors there. For the kind of work we are doing, there is somebody else. In fact, I used to say we are solving India's food problem. If four of us go away, we reduce the population." Few said money had anything to do with their decisions. Instead they stressed American "know-how" and the opportunities to do research and use equipment not available back home. An oceanographer from the Middle East said that he could not get work in his field back home after completing advanced studies in the United States. He said he would return home or go anywhere, even China, if it were the best place to do his work. This international theme was restated by a

German scientist working on an energy-conversion project: "I am by experience an internationalist. I consider the world my field of interest, everybody in the world the beneficiary of my concern."

The question remains whether the wealth of North American universities and corporations will ultimately benefit the entire world or just themselves and their countries as men and women like Dr. Sarkar decide whether to stay or go. That these scientists and physicians add to American prestige and power is beyond doubt.

April 8, 1977
Waltham, Massachusetts

After a year of working I wanted to go for higher studies and I really wanted to go to an advanced country just to look around and see how the things are. I got this admission and assistantship, but at that point my father died, in '63, early '64—I had some family responsibilities.

The structure in India is somewhat different than what you have here. I had my sisters who were not married, and marriage is a big deal there. I decided that I could not leave the responsibility I had for the family. So I completely cooled the idea of going for several years.

Then in '68 it occurred to me that maybe I should go out, maybe write to this university and see what they say now. I wrote back to them. They provided assistance. I said, "I'll go and study there two or three years and see how things go." In fact I came on a study visa. You could arrange five years.

Naturally I talked it over with the family. In my own family it really was no problem. My brother was really no problem; he quickly agreed. My mother was somewhat skeptical about it; she did not think I should go, but knowing that I had waited for so many years, and she is very negotiable, she really didn't object that much. My wife's parents were quite strong on this. They did not want us to go away and forget India completely. They had a feeling that we would not come back—come back in the sense of living there permanently. But we talked it over with them and basically they understood that I am going to fulfull my ambition—I'll not stay for long. And there was no main difficulty in convincing my wife; we had good communication. The child was only three years old, so we didn't have to ask him.

In the beginning, somehow it didn't look like to me a great step. The only difference was that I would be that much further away from home. I think if I had a choice that I had to come on my own money there is no way I could have come, because the money gets divided by a factor of eight or nine between there and here. That is one aspect of it. The other aspect is that you can't get that kind of foreign exchange released from the government. They just don't want to do that. So on my money I wouldn't have come.

How come you stayed here after you got your degree?

My feeling was that going to school was good—it gave me a certificate, gave me some background, all right. But I didn't get any idea about how the industry's operating. I planned to be in the area of research for the rest of my life. I really thought for me to take advantage of my stay here I really ought to *work,* really to get the firsthand experience. And then we decided I would work about three, four years and then go back.

I thought that three years is a long period originally. But you know, three years really gets you started and that's the reason we really have to postpone it. If it's '80 it gives me six, seven, eight years of working there. To a certain extent financial is one thing but more than that I think gives me enough experience. Really I feel I should be satisfied by then and if I'm not satisfied then, forget it, I'll never be. This is the lower limit.

Upper limit comes from the consideration that we have two children now. One is ten, the other is two and a half. So, I don't think I would like to impose my decision on my child. At sixteen, having been brought up here, he's at the age where he thinks what he's doing, at least *he* thinks that. He becomes completely Americanized. I am not saying that he is not now. He still has some habits because we try to inject on him. We observe the festivals, we observe the values, we have fairly good, in fact very good, interaction with the community from back home. Being a large group here we get together almost every weekend or so. So he does get pretty good exposure to our culture, our values. [But] my son now is roughly ten years old and he does not think the way I do. Our fairy tales are different. Our stories are different and our songs, poems are different. I am not saying that he will not be a misfit if he goes at twelve, but certainly he'll be a bigger misfit if he goes at sixteen.

I am saying we are planning to go back in '80, '81. I am not saying that we have got a plane ticket and we will go. We will probably review at that time. But I think if we decide not to go at that time then we are here for good.

Have there been any kinds of discrimination against you?

No. That is something, I really appreciate that very much. I never felt that I was discriminated against. In fact, I always felt that I got my share and more. I have heard people talk about it. Discrimination is something which has a very tight link with the economy of the country and I guess that that is one of the reasons that it is happening in Canada and why it is very severe in England. I am not saying it does not exist here, but to my knowledge I haven't seen any, at least in my life—that's the only one you can comment on. Everybody's circumstances are different. Maybe I am just lucky I met the right people.

Earlier I used to worry about my accent, which I have and I live with. Earlier I used to feel that maybe it's bad, maybe I should work on it. Very quickly I decided that's not the way to work. You can't change these things. You really can't. I'm sure that if you went to another country, you can't be one of those. We can be compatible. We can live happily, very friendly, but you don't have to be one of them to live there. I may be wrong.

Would you say from the point of view of India, the Indian economy, they have lost a great deal?

I feel that the point that the country has been losing a lot has been overemphasized. First of all, the way I think, I don't think the country has lost a heck of a lot if I stay away eight years and come back with better training. In fact they may come out winner. That's one aspect of it. Another aspect is I have already worked there. It's not a total waste. The other facet is our education is more or less completely subsidized by the government, so the number of people who go to colleges is much higher and some people feel that, I don't feel that, if I go back I will be displacing somebody. It's not there's a dearth of trained people there. There *are* people available. If I can get enough training, that can be useful. But for the point of view that the country has spent on me, I agree that they lost some. But part of it is very well paid for, for my work earlier, and maybe if I go back, it's paid for.

But many students leave at nineteen and they are never heard from again.

True. I think that is a total loss as far as India is concerned. If I did that I would feel guilty, in a way—guilty not in the sense that I am not doing the right thing. If I really look from a very broad point of view, after all, I am contributing to the good of the society. Why should it be for the country that I lived in? But I feel strongly that if the education is subsidized by the government, I think they have a point in expecting me to do something for them. Otherwise they have lost the money. Another aspect is, if I didn't go to school they might have trained somebody else. I think it's a valid point. But I don't believe that if I went to school there, I am bound to work the rest of my life without doing any betterment to myself, or without really doing what I want to do. I work on compromises, as you can very well tell.

DEBORAH PADMORE—
Trinidad Farewell

"You Always Have This Black Thing Hangin' Over Your Head"

Trinidad is a small, independent island country off the coast of Venezuela. Like most of the islands in the Caribbean, it has had a history of both colonialism and slavery. Between 1498 and 1797 the Spanish controlled Trinidad and its smaller sister island, Tobago. During the late 1770s the French had economic but not political control, and in 1797 the British took over. The native population was decimated in the first years of foreign occupation, and Africans were forcibly captured and brought to the island to operate a growing sugar-plantation economy. When the British gained control of Trinidad, abolitionism was a growing force, and in 1832 slavery was abolished, although an interisland slave trade continued.

In order to assure a stable and docile labor force, the British in Trinidad imported large numbers of indentured workers from India in the late nineteenth century. One hundred and forty-three thousand Asians entered Trinidad between 1845 and 1917.[1] By the end of World War I, the growing Indian nationalist movement began to protest Britain's treatment of Indian immigrants on the island. At the same time, a growing black nationalist movement in Trinidad indicated that independence and better economic conditions were on the minds of its people. In August 1962 Trinidad became independent.

British colonies in the Caribbean, like Jamaica, Barbados, and Trinidad-Tobago, have contributed to the United States immigrant population since the beginning of the Republic. Prince Hall, an ex-slave from

Barbados, fought at Bunker Hill; Denmark Vesey, from the Virgin Islands, tried to start a slave rebellion in the Carolinas during the early 1820s; Marcus Garvey, a Jamaican, formed the black-nationalist Universal Negro Improvement Association in the 1920s; Stokely Carmichael, a Trinidadian, was a major force behind the Student Nonviolent Coordinating Committee in the 1960s; and Shirley Chisholm is of West Indian origin.[2]

Black immigrants from the English, Spanish, and French Caribbean were living in New York and other major American cities in the early part of this century. Those from the British West Indies brought to the United States, a combination of British and African traditions. In fact, it was their British citizenship that allowed them to continue to enter the United States after the passage of the quota laws in the 1920s; they entered on never-filled British quotas.

Though entrance was easy, adapting to American society was not. As one early student of black immigration noted in the late 1930s, "The Negro enters in the dual role of Negro and immigrant."[3] Black immigrants carry the dual burden of being foreign and being black in a society where whiteness is prized. There is a new country, in some cases a new language, and there is also a different and discriminatory pattern of social relations. As Ms. Padmore said, "You always have this black thing hangin' over your head."

The rise in West Indian immigration to the United States since 1960 has been attributed to rising populations and economic problems, as well as changes in British immigration policy. After World War II, a growing number of British Commonwealth citizens from the Caribbean immigrated to the United Kingdom. By 1961 close to forty thousand West Indians were requesting permanent residency there. According to one study of Jamaican immigrants, those entering Britain were young, often skilled, and better educated than those back home. Almost half of them were women, seventy-five percent of whom left children on the islands.[4] During this same period a growing number of Indians and Pakistanis were also entering Britain. A slackening British economy could not absorb this new population growth. As more blacks and Asians entered England, a racial reaction set in and in 1962 the Commonwealth Immigrants Act was passed, placing strict limits on further immigration to Britain.

It is ironic that as various pressures led West Indians to seek their fortunes abroad, Britain began closing her doors and the United States and Canada began liberalizing their earlier racially oriented laws. Between 1966 and 1975 close to two hundred thousand people from Jamaica, Trinidad-Tobago, and Barbados entered the United States legally, with Jamaica accounting for about three-fourths of that figure.[5] At this time figures for all three countries are sharply rising.[6]

Deborah Padmore came to the United States from Trinidad in the early 1960s. She works as a secretary at an economic-opportunity agency in Cambridge, Massachusetts. Although her real ambition is to become a marine biologist, she is attending nursing school. She has one daughter, who lives in Trinidad.

When asked if she visited Trinidad frequently she replied that the $450 fare made it difficult to do so. "And you would be amazed at this anxiety that you have when you get on the plane to go back to Trinidad, hopin' that your friends would be there, and the place would be the same as you left it, and when you go back, it's not there. People have grown up; everything is changed."

July 26, 1976
Cambridge, Massachusetts

Who would want to write a book about immigrants? Everybody got the same thing to say—they want to go back home but—there's always this *but.* "Why don't you want to go back home if you're not satisfied with the United States?" And I think this is the struggle that you go through every day, havin' this yearnin' to go back since you came because, although you have lived here and you have accepted a lot of American customs, you still have ties with your *roots.* Take, for instance, me. I have been away since 1960; and I always think of Trinidad as when I left it. But then you go home periodically and you see that things have changed! It's not like what you left it as, but you still have that *yearnin'* to go back home and try to fit in, although *I* know I can't fit in. When I go back home, I'm too accustomed to this life here in America: getting up in the morning, goin' to work, hustlin', hustlin', hustlin'. I think it's something that I trained myself into, and I wouldn't be able to go back home and be relaxed as I was when I was there as a kid.

How did you happen to first get here?
I was married at that time. I got married at eighteen. My husband came to go to Howard University, and I followed after him. *An old*

story. [Laughs.] It was a big world, I wanted to see what it had in store for me. I think he felt the same way. He never got around to tellin' me. I ventured out, to learn as much as I could. It was rough.

It was about '61. Really at the height of everything, with Stokely Carmichael and the whole thing. I was not part of it. I was still learning. I was still in the grass roots, coming from Trinidad, not knowing *anything.*

You know, you have this *vivid* imagination of America being the most beautiful land in the world. You respected Americans, for some reason. They came down as tourists, and they portrayed America as a fantastic place to live in, where you always had money, and everything was beautiful. They tell you these stories, and it's like you *should* come here. Most of the time they came from places like Harlem, where you really had to save for five years to get a vacation around the '50's, '60's, and you're *not conscious* of this. You never hear them thinking of going to Paris or going to the Riviera, where *rich* people go. But they come down to the West Indies. They build you up. They give you this big impression that America is *it.* You never think about the racial tension and the intensity that you have to live with. They never talk about it. So I wanted to see for myself, and I saw a lot. I saw a great deal.

I went to Washington, D.C. My husband, he went to Howard. We got an apartment, and we lived there. [Later we moved to New York.] I worked and he worked. We went through our changes—a whole lot of them—and we just finally split up. I didn't stay with him that long, about five years, off and on, off and on.

I had just migrated from Trinidad; the atmosphere I was living in was *not* an American life-style. I'm not sure whether you are hip to Trinidad, but they do have a cosmopolitan culture. And you sit there with Indians, and you sit with Chinese children, and you sit there with so-called "Trinidad white people," and you never have a problem! You never *think* about it bein' a problem, because you are in this little country. When you come abroad, it takes you a while for you to see certain things.

At that time I didn't know what the hell was happenin'. I was hearin' so many things, and I couldn't *see* exactly where Stokely Carmichael was comin' from, where Rap Brown was comin' from. And even though you pick up a book and you read, you read, you read, things never did fall into place until after you started growin' and seein' things.

I'm not a racist. I cannot say that I'm a racist, that I hate people,

Deborah Padmore

white people, and that I *hate* the government, because the American government has done a lot for *me*—much more I think, than any other, or even my little country, will do for the people. I was able to go to school and get an education, which I know damn well my country would not be able to give. But there is good and bad in everything, and I don't think it's the government, really, I think it's the people.

Did breaking up with your husband have to do with you're being thrown into a whole new culture?

Well, it did and it didn't. Maybe if I was in Trinidad, I would have had to depend on him, he being the sole breadwinner of the family, because I know jobs are hard to get in Trinidad. And coming here and earning my own money made me more independent than I was born, and I was a very independent person. But that had a *lot* to do with it, coming here. I started working for my own money, and I started making a lot of friends and seeing and observing, reading a lot of magazines. Those things like *Redbook, Woman's Day,* they have a lot to contribute to divorces, too, you know. [Laughs.] You read them and you say, "Wow! What the hell's wrong with me! Why am I puttin' up with this shit? This man was goin' to school. I'm bustin' my ass to send him to school. He's screwin' all over me." Sometimes he slept home, sometimes he didn't. It got to a point where he gambled a lot, too, and well, of course, he was in America. I don't know where the man's head was at, to tell you the truth.

I think it was my husband who really eased me out of New York. He kept tormentin' me, tormentin' me, all the time, that I should come back to him.

I wasted too much time. If I had the man behind me, you know what would have happened? It would be cool sailin' for me, but then life is a different thing. You have to live it in stages. You can't push nothing, and things come along, just as you hoped they would. Now, looking back at it, I don't think I went through a lot. I think I made a good move coming to Boston. Seventeen years, you think you're in love, in love with what? I believe it was my mother and father both died. I thought I was very independent, and my sister got married, and I was sort of left alone. And I could remember me sayin', "What's the best thing for you to do? Get married." The first man came along I got married. I didn't stop and think who he was, where he came from, what's his background, anything. I don't think they make seventeen-

and eighteen-year-olds like that anymore. I think I was the last batch of the stupid ones.

I think Boston, Cambridge did a lot for me. More enlightenment, because I was away from my people in New York, and I was able to see the world. Being by myself, I had more time to meditate or concentrate, and I was able to see different people, and I learned a lot. It started fascinating me, how *could* one place be so different from another, and when it's not too far away, just four hours' ride? The workin' pressure in New York is not half as bad as here in Massachusetts.

What kind of pressure?

I'm talkin' about racial pressure. In New York, as a black person, you could work freely. But here, apart from you not being able to work as you want to, you always have this black thing hangin' over your head. You know, that you are *black*. I think if there is one place that reminds you of *who* you are is working in Boston. And this hostility that people have to acquire to *survive* in a small place like Boston. The ignorance that you hear, for a place with leadin' colleges, M.I.T. and Harvard.

I had a lot of experience here—especially as a worker. When I started working, I worked at the hospital. I was a technical assistant—*supposedly*. Ended up to be a charwoman. They would like to impress you that you are one notch on top of a nurse's aide, but break it down. They have you so uniformed. You have to have this pinstriped blue uniform. They keep you in your place. Apparently when the authorities come, they say, "Well, we have a couple of hundred black people. Look at *them*." Shit work! And the racist nurses. I don't know whether it's racism, stupidity, or just plain ignorance. Well, racism is ignorance, so I have to call it ignorance.

It was nasty—the way they treat the patients comin' in there, as though they were not supposed to come into a hospital. And if you are on welfare, they have to look down at you because you don't have money to come into [that hospital] so you will get the worst care possible. Very few doctors and very few nurses that I was with were sympathetic. They *push* for this power and recognition.

And the black people that come in there are supposed to go start in the kitchen. And if they had any potential at all to be anything else, they would have to go through this whole rigamarole even to get a transfer.

The minute you walk in there you think that these people goin' to help you. The only time they would get anxious or interested in you— if you had some rare disease or if you're the son of somebody that they want recognition from. It's just sickening.

But there are some nice people. They're hard to find, but somebody's out there. They have to lead this intense, nontrustin' life. This is something that the people in Trinidad do not live.

They never listen to anybody, Americans, never, to hear what people have to say—even around here. They call you a Turk. I don't know where the name derived from, but as long as you're a West Indian, you're a Turk. I do not know if it's jealousy, but West Indians have no place in America. They're not white, so they can't fit in with white people. And they're stupid, according to the black American. If I was takin' a poll, maybe I'll go around interviewin' people, but my *observations*—I do not know if it's because West Indians came here as skilled laborers. Most of them are. And the jobs that they can get, most Americans are not skilled. Only now, they are able to train black people, but before, you'll find a West Indian coming here as a carpenter, a painter, which he had to do.

I found so much ignorance when I came here. It was amazing. I was very much surprised that the standard of education was so low among black people, because in Trinidad, they tend to give you a British education, which covers everything, from A to Z. And I was surprised to see big people, grown people, not even knowing where Trinidad was. Since 1965 most black people are more aware.

Do you think you'll get citizenship some time?

I don't want citizenship. You still want to know where your roots are. I could tell you who my great-great-grandfather is. Although everybody came from Africa, those who landed in the West Indies were the much more fortunate ones. They came there first. The first stop was in Barbados, and Trinidad, and they probably kept their families together much more than when they were scattered throughout the South, although they had a lot of bartering slavery in Boston from Barbados here. I could still remember my great-grandfather, not really remember, but hear my mother talk about my grandfather and her father, and he talking about *his* father. And you know they had some sort of definite *link*. But when you hear people from America talk, they could only go back to one generation, or two generations, maybe. You don't see them gettin' that real link-up, "My father's father," unless they do some heavy research.

Do you think you'll bring your daughter here?

Tracy? She would come here on vacation, but I don't think America's a nice place to bring up a kid. She'd have no freedom. Maybe if I lived in the country where she is able to walk outside. And the crime rate is so high here. I don't think I would like her to go through the same shit that I went through. She has a big house in Trinidad, she has the nieces and nephews. And the freedom that she has. It isn't worth it. Especially in Boston, for her to go through that busin' business, it would just freak me out. I don't think that children should have to go through this bullshit in the first place. I think if they got some good teachers and put them in the school, the kids won't have to be bused, especially in places where people don't want you.

Look at the dangers these kids have to go through to go to different parts of the country. The stoning of buses. It's ignorance, plain ignorance. I can't see the head nor tail of it, up to now. And it's a big, wide world, and all of sudden, everybody's gainin' territory. You can't go down to South Boston, because South Boston is predominantly white; you can't go down to Roxbury, because Roxbury is predominantly black. So nonsensical.

I think that part of me still remains with me from Trinidad. That's still what remains with me. People not bein' able to integrate and talk to one another, because it's the life that you live, and everybody has their ups and downs. And poverty is something that everybody goes through, unless you are super rich. Poor black and poor white. Everybody's poor. I don't know what the fight is all about. Somebody of a different nationality than me, unless he's coming into rob *me*, then I might be defensive! Other than that, could I say that I hate this person because he's black, or I hate this person because he's white? It's very illiterate.

"BRIGITTE BESIMER"*—
"Illegal Alien"

There is a stereotype of the illegal alien—a young man, either Mexican, Latin, or West Indian. In fact, the genders, nationalities, and numbers of "illegals" in the United States are impossible to verify and can only be projected from the characteristics of those who are caught.[1] Numerical estimates range between one and twenty million.

Improperly documented immigrants are not new to American history. Arthur Miller's Italians who jumped ship to work on the New York docks in *A View from the Bridge* are now being replaced by those of other nationalities.[2] Immigration authorities continue to track them down.

In its 1974 *Annual,* the Immigration and Naturalization Service proudly declared the fiftieth anniversary of its border patrol. The patrol sees itself as exercising a patriotic service by capturing and deporting persons who have entered the United States illegally. Many of these "illegals" seem to be willing, however, to risk the possibility of arrest and deportation in order to contribute to their own, and their family's, economic survival.

In the *New York Times* of May 1, 1977, several writers tried to analyze the "illegal" phenomenon; all agreed upon its economic basis. James Sterba noted that a cleaning woman on the American side of the border can make three times as much money as a factory worker on the Mexican side; that unemployment and underemployment beset half of Mexico's population; and that the economic and population push of all of the countries south of the United States is a problem placed "on the nation's doorstep."[3]

The problem of "illegals" has hidden a number of real issues with which the United States government would rather not deal. "Illegals" often have served as scapegoats for the failure of the U.S. economic system to provide jobs and a growing economy for all of its people. Illegal immigration is also related to foreign policy. By supporting corrupt rulers, by backing them and American corporate interest with armed force, by not giving fair restitution for resources taken, U.S. foreign policy has helped to create illegal aliens in the Western Hemisphere. And in poor countries around the world where unequal distribu-

---

*"Brigitte Besimer" is a pseudonym.

tions of wealth, corrupt regimes, and growing populations exist, it is no wonder that immigrants, legal or illegal, find their way into a richer America.

The debate over "illegals" is bitter in the United States. Unions claim that "illegals" take away their jobs; others say that they are filling jobs Americans refuse to take. Some wish to see legislation protecting "illegals" from exploitation; others wish them deported and their employers punished. For now the words "illegal alien" exist as a racist code word for Latins and black West Indians. The questions of what legal status to grant those who have lived in the United States for many years, and what to do about future illegal immigration remain.

For two and a half years I tried to track down an undocumented person, and though television news and newspaper reports say that millions of "illegals" abound in the urban streets of the Northeast, Southwest, and Chicago, I was quite unsuccessful in finding one. Names would be given to me, but phones would be disconnected and addresses vacated. In the Los Angeles garment district, several Mexican women actually ran away from me, fearing I was from the Immigration service.

This is a somewhat extended forward to explain why, although all estimates are that Mexicans in the West and Southwest and Latins on the East Coast make up the bulk of the illegal population, I interviewed Brigitte Besimer, a Frenchwoman in her twenties. Brigitte is an "illegal". There are many people like her who legally enter the United States on a visitor's or student's visa and then disappear. Although Brigitte may not be typical of the largest numbers of the undocumented, her story tells something about what it is like to live under an illegal status in American society.

April 16, 1977
Cambridge, Massachusetts

I came here because I wanted to study [health foods]. I asked for a visitor visa because I thought I would be only there for six months. It's not recognized like a normal school, so I couldn't apply for a student visa. Now I've run out of my visa. I was not sure how long I'd be staying, so I didn't feel like going through the hassle of getting my papers renewed and stuff. Plus I was told that in order to have your visa, you had to have a certain amount of money, two or three thousand. You have to *prove* that you can support yourself without working. I didn't have that kind of money so I did not even try. So I stayed. It didn't really worry me. I thought when I want to leave I just leave. I didn't think I would ever get hassled.

Then I start traveling, and the first time I went to Key West. I hitch-hiked. It was the winter of '75. I had some problems. I almost got caught because I was hitchhiking on the highway and I was south of Washington, D.C., and the state police came by and asked me for my papers. I had my papers on me, but I did not want to show it to him. I gave him my name but when he asked me if my visa papers were together I told him, I had a visitor visa. Then he took me to the police station and he kept asking me all these questions over and over and I had to think of quick answers. I think that what saved me is that I was really positive. I was not scared, or at least I didn't let it show. I was very relaxed and smiling. Inside of me I was really praying. His job was only to give me a fine because I was hitchhiking on the highway. He didn't have to investigate into my papers.

He gave me a rough time, then he tried to call Washington, D.C., to get in touch with the FBI. He tried for two hours and he couldn't get through. Then he got in touch with somebody, an FBI guy. This guy came about an hour later, and I thought this time I'm not going to get out of the situation. He asked me the same question and I told him the same answer. I told him I left all of my papers in Key West because I didn't want to travel with my papers. I didn't want to take the chance that somebody stole my papers.

So, these guys from the FBI tried to call Washington, D.C., to try and check the computer? You know, to check when I came here and to see if my visa was all right. He couldn't because it was Easter, and it was the only day of the year that it's closed. He was really upset. He asked the state-police guy, "Can you keep her for two days, until Monday?" and the state police said, "No, I'm just not entitled to do that."

The guy from the FBI said, "I can't do it, either."

So the guy from the FBI said, "All right, we let you go, but I don't want you to hitchhike. Fly, whatever, take the bus. I don't want to see you again because if I see you again, you better be all right with your papers, because if you are not all right then I'll be really upset and you might end up in prison.

[Later, this officer,] after hassling me all afternoon, he felt like an asshole, I guess. He called to get the FBI guy and *nothing* came through! He felt very guilty, so he tried to make up for it.

I came close other times, but never with the FBI. Then I went to Key West, and there I had some problem to work. I was working in a restaurant. In order to work you have to have an ID card with your picture and your fingerprint and you have to go to the police station to get that—I guess because there is so much immigration there from Cuba. I switched jobs, got a false name, false Social-Security number.

How did you get a Social-Security number and do all that?[1]

Social-Security number, I knew the code. The code for the Social-Security number I just made up and I just asked for them to wait, then I got my ID. The first place I worked for a month. The second place I was working in a big chain restaurant. I asked them to wait. So I didn't work for a few months. They paid me minimum wages. In Florida it's like seventy cents an hour. Restaurant you make your money by tips. So they couldn't pay me lower than that.

I came to Key West first. I was only going to be a couple of weeks for vacation. It's just another world. So slow, and everyone takes his time. It's very mellow. I couldn't leave this place after two weeks.

I left around June and decided to go to Montana. There was a healing festival in Montana: massage and nutrition. Then I wanted to see the West Coast. So I left in June and started hitchhiking with a friend I met in Key West.

I was in Montana for about two weeks. Then I was hitchhiking through Oregon and Washington. I picked apples and cherries. Then I didn't have to have any papers—easy to get a job doing that—there is a lot of Mexican doing that. For the apple I worked a big company so they provide us with trailers, showers, a place to cook, bed. There were little cabins, too. I was with this friend from Key West. And then I left him, too, so I went by myself, and I was picked up by a bunch of girls who were picking apples, too. I had the most beautiful time. On the east side of Washington you have these very dry hills and this blue Columbia River. The sky is very blue, because you have no clouds. The whole valley is green, because you have all orchard.

When I went just north of Seattle I ran into a guy from Holland. He told me about how to get some papers—some false identification. He gave me this address and I wrote to this place. I gave them my name and this false information and gave the six dollars and then they send me ID.

I've been back to Boston for over a month now and I'm doing some housecleaning. I don't have to pay any tax. It's safe for me. There are three persons I am going to, three times a week. That's enough for me to live on. I don't mind it. I like it because I keep my hands busy but I can think, rather than waitressing or working in an office. Cleaning is not a problem, plus these are nice people. I go in different homes and see how people live. I can't complain. I just have to decide when I want to leave and which way.

What would happen if you decided to leave the ordinary way?

If I take a plane, they will see. I don't think they can actually put me in jail. They could, maybe, but I don't think they would. They would be glad I am leaving. But they would write it down and I wouldn't be able to come back, not if I wanted to come to the States and apply and get a visa. So, I don't want to do that. I am going to avoid this situation because you know eventually I might have to come here or I might want to come here. If I come back I will try to arrange it in such a way—I won't put myself in the same situation. I'll try to do it more legally if I come back. I know I will find a way. I just have to make up my mind. I'm not sure I want to go back now. I'm just stuck because I can't decide, that's all.

Did you ever think of trying to stay here permanently?

No, because I would like to go all over the world.

And then go back to France?

I'm not sure. I don't think I would like to settle down in the States. States is a good place to make money, but I don't think it is a good place to live. It's wild, it's dangerous. It's hard. I can see a lot of friends, a lot of people around me. They have been through bad trips, drugs; they have been taking heroin. I see a lot of my friends have been through this heavy thing—drugs is one of the big problems. Plus the Mafia is really controlling everything, almost, and pollution—I don't think it is a good place to live. But I know I would like to come back.

Do you ever feel like a criminal?

This land, the origin was Indian, and we didn't ask them, our ancestors did not ask them. Most of them came from Europe, like me, except it was 1600 or something. They just assumed it was their land, so I don't see how now they can say, "No. You can't come here." They have no right to do that, because they did it.

"LEE KI CHUCK"*—
From Korea to Heaven Country[1]

Ki is from Seoul, Korea. He came to the United States in 1973 with his father and settled in a Los Angeles suburb. He was then seventeen years old. Ki's father had fought in Vietnam and then tried to become successful in business in Korea before emigrating. His mother, his father's second wife, and his two stepbrothers remained in Korea until his father saved enough money by working in an auto shop to bring them to the United States. During those first months Ki missed his mother a great deal. He said, "I tried suicide so many times or ran away."

The first Koreans to come to the United States followed a pattern similar to that of Japanese and Filipinos—that is, via the Hawaiian plantations. Emigration was encouraged by the Korean government's opening of an immigration office in 1902, and the further backing of D.W. Desher, a plantation owner who recruited in Korea. Over 7,000 Koreans left for Hawaii between late 1902 and mid-1905, when the Korean government cut off emigration in order to protect its nationals from exploitation. After World War II, especially after the Korean War, many Koreans were able to enter the United States as "non-immigrants," that is, as immediate family of U.S. citizens. Most were wives or adopted children of U.S. servicemen. A high proportion of those Koreans entering between 1959 and 1965 became naturalized.[2]

When the Immigration and Nationality Act was revised in 1965 more Koreans with professional and technical skills entered the United States. Between 1967 and 1971, while the total number of Koreans went from near 4,000 a year to over 14,000, the percentage classified as "professional, technical and kindred workers" ranged between 17 and over 21 percent of those emigrating.[3]

Ki's parents practice acupuncture. He did not say whether either parent entered as a professional. Neither had studied Western or Orien-

---

*"Lee Ki Chuck" is a pseudonym.

tal medicine in Korea. But after hours of study in Japanese and Chinese, Ki's father began to practice acupuncture without a license in their home at nights after work. When his mother arrived, "She does not want to be a doctor, but my father made her. They argue a lot of the time. Acupuncture is cheap doctor in the Korea. But my mother understand at last because they find they can make money, and my mother studied, too." After moving to the New York area, Ki claims that his parents generally average $1,700 a week between them.

August 18, 1975
A New York suburb

Before, I was Oriental guy, right? But different society—everything is different—like girl friend and study and spending money and riding car.

I came here and I bought Pinto car. I was driving very crazy. One day my friend was driving crazy, Mustang, make follow me. I thought, "Americans are very lucky, they are always having good time." I was kind of hating inside. I never want to lose *anything*—even studies, sports, anything—I didn't want to lose to American. So I just beat him. After that time people know I am driving crazy. People just come to me, racing, so I raced every time. Then during last year, I wrecked up one car, first car, and I was *crazy*. I was racing with friend. I hit a tree. I have so many tickets from the police. [Laughs.] In a twenty-five-mile [zone], sixty miles I drove. I had so many warning tickets. I know that is very bad. You can't go to Harvard with these kind of tickets. I don't drive now anymore.

I have matured a lot since I got to this country. I smoke a lot, too. I used to smoke because I was curious—now one day, one pack. Every time I get up in the morning is so pain. And drinking. I found I like rock concert. So interesting, different. Like I go in the morning, 4:00. Those are nice guys I get drunk with, whiskey, go down to the beach and go swimming. Found a lot of crazy.

Actually my immigration was very hard. I had so many times crying. That was really a terrible time. I guess is all right now, really. I am so happy. And then, after my mother came here, my father was getting all right. They found I skip school so many times, getting bad, but they didn't tell anything to me. "Do whatever you want, but just don't be bad about it." They gave me another chance.

I'm still Korean. I was really trying to make good friend with American. I have a friend but I never think he is my best friend. American friend I can never make best friend. They just like "hi" friends. "Hi." "Hi."

What was your reaction to girls in this country?

Oh yeh, girls. When I was in Korea—like if I have girl friend—very innocent, talking about philosophy, society, politics, every time. It is hard to even touch hand there. You understand? Very innocent. This is Korea.

I met these few girls in this country, but I don't like them. They are more strong on the physical than I am. [Laughs.] Every time, is physical. Every time I try to talk to them about life, they say, "I think you are too smart. I don't think I can follow you." That's what everybody says.

I tried suicide. When I hit the tree, I was almost dead—fifty miles, I hit. But I didn't die. I was lucky—just a scratch and sore on the face. That was my fault. My friend, he couldn't stop his car, and he hit my car and the breaking window and spread out the glass. Insurance paid for car. Was total. And then after that, when I was getting really bad in the school—skipping school, drinking, doing marijuana outside—I come by home about 1:00. During school days, too. Sometimes I work. I make a lot of money. Like moonlight can make thirty, forty dollars, busboy, tips and they pay check, too, at the hotel. Make a lot of money, and then I can get whatever I want.

I can't face my principal. He's very nice but I couldn't face him so I just took twenty pills. Slept, but I didn't die. My mother didn't tell it to my father. Twenty, that's what I only regret, and my mother said, "You can die with twenty pills." But in the America, if you take sleeping pills a lot, you never die, but just the body inside is changed.

All of my friends in the Korea they still think I am having very good time. I don't tell them what happened to me. I have a car, and they think I am very rich.

If I come to America, I thought that America was really heaven country. I saw so many movie. I saw cars, everyone drives car. If I go to America, I can drive. I can watch TV, everything. I thought I was really heading to heaven. But that's wrong. You have to try to make heaven. Everybody still, everybody think all immigration come to this country. Before they come here they think of this country as heaven. This country, if you try, if you walk out, you can make money, you can be rich here. It's a really nice country, actually.

I used to be with a lot of friends, but now I am alone always. I didn't know what I am searching. I used a lot of philosophy book, but I can't find any answers. That's all American way. Everyone says I try too hard. Really, I want to make a lot of experience; I thought experience was good. If there is bad, don't even try. That's all I wanted to say to young people. I didn't expect I would smoke a lot like this. If there is a bad, don't even try, like racing cars, don't even try. You are going to have an accident. Is very bad.

You say I look like a quiet boy—but outside. Inside is very different.

"NGUYEN THI ANH"*—
After Vietnam

"I Believe the War Is Over"[1]

In the years following the collapse of American power in Southeast Asia, 145,000 South Vietnamese, Cambodians, and Laotians have entered the United States. Most are now unemployed, with thirty-six percent receiving some form of assistance from the United States government.[2] They arrived in the middle of a recession and at the end of the most controversial war in American history. Those who were evacuated and who have settled in the United States are living reminders of the strife-ridden war years and of the failure of U.S. policy in that part of the world since the Cold War.

The United States government began a parole program for Vietnamese orphans in March and April of 1975 when it became clear that the American-backed Saigon government could not withstand the approaching National Liberation Front forces. In late April, scenes of mass airplane, helicopter, and boat evacuations flashed across television screens and the front pages of American newspapers. During May and June most of the evacuated refugees were being moved from camps on Guam to army "reception centers" at Fort Chaffee, Arkansas, Indiantown Gap, Pennsylvania, and Elgin Air Force Base, Florida. From these centers the

---

*"Nguyen Thi Anh" is a pseudonym.

government matched individuals and families with American sponsors through the cooperation of charitable agencies.

In July 1975 an article in a Vermont newspaper announced the arrival of a Vietnamese woman and her two children under the sponsorship of a local couple. I was staying in Vermont, and I telephoned the couple to arrange an interview.

Nguyen Thi Anh is a petite woman in her twenties. When I first met her, she was shy and had obviously not been too well-informed about my mission. She was especially fearful of my pocket tape recorder, and I felt somewhat like a doctor with a needle assuring the patient that the instrument I was about to use was completely necessary and not really painful.

Anh was self-conscious about her English, but soon began to speak. She said that her husband left for Belgium in late 1971 to work as a clerk in the South Vietnamese embassy there. She and the children could not go along, so the couple were separated from 1971 to 1975. She went through the ordeal of the fall of Saigon and was evacuated with the children to Guam in late April 1975. After a stay in Fort Chaffee she took a secretarial job in Vermont with her sponsors.

Later in July Anh's husband, through the help of her sponsors, was reunited with the family in Vermont. I went to visit them. At that time Anh was happier, but even more shy. Her husband did most of the talking, discussing plans for jobs, a car, and a happy future.

Eight months later I returned to Cambridge from a trip to the West Coast. In my absence Anh had arrived at my doorstep, suitcases in hand. She, her husband, and the children had come to Boston, apparently without saying formal good-byes to their sponsors. Anh had hitchhiked alone across the city to my apartment. She said that she had had "no problem" with the sponsors, but that she and her husband were very lonely in Vermont. They had no neighbors, and the nearest village had a population of a few hundred in the winter months. They had never seen snow. Anh's husband, a slightly built man in his late twenties who had had visions of a clerk's job, cut wood for a living.

The Nguyens needed a place to stay. After being notified, the Catholic Charities of Boston made arrangements for them to receive Aid to Dependent Children, got Mr. Nguyen into a job-training program, and put up security for a month's rent. Anh was able to get a job as a stitcher. Her husband soon went in and out of a series of jobs.

When I spoke with Anh again it was June of 1976. She was under a great deal of stress, explaining that her husband was on the verge of a "breakdown." They had moved in and then out of some Vietanamese acquaintances' apartment and were now living alone in a section of Boston suffering from its own stresses as a result of the busing controversy. The Nguyen children, although not Catholic, had been placed in Catholic schools. Anh's husband was out of work and she was being trained as a keypunch operator. During the winter of 1977 she had flu for several months, becoming weakened and very depressed.

The Nguyen family's experience is fairly typical of Indochinese refugees. Despite the federal government's attempts to disperse them, most of the Southeast Asian refugees are settling into urban areas to live close to people from their own linguistic and national backgrounds. Many of them suffer from depression and anxieties over loss of, and separation from, their families. Some have committed suicide. More than five hundred have applied to the United Nations for repatriation.[3] At the same time, "boat people" escaping the new Vietnam in small craft hope to come to the United States.

July 9, 1975
The Green Mountains, Vermont

In 1954 I leave Hanoi and come to Saigon with my parents. We stayed from 1954 till now. I run away over there. I am twenty-nine. I was born in North Vietnam, and North Vietnam fall. I came to Vietnam and now South Vietnam. I come to States.

Many, many people doesn't like VC. When I stay in Saigon, when Da Nang is fall, from 28th March, I try to run away. All day outside not at home, looking for a way to come to here. Very hard time. I cannot sleep, I cannot eat, I cannot work, cannot do anything. You know Da Nang? Da Nang lose, and we worry. They say nothing, but I hear from American radio. They talk a little time in Vietnamese. So every day, everyone in Saigon try to hear that and everybody go to look for a way to come here to the States. We are very, very afraid of VC.

Some people like VC. Some people don't like VC. Before, the American government gave us a gun and everything to fight the VC, so we don't think that Saigon will lose. When the Americans left they give nothing so I think that Saigon will lose. When Da Nang lose, that's only one day and then everybody run away from Da Nang to Saigon. They said, "They're not far, not far." Everybody in my family, they don't like, because they come from Hanoi to Saigon. They mustn't eat, cannot sleep. Everybody got more skinny. They were scared.

Da Nang fall on the 28th of March, and on 29 April Saigon fall. So from 28th to 28th when I left Saigon, one month after this day, many, many people run out on the street to look for how we can get to go out of Vietnam. Many people who had many money had to pay five million Vietnamese piasters for one person to go out of Vietnam. From 28th March, the first people to go away from Saigon is a rich one. The somebody that is working at the Vietnamese government they go out of Saigon. Then us. We don't have money but we have some people to help us to go out.

That night everybody go to eat in the shop, in the market. Many people go to eat. They don't care. They think if VC coming they cannot eat, so they eat. [Laughs.] Everybody to spend money because if VC coming they cannot spend.

I went to talk with my boss. My American boss is U.S. contractor. He think that the VC only kill the big one—me they don't worry about. [Laughs.] But we don't like to stay with VC and we want to leave to come to States many years ago. I asked him. I come with him every day, every day, asking about if he please help me to go the United States. He say, "Wait. Wait." I have to wait for him long time. So on the 28th is the day Saigon lose, he picked up me. He helped me to put me on a plane to come to here.

When I left Saigon I just bring my two dictionaries and some clothes. [She points to two large volumes.] I don't worry about clothes. If I come here, if I make money I can buy clothes. I can't buy dictionaries, that's why I take it with me.

When I left Vietnam, I don't know that American will help us for food or looking for job. I didn't know what would happen for me in the future, so we just run away, that's all. But when I come here, I see Americans help us, so we are very very happy.

When I stay in Fort Chaffee, I see many many Vietnamese there, about 24–25,000 people. No problems. There are many people like me to stay there, not to go out. I don't want to be there. I understand that if I go out I'm going to be alone. Many thing will happen to me. Maybe something happens like the white skin American with the black skin American. I worry about that thing, so when I left Fort Chaffee I go to Chicago—I just cried.

From the first of July I here. I cannot hear from my parents, but I think in the future I try to work here to send some money to send for my parents because they are old.

I am very sad we have to leave. Very sad! I think it's better Saigon fell. It's better for Vietnamese over there now, because they will not die anyone. Is better for everybody to stay in Saigon now. But for me, I don't like VC.

I want to go back to see my parents. I think in the future I go back to visit. Long time ago the French come in Vietnam. After war with the French, Vietnamese and French are friends; now in the future Vietnamese and Americans will be friends, so we can go back. Vietnam is a very small country. We are very worried about war. We don't like war. When I was small we had to run from fighting and shooting. When I got older I hoped that there is no more war.

"MASHA"*—
Child of the Soviet Intelligentsia

"Everything Depends Just on Me"

Masha was born into a Jewish family in Kishinev, Moldavia, a Soviet republic bordering Rumania, formerly called Bessarabia. In April of 1903 Kishinev was the site of one of the worst pogroms against Jews in the history of modern Russia. It was unclear to me whether Masha was aware of this, since she often stressed her being "Russian" in culture rather than Jewish. Some time before their emigration Masha's mother and stepfather became Christian. Whereas the czarist pogroms of Kishinev precipitated the Russian Jewish exodus of the early part of the century, the Soviet policy of assimilation and Jewish harassment has led, at least in part, to a new exodus of Soviet Jews. Masha is a product of this new exile, and it was through Jewish agencies that her family was able to leave the Soviet Union. While many other national groups would also like to leave the Soviet Union, it has only been Jews who have been permitted to do so in large numbers.

Jews played major roles in revolutionary movements during the czarist era. Many consciously broke with Jewish traditions to aid the Revolution, and one of the first acts of the revolutionaries in March of

---

*"Masha" is a pseudonym.

1917 was to abolish legal restrictions on Jews.[1] But things did not always go well for Jews or other religious and national minorities under the Bolshevik regime. Constitutional guarantees not to oppress minorities and to respect the linguistic rights of non-Russians were not enforced. Soon after the Revolution state-supported atheism led to the suppression of religion in general, and the right of Judaism to continue as a functioning religion in particular.

The Soviet state does not, however, see Jews as members of a religious group, but as members of a nationality group. To balance ethnic diversity with communism, Soviet republics were set up, supposedly based on principles of nationality. Thus there is a Ukrainian SSR, an Armenian SSR, a Latvian SSR, a Turkmen SSR, etc. The Russian region, RSFSR, is theoretically just another national region. The government attempted to force Jews into this nationality scheme by constructing a Jewish national state on the Chinese frontier. The Biro-Bidzhan Project was a failure. Set up in 1927, it never attracted very many Jews.[2] In 1936 the Soviet government under Stalin forbade instruction in native languages in the schools. After World War II, besides having witnessed the obliteration of over one million Soviet Jews by invading Nazi troops, surviving Jews witnessed the Soviet suppression of the Yiddish press, theater, and Jewish schools. Jews, along with other religious groups, were forbidden the right to provide their young with religious education. Many rabbis and ritual leaders were arrested and deported in the 1920s, and Hebrew became the only language outlawed in the USSR.[3]

The aim of these policies was to assimilate all citizens into a Russian-dominated Soviet state. During this era and after, Jews were singled out and prosecuted for a variety of charges. As a result of fifty years of pressure, it is no wonder that many Soviet Jews are often not Jews at all.

Following the Six-Day War in Israel in 1967, the Arab defeat evoked contradictory responses from the Soviet government and the Jewish community. The government unleashed a propaganda campaign against Zionism, calling Israelis "Nazis." Many Jews began openly to identify with their Jewishness. A Repatriation Movement for a return to Israel became active.[4]

The Repatriation Movement of the years following 1967 staged sit-down strikes, published underground papers, and planned mass meetings around synagogues on holy days. In 1969, 3,207 Jews left the Soviet

Union; over 34,000 left in both 1972 and 1973. By 1971 many Jews, rather than immigrating to Israel, headed for the United States. This pattern has continued, so that although Israel remains a major destination, the United States by 1974 was receiving over twenty percent of all Soviet Jewish émigrés.[5] Included in these numbers are those Soviet Jews who first go to Israel and later change their minds, wishing to immigrate to the United States. The "drop outs," as they are pejoratively termed, include people like Masha and her family who, on reaching Rome, opted for the United States.

Although born a Jew, Masha is a daughter of the Soviet intelligentsia. Masha's parents are writers and intellectuals. They divorced when she was six years old, and her mother married a poet and moved to Moscow, where her stepfather's poems were circulated underground. She remained in Moldavia with her grandmother for about two years, until they joined her mother and stepfather. At fifteen, she and the three of them emigrated from the Soviet Union.

When I met Masha, she was a senior in a suburban high school. At present she is a university student. Her family is one of approximately 450 Soviet families who have settled in the Boston area in the 1970s.[6]

The new Soviet immigrants are often highly educated and may come to the United States not as dissidents or as religious Jews, but as people who want to "do better." They are not all of a heroic mold and often do not identify as Jews at all. It has been hard for agencies to place them, as American licensing requirements, social science, technology, and industry are vastly different from their Soviet counterparts.[7] As with other immigrants, the adjustments to American life have often brought great hardships. For members of the intelligentsia there is also the problem of finding a market for one's art, and the fear that economic necessity will force them to lose their true vocation. But it was a sense of hope, not of loss, which was expressed by Masha, a child of the intelligentsia.

January 24, 1976
Cambridge, Massachusetts

My father was a famous poet in Moscow. A lot of people knew about him, and during Khrushchev's time, when it was a little bit better, he very often spoke and read his poetry, but then when there was a new government, he didn't publish anything. They didn't let him publish anything after that. He published only one book, and all the rest of his poetry, it was circulating underground.

I know his poetry. He's not a political poet. You don't have to write something which is clearly, strictly opposed to the government. But everything that is really alive, everything that is really talented is opposed to the government.

My parents emigrated for political reasons. Once he was called into secret police and they asked him where he took the books he read and who gave him these books. He didn't want to answer them. He thought that it would be better for us to leave than for him to go to prison again. Under Stalin's time he was in prison and in exile in Siberia. He is really sick and he is fifty years old. He thought that he wouldn't be able to endure it. Another prison or another such experience would just kill him. It was a very hard decision.

A lot of people are emigrating because of repression of the Jews, but it wasn't—maybe partly—well, no, it wasn't the reason why we left. We had a lot of friends who left by this Mediterranean route who went to Israel. Maybe in the very beginning, we considered going to Israel, but then we decided, it didn't make sense. All of us have Jewish blood, but actually what is counted is *culture,* is languages, some other things. We decided we would go to America or Canada. My parents considered staying in Europe and maybe they will go to Europe.

People ask if it is true what they write about Soviet Jews, if what Solzhenitsyn writes is true. It is true. It's very hard to believe, but it is. One boy I knew, he went around Moscow in *yarmelke* and people had beaten him really badly for this and they told him, "Oh, you Jew." But, he was very proud of it and he showed to everybody the black spots on his face. And people have troubles when they wear Mogen Davids. There is a lot of Jewish discrimination, but not only Jewish, because they discriminate everybody who is against them.

Moscow synagogue is a kind of intellectual center. It's also quite dangerous to go there because there is always the police and they don't like gatherings of people. I was there once. It was before the Yom Kippur War in Israel. It was several weeks before we left Russia. There was a huge crowd of people. Usually, people never talk about politics in the streets. It's simply dangerous, especially about Israel. But this crowd before temple! Everybody was acquainted with each other and they talked about this Yom Kippur War. They really didn't try to hide their feeling because they knew that once they came to the temple they're already considered to be suspicious and to be antigovernment. Everybody thought, well, "If I would just be given permission to go to Israel and fight in the army." It was very inspiring, even for us. Police went around and said, "Don't gather. Don't gather." But still people stand aside when police came, and they joined hands when police left.

About leaving Russia, I was probably the most enthusiastic person in our family, because when I was thirteen or fourteen years old, I thought I'll go abroad, and all this foreign culture, Europe. I was very enthusiastic and my grandmother was, too, because I was. She told my parents that they have to leave only for me so that I could be free.

They were, they still are, Russian. They are not cosmopolitan, as I consider myself to be. And really, all their friends are there. All their life they were connected with Russian culture. They thought that things that they valued in their past life are not valued in Europe or in America. That's why they doubt about leaving.

We had to wait and we didn't know whether they will permit us. After requesting to emigrate we waited about five or six months. It was a very hard situation because my father ceased to earn money and my mother's wage was too small for us to live on. At that time he earned money by translations, and the government paid him. But after he asked for permission to go they began to consider him a "bad man"; therefore, they wouldn't give him work. Some of our friends, they wait eight months and nine months, and then they are told that they are not permitted to go. We really didn't know what would happen to us. Life is very hard for people who are refused to go. Nobody will give them a job. Mostly they have to go to work like to the laundry. It's not considered that bad in America, but in Russia it really makes difference. A person who has Ph.D., he usually works on his level.

Several times we'd have incidents, not secret police but other police came to us and they asked us something. I don't know whether it was connected with our wish to emigrate.

I didn't tell anyone. And it was very convenient that I was not a member of Comsomol. All the time I avoided entering. Everyone wants to enter party because unless you are a member you can't enter university or you can't do anything. Because I wasn't a member, the school didn't know that I was leaving. I just came the last day and asked for my papers, told them that I was leaving and didn't say any more.

There are two streams. In Vienna, Austria, they are divided. There is one stream of people who go to Israel and there is another who are just going to immigrate somewhere. They do not consider themselves Jews, they just want to get out of Russia. These people go to Rome. People from Rome go either to Canada or to America.

We stayed in Rome at least three or four weeks. From Italy we flew to New York. Our organization, HIAS, it distributes people, to Boston or to New York. We did ask to come here because we thought Boston was a cultural center, seat of intellectuals [laughs], and we had a friend here who taught at a university.

We just landed in New York and our friends met us in the airport. We sat in the taxi. We were five minutes away from airport and then we saw a car accident. It looked just like in the movies. All these people, in the blood, they flew from the car. It *shocked* me, like real American film. It was my first impression.

The next day I went with a friend of mine, we went in to Manhattan. It was the first time I've ever seen an American crowd. We went to Broadway. I felt so alien, like I have never felt in Rome. These people, they did not look at each other; they just went. I was frightened because I felt that they were very mechanical, and they weren't alive. Maybe it's my fantasy, but I thought, nobody smiled. Maybe it's just stereotype; maybe I have just read too many anti-American articles, but first day I was really shocked. I have been often to New York and it was OK. Maybe I got accustomed to it; first it was just terrible.

After two days HIAS bought us a ticket and we went to Boston, and some people met us, our friends and some representatives from HIAS and even some people from the newspaper. They brought us to our apartment. I expected something incredible. I thought American should be so different from Europe. I came here and it was not that drastically different.

School was incredible, I couldn't believe it but all my teachers and guidance counselors and everybody was so nice. It was just unbelievable how lucky I was. I guess my school is a very good school, but everyone was very helpful.

Kids were so strange, even more strange than in Italy. In Russian school everybody is in uniform. Everybody watches you. In this school I see the kids that lay on the floor or the corridor and we had to go around them. I thought just "ZOO." Then it was all right.

Most of everything I heard about America was wrong stereotype. When I was in Europe I thought that New York should be skyscrapers and cowboys, and it was not so. I heard a lot of the drugs problems. I always hear that somewhere this kid is smoking and this kid is selling drugs, but I have never seen them. I was walking from one class to another and there are very often standing couples of two young people and kissing in the door. I was very embarrassed because I was late to my class and I couldn't tell him just "Get out, I have to enter this door." And I just stood and looked somewhere else till they will stop kissing. It seemed so normal that they were kissing. I really didn't know how I should behave. I just wasn't accustomed to that.

I heard from many people that American youth is *depraved*. I think that is ridiculous. In Russia nobody would ever stand like that in front of everybody, and it's not because Russians are more higher cultured, but because administration wouldn't let it. Everybody would laugh at the kids who would stand together on a staircase, and say something and the teachers would say something; they would show that it is not appropriate.

I don't have deep relationship with anybody but I know a few people. When I came I was in high school and they knew each other maybe in the elementary school or in the high school. Well, it's hard to enter the group at such an old age as sixteen. I don't meet anybody like after school. But I say "Hi" to all the kids.

School, it's not just everybody is friendly with everybody. There are levels. It's very clear in the lunchroom. On the left there are black kids and on the right there are Jewish kids and somewhere else there are kids from Israel and somewhere else there are Spanish kids and somewhere else there are the school intellectual elite. Usually I sit by myself, except there are a few other Russian kids and we sit by ourselves. The intellectual kids have their own group and they have their own connections. Although they feel very good about me, actually they don't know me. I hope it will be different in the university because there everybody does not know each other.

Do your parents work now?

My mother works in a university library. It's not her job. In Russia she was a very high specialist in bibliography. She was a librarian, but she didn't do just the typical job. She is a very high-class professional. My father writes and sends in articles. Now he is more writing essays on history and literature, in Russian. It doesn't make sense for him to write in English because first, he doesn't know English. There is a new Russian newspaper in New York and a magazine in Paris and there are a few magazines in Germany. The problem is that they don't pay much. He has got a grant from some kind of foundation, but most of what we live on is my mother's wage. We live just about the same as we lived in Russia. In comparison with Americans we live very poorly, but I just don't care.

[My father] feels very lonely here. He speaks six or seven hundred English words, all misplaced, even worse than me.

Of course classes do exist in America. In Russia we—well, my parents—they belong to a certain class of people and here we came, we didn't come to the same class. Like in Moscow, friends of my father's are artists and writers and here we don't usually meet these people. Like my father knows a few of them but we didn't enter the same circle. Well, it's usual with immigrants, I guess, from what I read about other immigrations. But with me, everything depends just on me, just how gifted and how talented I am.

I really don't know what I want to do in the future. I guess everything depends on my occupation. Right now I'm interested in European history. Probably I would like to live in America. Probably I would like to travel and to live in Europe three months a year. Still I would like to live in America because it is the only really secure place in the world. I know I change my mind all the time, so I don't know.

I hardly think it will be possible to return. I'd like to go sometime, but just as a tourist, to see my friends. I don't think I will ever be permitted to go there. Definitely I cannot go before I am a citizen of the United States because before I am a citizen they can do anything with me they want.

Maybe the economic obstacle is very difficult for my parents, but I have never participated in the economic life of my family. I think probably my parents feel very insecure with no steady job for their level. Probably it is a little bit disappointing that I can't enter the group I want to enter. It's sort of frustrating not having friends, but I guess it will change next year.

NOTES

PART I NEW BEGINNINGS: 1900-1929

1. Niles Carpenter, *Immigrants and Their Children: 1920,* Census Monograph VII (Washington, D.C.: U.S. Government Printing Office, 1927), Table 18, p. 26, and Table 3, p. 6.

2. U.S. Department of Justice, *1975 Annual Report: Immigration and Naturalization Service,* Table 11, p. 55, and Table 1, p. 31.

3. In the 1830s, 50,000 residents of the British Isles left for Canada; 70,000 British, Irish, and Germans left for the United States. The peak years for British immigration were between the 1870s and the 1880s, in which from one-half to one percent of the population emigrated. Philip Taylor, *The Distant Magnet: European Emigration to the U.S.A.* (New York: Harper & Row, 1971), pp. 21, 22, 25, 42-43.

4. Leonard Dinnerstein and David M. Reimers, *Ethnic Americans: A History of Immigration and Assimilation* (New York: Dodd, Mead & Co., paperback edition, 1975), p. 13.

5. Taylor, *The Distant Magnet,* pp. 70-86.

6. Between 1868 and 1914 no fewer than 10,000 Scandinavians arrived every year. *Ibid.,* p. 27.

7. U.S. Bureau of Census, *Historical Statistics of the United States: From Colonial Times to 1957,* p. 62; also in Carpenter, *Immigrants and Their Children,* p. 155.

Minnie Kasser Needle

Introduction

1. Oscar and Mary F. Handlin, *A Century of Jewish Immigration to the United States* (New York: American Jewish Committee, 1949, reprinted from the American Jewish Year Book), p. 12.

2. Samuel Needle (Joseph's nephew) said that the family name had been Noodle and Joseph's brother's (his father's) name had been Aaron. The family name was Anglicized to Needle, his father's name changed to Harry.

Oral History

1. Peruke are wigs made especially for Jewish women. When Orthodox women marry, they are required by Jewish law to shave their heads and use the wigs, which are very plain.

2. Young maid from Galicia.

3. I know.

4. Minnie admitted that she was older than Joseph, but it appears that she was able to lie about her age on her naturalization papers. Joseph's papers cite his birthdate as August 20, 1889; Minnie's, April 22, 1889. My guess is that his is correct and hers, we will never know.

5. June 17, 1911.

6. An earlier time she said, "I told your grandfather to go to the drugstore to get something. He said he wouldn't go, that he was embarrassed. So I told him, 'Sleep over there.'"

7. An optometrist.

8. Credit union. The wedding took place in September 1938.

9. Inducted February 13, 1943. Served two and a half years.

10. Gentiles. Her statement about Ruth is untrue; she is very active in her synagogue.

Catherine Moran McNamara

Introduction

1. U.S. Department of Justice, *1974 Annual Report: Immigration and Naturalization Service,* Table 13, pp. 56–57.

2. William Shannon, *The Irish in America* (New York: Macmillan, 1966), pp. 1, 45–47.

3. Marcus Lee Hansen, *The Immigrant in American History* (Cambridge: Harvard University Press, 1940; reprint edition, New York: Harper & Row, 1964), ch. 2, including pp. 30–32.

4. Oscar Handlin, *Boston's Immigrants: A Study in Acculturation* (Cambridge: Harvard University Press, 1941; reprint paperback edition, New York: Atheneum, 1974), ch. 2.

5. *Ibid.,* ch. 7, especially pp. 187–89.

Nicholas Gerros

Introduction

1. Theodore Saloutos, *The Greeks in the United States* (Cambridge: Harvard University Press, 1964), pp. 30–38.

2. *Ibid.,* p. 110; Theodore Saloutos, *They Also Remember America: The Story of the Repatriated Greek-Americans* (Berkeley: University of California Press, 1956), Table 1, pp. 30, 50.

3. Henry Pratt Fairchild, *Greek Immigration to the United States* (New Haven: Yale University Press, 1911), pp. 202, 258–59.

Oral History

1. Castle Island was not a receiving center after 1890. He must have landed on Ellis Island.

2. Jordan Marsh Company in Boston.

Philip and Theresa Bonacorsi

Introduction

1. Joseph Lopreato, *Italian Americaus: Ethnic Groups in Comparative Perspective* (New York: Random House, paperback, 1970), pp. 33–35.

2. Between 1880 and 1910 Italian population rose more than six million despite mass migrations which occurred. Taylor, *The Distant Magnet,* p. 51.

3. Until 1900, Italian immigration to Latin America was larger than immigration to the United States. Brazil and Argentina were the most important destinations. *Ibid.,* p. 60.

4. Richard Gambino, *Blood of My Blood: The Dilemma of Italian-Americans* (Garden City, N.Y.: Doubleday & Co., Inc., Anchor Books, 1975), p. 84.

5. "From 1908 through 1916, 1,215,998 Italians left the United States. This back-and-forth migration however, virtually ceased by the mid-20's after the quota system went into effect." Dinnerstein and Reimers, *Ethnic Americans,* p. 39.

6. Samuel Yellen, *American Labor Struggles: 1877-1934* (New York: Monad Press ed., 1974; copyright 1936 by Samuel Yellen), pp. 171–204. Also, see Elizabeth Gurley Flynn, *Rebel Girl: An Autobiography—My First Life 1906-1926* (New York: International Publishers, 1973 ed.), pp. 127–51.

Mose and Joe Cerasoli

Introduction

1. Paul Demers, "Labor and Social Relations of the Granite Industry in Barre" (study, Goddard College, Plainfield, Vt., May 1974), pp. 1–16.

2. A U.S. Health Department study conducted in 1957 showed that 86 percent of the deaths of granite stonecutters in 1921 were the result of tuberculosis-related silicosis. Demers, *ibid,* pp. 52–55.

Oral History

1. The battle for the unification of Italy was fought during the 1860s.

2. Labor slang for out of work.

3. The American Plan of Employment was an antiunion tactic used by employers during the 1920s. American Plan companies did not hire union men and women.

"Moshe Lodsky"

Introduction

1. Moses Rischin, *The Promised City: New York's Jews, 1870-1914* (Cambridge: Harvard University Press, 1967, ed.).

2. *Ibid.,* pp. 65–67.

Oral History

1. A dowry.

2. Roughly, "A lot of trouble is half the victory."

3. An expanded Hebrew Immigrant Aid Society (HIAS) was organized in 1909 to help Jewish immigrants in transit and after they arrived in the United States. At that time it was one of many charitable institutions. Rischin, *The Promised City,* ch. 6, "Philanthropy versus Self-Help."

4. Praying done in the home or in synagogue. The prayers are sung or spoken as the person rocks rhythmically back and forth. Traditionally, religious garments are worn.

5. A person from the same village in the old country (pl., *landslayt*).

6. Or the *Morgen Journal*, a Yiddish morning paper founded in 1901 and well known for its ads. See Rischin, *The Promised City*, p. 123.

7. Vermin.

8. The Amalgamated Clothing Workers Union was founded in 1914.

9. Talking a lot, gabbing.

Valeria Kozaczka Demusz

Introduction

1. William I. Thomas and Florian Znaniecki, *The Polish Peasant in Europe and America* (New York: Alfred A. Knopf, 1927), vol. II, "Emigration from Poland," pp. 1483–1504, and "The Polish American Community," especially p. 1511.

Oral History

1. Don't you speak Polish?

2. Scene of summer clashes between members of the black Roxbury and the white South Boston communities.

3. Referring to the school busing crisis.

Richard O. Lim

Introduction

1. Carey McWilliams, *Factories in the Fields: A Story of Migratory Farm Labor in California* (Santa Barbara, Calif.: Peregrine Publishers, Inc., 1971 ed.), "The Chinese," pp. 66–80.

2. Victor G. and Brett de Bary Nee, *Longtime Californ': A Documentary Study of an American Chinatown* (Boston: Houghton Mifflin Co., Sentry edition, 1974), pp. 55, 409–10.

3. *Ibid.*, p. xix and Part I: especially pp. 19, 55–56.

Oral History

1. The On Lok Health center is a multiethnic health care facility catering mostly to the elderly.

Natsu Okuyama Ozawa

Introduction

1. McWilliams, *Factories in the Fields*, "Our Oriental Agriculture," pp. 103–33.

2. William Petersen, *Japanese Americans: Oppression and Success, Ethnic Groups in Comparative Perspective* (New York: Random House, 1971), p. 196.

3. T. Iyenaga and Kenoske Sato, *Japan and the California Problem* (New York: G. P. Putnam's Sons, 1921), p. 133.

4. Roger Daniels, *The Politics of Prejudice: The Anti-Japanese Movement in California and the Struggle for Japanese Exclusion* (Berkeley: University of California Press, 1963; reprint edition, Gloucester, Mass.: Peter Smith, 1966), pp. 44–45.

5. Roy L. Garis, *Immigration Restriction: A Study in the Opposition to and Regulation of Immigration to the United States* (New York: Macmillan, 1927), pp. 339–41.

6. Petersen, *Japanese Americans*, pp. 66, 72–81.

7. Michi Weglyn, *Years of Infamy: The Untold Story of America's Concentration Camps* (New York: William Morrow & Co., Inc., 1976), p. 71, from Memorandum, Francis Biddle to Franklin Roosevelt, February 20, 1942, OF 4805, Franklin D. Roosevelt Library, Hyde Park, N.Y.

8. About 110,000 people were evacuated but 120,000 came under War Relocation Authority custody according to WRA statistics. *Ibid.*, p. 21. In Canada, internment occurred for 23,000 members of the West Coast community of Japanese descent; 75 percent were Canadian citizens. *Ibid.*, p. 56.

9. *Ibid.*, p. 276; also, Petersen, *Japanese Americans*, pp. 104–108.

10. Petersen, *Japanese Americans*, p. 87; and Weglyn, *Years of Infamy*, pp. 134–55.

11. Petersen, *Japanese Americans*, pp. 104–108.

12. The *Endo, Korematsu,* and *Hirabayashi* Cases. Weglyn, *Years of Infamy,* pp. 223–28.

Oral History

1. The entry port in San Francisco for immigrants arriving by sea. Many Asians were held here or deported. Its function was similar to that of Ellis Island in New York Harbor.

Willie Barientos

Introduction

1. The Pilipinos in America History Workshop, ed., *Iriri Ti Pagsayaatan Ti Sapasap: A Reader on the History of Pilipinos in America* (San Franciso: San Francisco State University, Asian Studies Dept., 1975), p. 257.

2. In 1934 Congress passed an act promising the islands independence in ten years and setting a Filipino quota at fifty.

3. Louis Bloch, "Filipino Immigration Statistics 1923–1935," in *Reader on Pilipinos,* pp. 237–39; also, Carey McWilliams, *Brothers Under the Skin* (Toronto: Little, Brown & Co., 1964), ch. 2. Slightly different figures but the same point.

4. McWilliams, *Factories in the Fields*, pp. 131–33.

5. John Gregory Dunne, *Delano* (New York: Farrar, Straus & Giroux, 1971), p. 3.

6. Michael Buraway, "The Functions and Reproduction of Migrant Labor," *American Journal of Sociology* 81 (March 1976): 1073–1074.

Oral History

1. Figures vary depending upon sources used. Peak years were 1926 and 1929 for Filipinos admitted to California via San Francisco. One total for the 1929–35 period is 301,543, based on Bloch, "Filipino Immigration Statistics," and statistics from the U.S. Department of War, both in *Reader on Pilipinos,* pp. 236–38.

2. There were no Filipino quotas until 1934. In 1946, the quota of fifty per

year was doubled. Numbers of Filipino immigrants have been up since 1965, with a high proportion being in the scientific and technical fields.

3. Filipino term of respect.

4. Doing housework in someone's home and going to school.

5. As a result of agitation and the 1965 Delano grape strike, Senate Hearings were held in Delano in early spring 1976. Selections from Hearings of the U.S. Senate Subcommittee on Migratory Labor, 89th Congress, 2nd sess., cited in Matt S. Meirer and Feliciano Rivera, *Readings on La Raza: The Twentieth Century,* American Century Series (New York: Farrar, Straus & Giroux, Hill and Wang, 1974), pp. 195–204.

PART II. SURVIVORS: 1930-1945

1. Elizabeth J. Harper and Roland F. Chase, *Immigration Laws of the United States,* 3rd ed. (Indianapolis: Bobbs-Merrill, Inc., 1975), pp. 10–11. The anti-anarchist and anti-Communist legislation had a strong anti-Semitic tinge. Other targets were Germans thought to be insufficiently patriotic during World War I, and potential foreign radical organizers for organizations like the IWW.

2. Many Asians continued to be excluded, but people from North and South America were not.

3. John Higham, *Send These to Me: Jews and Other Immigrants in Urban America,* "The Politics of Immigration Restriction" (New York: Atheneum, 1975), p. 54.

4. *Ibid.,* p. 55, citing John B. Trevor, *An Analysis of The American Immigration Act of 1924* (New York: Carnegie Endowment for International Peace, 1924), p. 62.

5. *1975 Annual Report: INS,* Table 1, p. 31. For the implications of restrictionism and racism in these years, see Henry L. Feingold, *The Politics of Rescue: The Roosevelt Administration and the Holocaust, 1937–1945* (New Brunswick, N.J.: Rutgers University Press, 1970); Arthur D. Morse, *While Six Million Died* (New York: Random House, 1968); John Morton Blum, *V Was for Victory: Politics and American Culture During World War II* (New York: Harcourt Brace Jovanovich, 1976).

Araxi Chorbajian Ayvasian

Oral History

1. The second meeting was to clarify some of the material discussed earlier. I have combined the two meetings into one history. Strictly speaking, I realize this has some historical problems, especially in this case, when the meetings are over a year apart. This is a liberty I took for the sake of the narration.

2. Dates are incorrect. 1890 should be 1894, and 1907 should be 1909.

3. Sometimes spelled Meskne and Der-el-Zor. These are both cities on the Euphrates River. The city of Zeytoun is also spelled Zeiton, and Marash, Maras.

"Andrés Aragón"

Introduction

1. Patricia W. Fagan, *Exiles and Citizens: Spanish Republicans in Mexico* (Austin: University of Texas Press, 1973), p. 32. When the French borders were opened early in 1939 there were 240,000 men, women, and children, including 10,000 wounded. Then, between February 5th and 10th, 250,000 additional members of the Republican Army crossed the border. Hugh Thomas, *The Spanish Civil War* (New York: Harper & Row, Harper Colophon Books, 1963 ed.), p. 575.

2. Fagan, *Exiles and Citizens*, pp. 22–39.

3. On the Haymarket Affair, see John Higham, *Strangers in the Land: Patterns of American Nativism 1860-1925* (New Brunswick, N.J.: Rutgers University Press, 1955), p. 54, and Yellen, *American Labor Struggles*, "Haymarket," pp. 39–71.

4. Higham, *Strangers in the Land*, pp. 229-33, and chs. "Crusade for Americanism" and "The Tribal Twenties." Also see William Preston, Jr., *Aliens and Dissenters: Federal Suppression of Radicals, 1903-1933* (Cambridge: Harvard University Press, 1963).

Oral History

1. Brackets in this oral history are additions suggested for clarity by "Dr. Aragón."

2. Cultural militia.

3. *Armas y Letras*, or, rifles and letters.

4. When Madrid came heavily under siege in late October 1938, the Republican government made the decision to reestablish itself in Valencia and left Madrid on November 6. Thomas, *The Spanish Civil War*, pp. 319-20.

5. *Grupo* Pablo Iglesias.

6. Américo Castro was born in Rio de Janeiro in 1885 and was a historian and literary scholar. He died in 1972.

Anna Foa Yona

Introduction

1. The first Nazi deportations of Jews from Rome began in October of 1943. Over one thousand of eight thousand Roman Jews were rounded up and sent to Auschwitz. Lucy Dawidowicz, *War Against the Jews. 1933-1945* (New York: Holt, Rinehart and Winston, 1975), pp. 368-71.

Oral History

1. See Elizabeth Wiskemann, *Italy* (London: Oxford University Press, 1947), p. 67. Also see Gaetano Salvemini, *Under the Axe of Fascism* (New York: The Viking Press, 1936).

2. October 1935. This is confirmed in D.A. Binchy, *The Church and State in Fascist Italy* (London: Oxford University Press, 1941), pp. 611-13.

3. Marshall Pietro Badoglio was commissioned by the king to form a new government after the effective Allied invasion of Italy, beginning in July of 1943, and the deposing of Mussolini. More German troops were sent to Italy. Rome did not fall to the Allies until June of 1944.

Carl Cohen

Introduction

1. The largest number of any national group of immigrants coming in the nineteenth century were Germans, who settled primarily in the Midwest. Under the Johnson-Reed act of 1924, only 25,814 Germans could enter per year.

2. Israel Pocket Library, *Holocaust* (Jerusalem, Israel: Keter Books, 1974, originally published in the *Encyclopedia Judaica*), Jacob Robinson, "The History of the Holocaust," pp. 1-59.

3. Dawidowicz, *War Against the Jews,* pp. 48-69, 100-104.

4. "In 1938 'emigration' was a euphemism for 'expulsion.' Once the war began, 'evacuation' became a euphemism for 'deportation,' which, in turn, signified transportation to a place of death." *Ibid.,* p. 106.

5. Robinson, in *Holocaust,* p. 54.

Oral History

1. Also included in the text is a brief selection from a tape made at Newton North High School in Newton, Massachusetts, in late March of 1975. A few paragraphs from this tape were added to the section discussing Buchenwald.

2. His wife was released shortly thereafter.

3. Baeck was an important moral and religious philosopher as well as a writer and a liberal Jewish rabbi.

4. A concentration camp for the elderly at Wannsee in Bohemia. It was the only camp to allow visitors and was a place for those "whose disappearance would prove embarrassing to the Germans in case of international inquiries about their welfare." Most inmates went from there to Auschwitz. Dawidowicz, *War Against the Jews,* p. 137.

PART III.   NEW GENERATIONS: 1946 through the 1970s

1. Richard Irwin, "Changing Patterns of American Immigration," *International Migration Review* 6 (Spring 1972): 27, Table 5.

2. Between June of 1964 and June of 1975 women outnumbered men by at least 20,000 in every year. From every continent, women outnumber men in the 1975 immigration figures. In 1975 over 205,000 females came, and 132,000 were between the ages of ten and thirty-nine. *1975 Annual Report: INS,* Table 9, and Table 10, p. 53; also in Irwin, "Changing Patterns," Table 4, p. 22.

3. Irwin, "Changing Patterns," pp. 22-23.

4. Dinnerstein and Reimers, *Immigration and Assimilation,* p. 83.

5. *Ibid.,* pp. 84-85. Harper and Chase, *Immigration Laws,* pp. 38-39; also see Austin T. Fragomen, Jr., "1976 Amendments to Immigration and Nationality

Act," *International Migration Review* 9 (Spring 1977): 95-100. There are seven preference categories. Family and relative preferences are #1, 2, 4, 5. Occupational preferences are #3 and 6, #3 being immigrants in the "professions" and #6 being "other workers." Preference #7 is for "conditional entrants," in most cases, refugees. "Non-preference immigrants" include "private bill cases." Others in this status are students, visitors, and ambassadors not intending to immigrate. *1975 Annual Report: INS*, Table 35, pp. 9, 45.

6. In fact, the refugee category in the seventh preference was defined by law as anti-Communist escapees from non–Western Hemispheric countries.

7. Gunnar Myrdal, *An American Dilemma: The Negro Problem and Modern Democracy*, 2 vols. (New York: Harper, c. 1944).

8. *Wall Street Journal*, June 18, 1976.

"Anton Tamsaare"

Introduction

1. Some 30,000 Estonians left from 1939 to 1943, but a large number fled late in 1944 as the Soviets entered Estonia. Jaan Pennar, Tönu Parming, and P. Peter Rebane, eds., *The Estonians in America 1627-1975: A Chronology & Fact Book* (Dobbs Ferry, N.Y.: Oceana Publications, Inc., Ethnic Chronology Series No. 17, 1975), p. 27.

2. Refugee figures from UNRRA and IRO are incomplete, inasmuch as many refugees did not deal with these organizations. Anthony Bouscaren, *International Migrations Since 1945* (New York: Frederick A. Praeger, 1963), pp. 31-32.

3. Julius Epstein, *Operation Keelhaul: The Story of Forced Repatriation from 1944 to the Present* (Old Greenwich, Conn.: Devin-Adair Co., 2nd ed., 1974), p. 23.

4. Anthony Bouscaren, *International Migrations Since 1945* p. 35.

5. *Ibid.*, p. 68.

6. Howard Blum, *Wanted: The Search for Nazis in America* (New York: Quadrangle, New York Times Book Co., 1977). Also see Dorothy Rabinowitz, *New Lives: Survivors of the Holocaust Living in America* (New York: Alfred A. Knopf, 1976), ch. 1.

Thomas Blatt

Introduction

1. Raymond Aron, "The Meaning of Destiny," in Tamas Aczel, ed., *The Years After: The Hungarian Revolution in the Perspective of History* (New York: Holt, Rinehart and Winston, 1966), p. 23.

2. *Ibid.*, Arthur Koestler, "The Ubiquitous Presence," p. 205.

3. Harper and Chase, *Immigration Law*, pp. 27-28.

4. Alexander S. Weinstock, *Acculturation and Occupation: A Study of the 1956 Hungarian Refugees in the United States* (The Hague: Martinus Nijhoff, 1969), p. 39.

5. Leslie Konnyu, *Hungarians in the United States: An Immigration Study* (St. Louis: The American Hungarian Review, 1967), pp. 21-22, 55-57.

Oral History

1. His mother died in 1966.

Rodolfo de León

Introduction

1. Citing INS figures, the *New York Times* noted that 213,000 Cuban refugees were permanent residents, fifty percent of whom were living in the Miami area, thirty percent in the New York–New Jersey area. "Visas of Refugees Expedited," *New York Times,* Sept. 20, 1976.

2. Richard R. Fagan, Richard A. Brody, and Thomas J. O'Leary, *Cubans in Exile: Dissaffection and Revolution* (Stanford: Stanford University Press, 1968), pp. 4–5.

3. This agency was set up in February 1961 and has spent $1.1 billion for medical and social services as well as resettlement aid. "End of Cuban Refugee Program Recommended by Federal Panel," *New York Times,* Sept. 21, 1976.

4. Lee Lockwood, *Castro's Cuba, Cuba's Fidel* (New York: Macmillan, 1967), p. 250.

Oral History

1. Prior to the revolution, Castro built his base in the Sierra Maestra Mountains.

2. Camilo Cienfuegos fought with Fidel in the Sierra and became commander-in-chief of the army. He died in a plane crash in October of 1959.

3. The 26 July Movement—Castro's revolutionary movement's name. From the July 26, 1953, attack on the Moncada Barracks.

4. Castro was in Camagüey on the fourth, in Havana the eighth. Hugh Thomas, *Cuba: The Pursuit of Freedom* (New York: Harper & Row, 1971), pp 1032–33.

5. Hook leg.

6. Literally, worms. People against the revolution.

7. Squealers.

8. The Bay of Pigs, or Battle of Cochinos Bay, began on April 15, 1961, when a group of Cuban exiles, actually financed and trained by the United States, invaded Cuba. Those picked up between the fifteenth and the seventeenth included 2,000 CIA agents and 20,000 counterrevolutionary sympathizers. Thomas, *Cuba,* pp. 1355–71.

9. "Upward the masses of the world."

10. Peasants.

"Elana Christopoulous"

Introduction

1. Stephan Thernstrom calls children like these, "*de facto* second generation." See Stephan Thernstrom, *The Other Bostonians: Poverty and Progress in the American Metropolis* (Cambridge: Harvard University Press, 1973), p. 120.

2. From Asia the figure is 57.4 percent for relative preference. Asian occupa-

tional preference in 1975 is 22.9 percent and Europe's, eleven percent. *1975 Annual Report: INS*, p. 5.

3. *Ibid.*, table 13, p. 64, and Table 6, p. 36.

Antonio Cardoso

Introduction

1. *1974 Annual Report: INS*, Table 13, pp. 57–58. Several problems exist with the statistics on Portuguese immigration: (1) island and mainland immigration is not differentiated as yet in INS figures; (2) seamen and others entering illegally are not recorded; (3) people from the Cape Verde Islands are sometimes listed in African, not Portuguese, figures. For better statistical breakdowns and for the major study on Portuguese Americans, see Francis M. Rogers, *Americans of Portuguese Descent: A Lesson in Differentiation* (Beverly Hills, Calif.: SAGE Publications, 1971), esp. pp. 28, 32, 34–36.

2. Rogers, *Americans of Portuguese Descent*, p. 26.

3. See listing of thirty-two churches in southern New England and several others in New Jersey and California. All but six of the New England churches were set up prior to 1930. National parishes were common among most of the major Catholic immigrant groups in the United States, not only among the Portuguese. *Ibid.*, pp. 27, 29, 34. Also, James P. Adler, *The Portuguese: Ethnic Minorities in Cambridge*, vol. 1, in the series Ethnic Minorities in Cambridge (City of Cambridge, 1972). For the history of Azorean immigrants, look for a pair of books from Francis M. Rogers.

4. Rogers, *Op. Cit.*, pp. 32–33.

5. *1975 Annual Report: INS*, Table 14, p. 159, and Table 12A, p. 53.

6. Rogers citing Portuguese figures, Table 5, p. 36.

Graciela Mendoza Peña Valencia

Introduction

1. Albert Prago, *Strangers in Their Own Land; A History of Mexican Americans* (New York: Four Winds Press, a division of Scholastic Magazine, Inc., 1973), p. 105, also pp. 84–104.

2. Matt S. Meier and Feliciano Rivera, *The Chicanos: A History of Mexican Americans* (New York: Hill and Wang, paper, 1972), pp. xii–xiv.

3. *1974* and *1975 Annual Report: INS*, Table 19, p. 79. Figures do not differentiate between one Mexican going back and forth across the border daily, as many do, and a Mexican coming to the United States for an extended visit; thus the inflated number.

4. Report by the Select Committee on Western Hemisphere Migration. Washington: U.S. Government Printing Office, 1968, in Matt S. Meier and Feliciano Rivera, *Readings on La Raza: The Twentieth Century* (New York: Hill and Wang, paper, 1974), pp. 204–208. For an analysis of areas from which undocumented immigration originates and possible solutions plus a brief history of the con-

tinuing nature of this phenomenon, see Jorge A. Bustamente, "Undocumented Immigration from Mexico: Research Report," *International Migration Review* 11 (Summer 1977): 149–89.

5. The Bracero Program admitted temporary farm workers into the United States. Public Law 78, as it was called, thus allowed more than 4.5 million Mexicans to be legally contracted. Richard B. Craig, *The Bracero Program: Interest Groups and Foreign Policy* (Austin: University of Texas Press, 1971), p. ix.

6. *1974* and *1975 Annual Report: INS*, Table 27B.

Alma Mejia Uminsky

Introduction

1. *1975 Annual Report: INS*, Tables 13 and 14, pp. 63–65.

"Dr. A.L. Sarkar"

Introduction

1. *1975 Annual Report: INS*, Table 13, p. 63, and Table 8, p. 44.

2. Asian immigration in the professional and technical categories was up 500 percent between 1964 and 1969. The Committee on the International Migration of Talent, *Modernization and the Migration of Talent* (U.S.A., A Report from Education and World Affairs, 1970), p. 3. For an economic analysis of the problem of talent migration, see Brinley Thomas, *Migration and Economic Growth: A Study of Great Britain and the Atlantic Economy* (Cambridge, England: University Press, second edition, 1973).

3. For the general debate, see Walter Adams, ed., *The Brain Drain* (New York: Macmillan, 1968).

Deborah Padmore

Introduction

1. Eric Williams, *History of the People of Trinidad and Tobago* (London: Andre Deutsch, 1962), chs. 8 and 9. Figures from Robert D. Crassweller, *The Caribbean Community: Changing Societies and U.S. Policy* (New York: Praeger, 1972), p. 222.

2. Tony Best, "West Indians and Afro-Americans: A Partnership," *The Crisis* 82 (December 1975): 391.

3. Ira De A. Reid, *The Negro Immigrant: His Background, Characteristics and Social Adjustment, 1899-1937* (New York: Arno Press and the New York Times, reprint, 1969, first printing Columbia University Press, 1939), p. 215. This is the only full-length study on black immigrants. See also Florette Henri, *Black Migration: Movement North 1900-1920* (Garden City, N.Y.: Doubleday Anchor Press, 1975).

4. This study was done on a sample of Jamaicans preparing to leave the island. O.C. Francis, "The Characteristics of Emigrants Just Prior to Changes in British Commonwealth Immigration Policies," in F.M. Andic and T.G. Mathews, eds.,

The Caribbean in Transition: Papers on Social, Political and Economic Development, Second Caribbean Scholars' Conference, Mona, Jamaica, April 14–19, 1964 (Rio Piedras, Puerto Rico: Institute of Caribbean Studies, University of Puerto Rico, 1965), pp. 91–121, esp. 119–21.

5. A high proportion of West Indians coming to the United States in recent years are professional and technical workers. Between 1960 and 1972, forty-seven percent were in this category, seventy percent being in medical fields. Ransford W. Palmer, "A Decade of West Indian Migration to the United States, 1962–1972: An Economic Analysis," *Social and Economic Studies* 23 (December 1974): 571–87, esp. 572–76.

6. *1975 Annual Report: INS,* Table 14, p. 65.

"Brigitte Besimer"

Introduction

1. For a critique of the media and its reporting in this area, see Susan Jacoby, "Immigration and the News Media: A Journalistic Failure," Proceedings of the National Consultation on Undocumented Migrants and Public Policies, reprinted in *Migration Today* 5 (April 1977): 20–22.

2. Arthur Miller, *A View From the Bridge* (New York: Bantam Library of World Drama, paper, 1967).

3. James P. Sterba, in "Aliens: Where They Come From, What Awaits Them," "From Mexico to Hard Times in the Southwest U.S.," *New York Times,* May 1, 1977, Sec. 4, p. 3. See also Robert Lindsey, "A Falling Peso Spurs Illegal Immigration," *New York Times,* Jan. 9, 1977, p. 43.

Oral History

1. For problems in authenticating documents, see James P. Sterba, "Bogus Documents Hamper Drive on Illegal Aliens," *New York Times,* Aug. 22, 1977, pp. 1, 14.

"Lee Ki Chuck"

Introduction

1. In Korean, the first name, Lee, is the surname, Ki is the first name, and Chuck is similar to a middle name. Locations have been changed.

2. Hyung-chan Kim, "Some Aspects of Social Demography of Korean Americans," *International Migration Review* 8 (Spring 1974): 28–30, 35.

3. Between 1959 and 1966 the range was between 4.7 and 14.3, 1966 and 1963 being the only years having double digits. *Ibid.*

"Nguyen Thi Anh"

Introduction

1. The words "I Believe the War Is Over" are from a song by the same name by Phil Ochs.

2. Douglas Kneeland, "Indochinese Refugees Now A Displaced Underclass," *New York Times,* Sunday, July 10, 1977, Sec. 4, p. 5.

3. *Ibid.*

"Masha"

Introduction

1. S. Ettinger, "The Jews in Russia at the Outbreak of the Revolution," in Lionel Kochan, ed., *The Jews in the Soviet Union Since 1917* (London: Oxford University Press, 1970), p. 14.

2. *Ibid.,* Chimen Abramsky, "The Biro-Bidzhan Project, 1927-1959," pp. 62-75.

3. *Ibid.,* Joshua Rothenberg, "Jewish Religion in the Soviet Union," p. 167.

4. *Ibid.,* Zev Katz, "After the Six Day War," pp. 322-23.

5. Barry P. Levenfeld, "Recent Soviet Immigration" (B.A. thesis, Harvard College, April 1976), pp. 1, 21; p. 49, Table 4.

6. Susan Quinn, "Voyages: For Soviet Jews in Boston the Journey to Freedom Has Just Begun," *Boston Magazine* (March 1977): 64.

7. Betsy Gidwitz, "Perceptions and Problems of Soviet Jewish Emigrés: Factors in Their Adjustment to Conditions in Israel and the United States," prepared for delivery at the Midwest Slavic Conference, Ann Arbor, Michigan, 6 May 1977, pp. 2-9, 17; and Levenfeld, "Recent Soviet Immigration," p. 24.

BIBLIOGRAPHY

Copies of the original tapes of the following people are on file at the Arthur and Elizabeth Schlesinger Library on the History of Women in America at Radcliffe College, Cambridge, Massachusetts: Minnie Needle, Catherine McNamara, Philip and Theresa Bonacorsi, Valeria Demusz, Natsu Ozawa, Araxi Ayvasian, Anna Yona, and Kyoko Takayanagi.

The following bibliography is general in nature. For more information consult the footnotes.

IMMIGRATION AND ETHNICITY

Adamic, Louis, *From Many Lands* (New York: Harper & Bros., 1940).

Adams, Walter, ed., *The Brain Drain* (New York: Macmillan, 1968).

Appel, John J., ed., *The New Immigration* (New York: Jerome S. Ozer, 1971).

Bouscaren, Anthony T., *International Migrations Since 1945* (New York: Praeger, 1963).

Dinnerstein, Leonard, and Frederick Jaher, eds., *The Aliens* (New York: Appleton-Century-Crofts, 1970).

Dinnerstein, Leonard, and David M. Reimers, *Ethnic Americans: A History of Immigration and Assimilation* (New York (?): Dodd, Mead & Co., 1975).

Glazer, Nathan, and Daniel Patrick Moynihan, *Beyond the Melting Pot* (Cambridge: M.I.T. Press, 1963).

Greeley, Andrew, *Why Can't They Be Like Us?* (New York: E.P. Dutton & Co., 1971).

Handlin, Oscar, *The Uprooted* (New York: Grosset & Dunlap, 1951).

Hansen, Marcus Lee, *The Immigrant in American History* (Cambridge: Harvard University Press, 1940).

Higham, John, *Send These to Me: Jews and Other Immigrants in Urban America* (New York: Atheneum, 1975).

——, *Strangers in the Land: Patterns of American Nativism 1860-1925* (New Brunswick, N.J.: Rutgers University Press, 1955).

Hutchenson, E.P., *Immigrants and Their Children, 1850-1950* (New York: John Wiley & Sons, Inc., 1956).

Isaacs, Harold R., *Idols of the Tribe: Group Identity and Political Change* (New York: Harper & Row, 1975).

Jones, Maldwyn Allen, *American Immigration* (Chicago: University of Chicago Press, 1960).

Novak, Michael, *The Rise of the Unmeltable Ethnics* (New York: Macmillan, 1972).

Soloman, Barbara, *Ancestors and Immigrants: A Changing New England Tradition* (Chicago: University of Chicago Press, 1972 ed.).

Taylor, Philip, *The Distant Magnet: European Emigration to the U.S.A.* (New York: Harper & Row, 1971).

Thernstrom, Stephan, *The Other Bostonians: Poverty and Progress in the American Metropolis, 1880-1970* (Cambridge: Harvard University Press, 1973).

SELECTED WORKS ON IMMIGRANT GROUPS

ARMENIANS

Arlen, Michael, *Passage to Ararat* (New York: Farrar, Straus and Giroux, 1976).
Hartunian, Abraham H., *Neither to Laugh Nor to Weep*, translated by Vartan Hartunian, (Boston: Beacon Press, 1968).

CHINESE

Kingston, Maxine Hong, *The Woman Warrior: Memoirs of a Girlhood Among Ghosts* (New York: Alfred A. Knopf, 1977).
Lyman, Stanford M., *Chinese Americans* (New York: Random House, 1974).
Nee, Victor G., and Brett de Bary, *Longtime Californ'; A Documentary Study of an American Chinatown* (Boston: Houghton Mifflin Co., 1974).

CUBANS

Fagan, Richard, Richard A. Brody, and Thomas J. O'Leary, *Cubans in Exile* (Stanford University Press, 1968).
Thomas, Hugh, *Cuba: The Pursuit of Freedom* (New York: Harper & Row, 1971).

FILIPINOS

Pilipinos in America History Workshop, *A Reader on the History of Pilipinos in America* (San Francisco: Asian Studies Department, 1975).

GERMANS AND OTHER CENTRAL EUROPEANS

Fermi, Laura, *Illustrious Immigrants: The Intellectual Migration from Europe, 1930-1941* (Chicago: University of Chicago Press, 1968).
Fleming, Donald, and Bernard Bailyn, eds., *The Intellectual Migration: Europe and America, 1930-1960* (Cambridge: Harvard University Press, 1969).

GREEKS

Saloutos, Theodore, *The Greeks in the United States* (Cambridge: Harvard University Press, 1964).
——, *They Remember America: The Story of the Repatriated Greek-Americans* (Berkeley: University of California Press, 1956).

HUNGARIANS

Aczel, Tamas, ed., *Ten Years After: The Hungarian Revolution in the Perspective of History* (New York: Holt, Rinehart and Winston, 1966).
Kosa, John, *Land of Choice: The Hungarians in Canada* (Toronto: Toronto University Press, 1957).

IRISH

Handlin, Oscar, *Boston's Immigrants: A Study in Acculturation* (New York: Atheneum, paper ed., 1974).
Shannon, William V., *The Irish in America* (New York: Macmillan, 1966).
Wittke, Carl, *The Irish in America* (Baton Rouge: Louisiana State University, 1956).

ITALIANS

Gambino, Richard, *Blood of My Blood: The Dilemma of the Italian-Americans* (Garden City, N.Y.: Doubleday, 1974).

Gans, Herbert J., *The Urban Villagers: Group and Class in the Life of Italian Americans* (New York: The Free Press, 1962).

Lopreato, Joseph, *Italian-Americans* (New York: Random House, 1970).

JAPANESE

Hosokawa, Bill, *Nisei: The Quiet Americans* (New York: William Morrow & Co., 1969).

Petersen, William, *Japanese Americans: Oppression and Success* (New York: Random House, 1971).

Weglyn, Michi, *Years of Infamy: The Untold Story of America's Concentration Camps* (New York: William Morrow & Co., 1976).

JEWS

Dawidowicz, Lucy, *The Golden Tradition: Jewish Life and Thought in Eastern Europe* (Boston: Beacon Press, 1968).

———, *The War Against the Jews: 1933–1945* (New York: Holt, Rinehart and Winston, 1975).

Howe, Irving, *World of Our Fathers* (New York: Harcourt Brace Jovanovich, 1976).

Kochan, Lionel, ed., *The Jews in the Soviet Union* (New York: Oxford University Press, 1970).

Kramer, Sydelle, and Jenny Masur, eds., *Jewish Grandmothers* (Boston: Beacon Press, 1976).

Rabinowitz, Dorothy, *New Lives: Survivors of the Holocaust Living in America* (New York: Alfred A. Knopf, 1976).

Rischin, Moses, *The Promised City: New York's Jews, 1870–1914* (Cambridge: Harvard University Press, 1962).

MEXICANS

Meier, Matt S., and Feliciano Rivera, *The Chicanos: A History of Mexican Americans* (New York: Hill & Wang, 1972).

———, eds., *Readings on La Raza: The Twentieth Century* (New York: Hill & Wang, 1974).

POLES

Thomas, W. I., and Florian Znaniecki, *The Polish Peasant in Europe and America*, 2 vols. (New York: Alfred A. Knopf, 1927).

Wytrowal, Joseph A., *Poles in American History and Tradition* (Detroit: Endurance Press, 1969).

PORTUGUESE

Rogers, Francis M., *Americans of Portuguese Descent* (Beverly Hills, Cal.: Sage Publications, 1974).

SPANISH EXILES

Fagan, Patricia, *Exiles and Citizens: Spanish Republicans in Mexico* (Austin: University of Texas Press, 1973).

Thomas, Hugh, *The Spanish Civil War* (New York: Harper & Row, 1961).

WEST INDIANS

Crassweller, Robert D., *The Caribbean Community: Changing Societies and U.S. Policy* (New York: Praeger, 1972).

Reid, Ira De A., *The Negro Immigrant: His Background, Characteristics and Social Adjustment, 1899–1937* (New York: Columbia University Press, 1939; reprinted ed., New York: Arno Press and the New York Times, 1969).

Williams, Eric, *The History of the People of Trinidad and Tobago* (London: Andre Deutsch, 1962).